THE GREEK ISLANDS

Publishers: George A. Christopoulos, John C. Bastias

Translation: Alexandra Doumas
Managing Editor: E. Karpodini-Dimitriadi
Art Director: Angela Simou
Special photography: N. Desyllas, N. and K. Kontos,
A. Rodopoulos, Y. Skouroyannis, Sp. Tselentis
Maps: D. Tsopelas
Phototypesetting: F. Panagopoulos & Co

Printed and bound by Ekdotike Hellados S.A., Athens

THE GREEK ISLANDS

A traveller's guide to all the Greek Islands

E. KARPODINI-DIMITRIADI, Ph.D.

Archaeologist

EKDOTIKE ATHENON S.A.

Athens 1990

ISBN 960-213-064-4
Copyright © 1987
EKDOTIKE ATHENON S.A.
1, Vissarionos St., 106 72 Athens
Printed in Greece

CONTENTS

INTRODUCTION

Betwixt sky and sea, drenched in sunshine and salty spray, like precious pearls the isles of Greece rise at random from the sea. Large and small, with "seaward and landward towns", frequently fortified and even with castles, with lilliputian white villages, noble mansions and humble dwellings, steep cobbled streets, vines and olive trees, windmills and countless churches, their charm is irresistible, an open invitation for the visitor to get to know them better.

It is no easy task to describe the beauty of the islands with their age-old history, remnants of monuments of all eras, legends interwoven with the past, bringing it to life with every step. Each island is a story in itself. That, in the words of the poet Odysseas Elytis, "Greece rests on the sea", is indeed true, for 3/4 of the landmass of Hellas is lapped by the sea and only 1/5 of this area, some 25,000 sq. km., are islands. There are over 3,000 isles and islets, of which only 167 are inhabited, the majority scattered throughout the Aegean Sea. These we have divided into nine groups. To the south lies Crete, the largest island of all; in the centre, almost at the heart of the Aegean, are the Cyclades, a group of islands large and small. Southeast, yet another archipelago, the Dodecanese; to the north the islands of the East Aegean and even further north those of the North Aegean, close to the

shores of Thrace. Yet another large island, Euboia, skirts the coast of the Greek mainland and northeast of it lie the Sporades. Last but not least, between the Peloponnese and Attica, are the isles of the Saronic and Argolic gulf.

West of the mainland are the Ionian islands with their infinite variety of landscapes and monuments. And the little islands to the south of the Peloponnese (belonging administratively to Piraeus) Kythera, Antikythera and Elafonissos are considered together with the Ionian islands.

The main departure points for the islands are Athens, with which there are air connections, and Piraeus. Boats leave Piraeus for the islands of the Saronic and Argolic gulf, the Cyclades, Crete, the Dodecanese, the islands of the East and North Aegean and Kythera, while those from Patras and Igoumenitsa serve the Ionian isles.

With their picturesque landscapes, mild climate, lovely beaches and host of monuments, the islands attract thousands of visitors seeking relaxing and interesting holidays.

This book is intended to give the visitor an overview of the islands' past history, as well as their contemporary aspect, so that he may enjoy their sea and sunshine and unique natural environment in the midst of hospitable folk.

THE ISLANDS OF THE SARONIC AND ARGOLIC GULF

The islands of the Saronic and Argolic gulf are located between the northeast shores of the Peloponnese and the west coast of Attica, being referred to as the islands of the Argosaronic gulf for brevity. They are Salamis, Aegina, Hydra, Poros and Spetses, all of which attract a considerable number of visitors, especially at weekends and during the summer months. There are several boats a day from Piraeus as well as from the Argolid, most convenient for those vistors wishing to spend a few hours of peace and quiet in their soothing environment.

The main features of all these islands are their pretty villages, delightful beaches, dazzling white houses retaining elements of vernacular architecture and narrow cobbled streets. Their past is rich in mythological and historical tradition, intimately associated with the sea. Yet each has a personality distinctly its own.

Salamis —at the entrance to the gulf of Elefsis— is renowned for the epoch-making naval battle (480 BC), between the Greeks and Persians. Aegina, with its ancient nautical tradition, first capital of the newly-established Greek state, has idyllic beaches and many monuments. Poros, in antiquity the island of Poseidon, is famed for its verdant vegetation. Spetses combines its special place in Modern Greek history, on account of its illustrious maritime tradition and past glory, with its old-world tranquility and golden sands. Hydra, equally famous for its prowess in seafaring, with its impressive mansions attesting its former prosperity, also has a unique terrain.

◄1. Fishermen on Leros.

◄2. Paros. View of the harbour.

3. Aegina. View of the harbour.

4. Hydra. Island of the Saronic gulf with a unique landscape.

Salamis

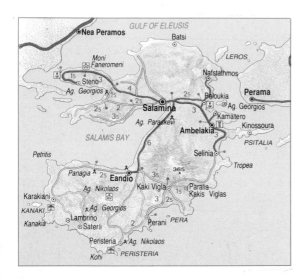

GEOGRAPHY. Situated in the gulf of Eleusis (Elefsis), 95 sq. km. in area, length of coastline 104 km. population 28,574. Capital Salamina (Koulouri). There are connections between the island and Piraeus but most of the car and passenger ferries ply the route from Perama to Paloukia (the island's harbour), from 05.00 hours until midnight every day. There are smaller harbours in the south and east of the island, Selinia, Kaki Vigla and Peristeria. Salamis is a rather flat island with a few mountainous eminences (highest peak Mavrovouni, 365 m. a.s.l.) and the population is mainly engaged in agriculture and seafaring. Since it is so near Athens, Salamis is popular with visitors, especially at the weekends, who mainly congregate on the south side of the island.

HISTORY. According to mythological tradition the island was named after the nymph Salamis. From the ancient sources it is known to have participated in the Trojan War and, in historical times, was a bone of contention between the Athenians and Megarites. The most famous event in its historic past was the naval battle fought in its waters in 480 BC, between the Greeks and the Persians, decisive for the outcome of the Persian Wars and Greece's independence.

SIGHTS-MONUMENTS. In the small Archaeological Museum at **Salamina**, the main town, finds associated with the island's past, going back to Mycenaean times, can be seen. From Salamina one can visit various other parts of the island, such as the **Phaneromeni Monastery,** about 6 km. away on the northwest coast, which attracts many pilgrims. The tiny church preserved within the monastery is actually the original building, founded in the 11th century. The present katholikon, built in the 18th century, houses several valuable icons. The **Monastery of St. Nicholas,** also of 18th century date, on the west coast near Moulki and the Byzantine chapel of **St. John Kalyvitis**. This village is also known as *Aianteio,* since it is the location of the city of Aiantas, hero of the Trojan War. On the northeast side, at **Ambelakia,** there are some traces of the Classical acropolis, for the island's capital was evidently in this area in those days. Most vistors converge on **Moulki** in the west, **Ambelakia** in the east and **Selinia,** the leading summer resort. There are refuelling facilities for boats in the harbour, as well as some hotels for the accommodation of visitors.

5. The island of Salamis. Aerial photograph.

5

Aegina

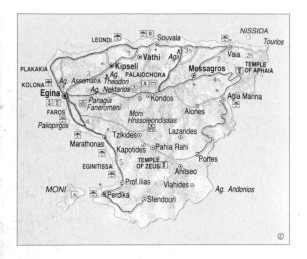

GEOGRAPHY. Situated almost in the middle of the Saronic gulf, its harbour, Aegina, is only 16 nautical miles from Piraeus. The island, 83 sq. km. in area, 57 km. of coast, 11,177 inhabitants, has daily car and passenger ferry and several hydrofoil (Flying Dolphin) connections with Piraeus per day. During the summer months their frequency is increased and additional passenger services operate between Piraeus and the harbours of Souvala and Aghia Marina. Throughout the year there are links with Hydra, Spetses, Methana and Poros and in the summertime there are hydrofoils to Methana, Hydra, Poros, Hermioni, Spetses and Tolon, Nauplion. A fertile island with mild climate, several flat tracts of land and some hills (highest peak Oros, 532 m. a.s.l.), it was one of the first to develop as a tourist centre. Not only has it idyllic beaches and picturesque villages, its comprehensive tourist facilities include a yacht marina in the harbour of Aegina. All in all an ideal holiday spot.

HISTORY. Inhabited since antiquity, Aegina was named after the homonymous nymph, most beloved of the daughters of the river god Asopos. Its history goes far back into Neolithic times, for the first settlements on the island date to around 3000 BC, more specifically at the site of Kolona, northwest of the present town. Remains have also been found at Aghia Marina. In the Bronze Age (2500 – 2000 BC) colonisers arrived from Karia in Asia Minor and settled here. Shortly afterwards (2000 –

1600 BC) Achaeans came from the Peloponnese. Finds brought to light in the course of excavations by the German Archaeological Institute indicate that the Aeginites were involved in marine and mercantile activities as early as 1800 BC and their produce, as well as their pottery, was traded in Crete, the Cyclades and the Greek mainland. A member of the Amphictyony of Kalaureia (8th – 7th century BC), Aegina was a rival of Athens and in the mid–6th century BC was the first Greek city to mint its own coinage, which had a wide circulation in commercial markets of that time until Athens struck its own tetradrachm. Experienced seafarers, the Aeginites played a vital role in repelling the Persians during the Persian Wars, after which Athens emerged as the new naval power, sovereign of the sea. In 456 BC the island was taken by the Athenians and for short intervals also belonged to the Spartans, Thebans, Macedonians and Romans (133 BC) who sold it to king Attalos of Pergamon. In Byzantine times successive piratical raids forced the inhabitants to retreat into the hinterland where they built Palaiochora. In 1537, however, it was attacked by Barbarossa, the male population decimated and the women and children sold into bondage. The island remained deserted until it was resettled by the Turks. During the 1821 Revolution many freedom-fighters sought refuge on Aegina and in 1828 the first government of the liberated Greek state was established there.

SIGHTS-MONUMENTS. In ancient times the island was famed for its school of sculpture and for the cult of **Aphaia**, whose sanctuary stands on an eminence some 4 km. from Aghia Marina. Twenty-four columns from the peristyle of the temple, regarded as one of the most beautiful in antiquity, are preserved, as well as part of the restored cornice and two columns of the pronaos. There are also remains of the buildings used by the priests, the propylaia and the foundation of an altar. The sanctuary was enclosed by a peribolos which included a propylon, priests' house, altar and peripteral temple of the goddess with wonderful sculpted pediments in Parian marble. This decoration was removed by Prince Ludwig of Bavaria in 1813 and is nowadays housed in the Munich Glyptothek. Today all that survives of the an-

6. *Aegina. The temple of Aphaia, one of the most important in antiquity.*

7. *Aegina. An island with lovely countryside and idyllic beaches.*

6

7

cient temple are a few columns and remnants of other buildings within the sanctuary. Finds from Aphaia, as well as from other historical sites on the island, are exhibited in the Archaeological Museum in the main town. Ruins of the Archaic temple of Apollo still survive at Kolona, while at the port there are remnants of the ancient harbour installations. In the immediate vicinity of the town, on the way to the village of **Aghioi Asomatoi** (1.5 km.) stands the church of **Sts. Theodore** or **Omorphi Ekklesia** (Lovely church), founded in 1282 by an Athenian family and adorned with important wall-paintings. Also significant is the church of the **Dormition of the Virgin** in the monastery of that name in the village of Tsikides (6 km. south of Aegina). Of the many monasteries and churches on the island that most frequently visited is **St. Nektarios** (6 km. east of Aegina), built in 1904 by the Bishop Pentapoleos who died there in 1920 and was canonised in 1961. On the 9th of November, the anniversary of his death, pilgrims flock to the island. The nearby **monastery of St. Catherine** stands on the site of an ancient temple of Aphrodite and, a short distance beyond, the Byzantine town of **Palaiochora** where the islanders sought protection from marauding pirates during the 9th and 10th centuries.

To the north of Paliochora (approx. 5 km.) is the region of **Souvala,** one of the island's many holiday resorts from where one can visit **Aghioi**, **Vaia** and **Mesagro**, a village with a tradition of pottery making. About 6 km. south of this village is Aghia Marina, very popular with holidaymakers because of its sparkling sea and characteristic island atmosphere. West of Aghia Marina is the village of **Alones** and on the southwest coast of the island (approx. 10 km. from Aegina) the quaint fishing village of **Perdika** from where one can take a boat to the opposite islet of **Moni** with its lush vegetation. All the beaches on the island (north and south) are accessible by local bus and are fine for swimming and fishing. There is a daily boat service between Aegina and the neighbouring isle of **Angistri**, another favourite tourist haunt, particularly during the summer months. Aegina is equipped to cater for visitors; there are several hotels (many in town, by the harbour and at Aghia Marina), as well as rooms and apartments for rent.

8

9

8. Aegina. The harbour.

9. Aegina. Another view of the harbour.

Poros

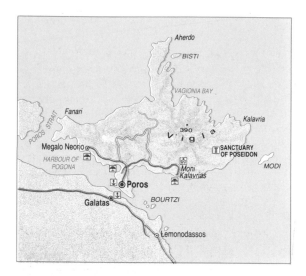

GEOGRAPHY. At the very edge of the Saronic gulf, clinging to the east coast of the Peloponnese, Poros is more like a peninsula than an island. 29 nautical miles from Piraeus, 23 sq. km. in area, it has 43 km. of coast and a population of 3, 929. Boats from Piraeus come here via Aegina and Methana, as do the hydrofoils. There is also a direct link with Galatas on the coast of the Peloponnese. Connections with the islands of Hydra and Spetses and, during the summer months, hydrofoils to Tolo, Nauplion and Hermione and twice a week to Leonidion, Kyparissia and Monemvasia. A verdant island with some hills (highest peak Vigla, 390 m. a.s.l.), it is an ideal spot for quiet holidays and romantic excursions.

HISTORY. Poros actually comprises two islands, linked by a very narrow isthmus. In antiquity these were known as Sphairia and Kalaureia, the latter being the birthplace of Theseus, according to mythological tradition. Here too one of the greatest orators of antiquity, the Athenian Demosthenes, met his death. Throughout the 7th century BC Poros was the centre (Kalaureia) of an amphictyony of seven cities. In the ensuing centuries its fate was much the same as that of the other islands. It played an active role in the Greek War of Independence in 1821 and the first naval dockyard was installed here in 1830.

SIGHTS-MONUMENTS. In antiquity Poros was the centre of the Amphictyony of Kalaureia and seat of the very important sanctuary of **Poseidon**, which has been revealed in the course of excavations at **Vayonia** on the north side of the island, 8 km. from the main town. Virtually no traces remain of the famous temple of Poseidon in which the orator Demosthenes sought refuge and committed suicide by taking poison. However, from this area, known as *Palatia* by the locals, there is a unique view over the open sea and the coast of Troizinia opposite. About half an hour to the south of the ancient sanctuary is the **monastery of Zoodochos Pege** (Life-giving source). The dominant feature in the monastery church is its gilded iconostasis which dates to the 18th century. Poros is an island small enough for one to ramble over, to enjoy its shores and sea, particularly on the south side, as well as its capital, **Poros**, which still remains a charming island town with its two-storey houses, waterfront cafés, patisseries and restaurants, not to mention its clock-tower. There is also an Archaeological Museum. Poros has a distinctive ambience, due in large part to its green natural environment and many trees, often growing right at the water's edge. One of the loveliest spots on the island is the west coast (*Megalo Neorio*). There are day trips from Poros to the archaeological sites of the Argolid (Epidaurus, Nauplion, Mycenae) and excursions to Troizinia with its remains of an-

12

10

10. Poros. A picturesque corner.

11. Poros. Another characteristic view.

12. Poros. View of the harbour with the clocktower.

cient Troezen where the tragic myth of Hyppolytos and Phaedra was enacted. Lemonodassos (lemon forest), east of **Galatas** is an area full of orange and lemon groves and at nearby **Alyki** the islanders usually bathe. Equally beautiful, however, are the coves of **Askeli** and **Monastiri**. All beaches can be reached by bus and for those with a boat there are any number of unfrequented beaches and nearby islets. Accommodation is available in hotels, pensions, rented rooms and furnished flats.

11

Hydra

GEOGRAPHY. With its cosmopolitan atmosphere and constant throng of tourists, Hydra is quite unlike the other islands of the Argo-saronic gulf. 50 sq. km. in area, with 56 km. of coast and 2,723 inhabitants, its main town is also called Hydra. There are daily boat and hydrofoil connections with Piraeus, 36 nautical miles away, as well as with Aegina, Methana, Poros, Spetses and Hermione. During the summer there is a hydrofoil link with Tolo, Nauplion and Porto Cheli, and twice a week with Monemvasia and Leonidion. Tourist facilities are of a high standard and there is a yacht marina in the harbour. Hydra is also exceptional on account of its unique landscape, differing from that of the other islands in that it is rocky and barren (highest point Eros, 593 m. a.s.l.).

HISTORY. It was known in antiquity as Hydraia and there was a Mycenaean settlement to the west of the present town, as excavations have revealed.

In Homeric times it was dependent on Mycenae and later on Hermione which, according to Herodotus, sold the island for 100 talants to exiled Samians. It seems that during the Byzantine era it experienced a floruit, as evident from finds at the locality of Episkopi on the island's west coast. However, its greatest acme was achieved in more recent times, particularly during the 17th and 18th century when its inhabitants amassed a considerable fleet of vessels, both large and small, which voyaged throughout the Mediterranean. This fleet and its experienced crews comprised the Hydriote contribution to the Struggle for Independence in 1821. The island's nautical tradition continued into modern times even though many of its inhabitants moved to Piraeus or emigrated to America. Nowadays there is a Merchant Navy Academy here.

SIGHTS-MONUMENTS. The old harbour with its canons and imposing bourgeois residences dominating the landscape also bear witness to its great maritime tradition. The houses are built amphitheatrically, many have been refurbished in the original style and have preserved their interior decoration, often reminiscent of renaissance mansions in miniature. Of these the Voulgari mansion on the west flank of the harbour, that of Kountouriotis further up, Tombazis' adjacent to that of Voulgaris, as well as those of Votsi and Koulouris are particularly impressive. A branch of the School of Fine Arts is accommodated in the Tombazis mansion, a Home for the Aged in that of Kriezis and the Merchant Navy Academy in the Tsambados residence. The Museum houses archival material related to the 1821 Revolution. Of the many important churches and monasteries on the island, mention should be made of the cathedral (metropolis), dedicated to the Dormition of the Virgin and built in 1765, with its marble iconostasis and numerous icons (including one the Neomartyr Constantine of Hydra). On the east side of the island, beside the bay of **Mandraki** (3 km. from the harbour) stands the monastery of the Holy Trinity and to the northeast that of St. Nicholas and St. Matrona, on the highest peak of the island the monasteries of Prophet Elijah (circa 1800) and St. Eupraxia (circa 1800). Next to the lighthouse (Faros) (at the northeast tip of the island) is the monastery of the Dormition or the Virgin Zourva. The regions of **Kaminia**, **Vlychos** and **Molos** are particularly picturesque and from here one can climb up to Episkopi (on the south side), site of the Byzantine town. In general only a few beaches are suitable for swimming (**Mandraki, Kaminia, Vlychos, Molos, Bisti**) and access to these is by small boat. There are refuelling facilities in the harbour. Visitors may stay in hotels (mostly in town) and a limited number of rooms and apartments for rent. Hydra is girt by numerous rocky islets, the largest of which is Dokos.

13. Hydra. A corner of the harbour at dusk.

14. Hydra. Another view of the harbour.   *15. Hydra. Mandraki.*

14

15

16. Hydra. The harbour and town with its
impressive mansions.

16

Spetses

GEOGRAPHY. Located at the entrance to the Argolic gulf, Spetses, which is also the name of its main town, is 22 sq. km. in area, has 29 km. of coast and has a population of 3,708. Some 52 nautical miles from Piraeus, the island is extremely close to the Peloponnese, being only 2 nautical miles from Kosta, from where visitors are conveyed in speed boats. There are also passenger ferries and hydrofoils from Piraeus and connections with the other Argosaronic islands, as well as with Hermioni and Porto Cheli, again by boat and hydrofoil. During the summer additional services link Spetses with Tolo, Nauplion, Leonidion, Monemvasia and three times a week with Neapolis and Kythera. Cars are prohibited on the island and the only means of transport are the bus and horse-drawn carriages. One may also travel by small caiques or by "taxi", that is speedboats departing from the harbour, Dapia, for picturesque beaches and bays. The island is rich in natural beauty and is an ideal place for both quiet and cosmopolitan holidays.

HISTORY. During antiquity Spetses was known as *Pityoussa* and, as finds from excavations at Aghia Marina testify, was inhabited in the Early Bronze Age (2500 – 2000 BC). The ancient city was located at *Kastelli,* a short distance from the present harbour. Little else is

known of the island's past history. In more recent times Spetses, like Hydra, developed to a notable naval power and, Psara, its fleet played a major role in the 1821 Revolution. Captain Laskarina Bouboulina is one of the legendary figures of the Struggle for Independence and her bones repose in the local museum. The interior of her house is preserved just beyond the harbour. The heart of Spetses is its quaint little harbour, Dapia, with its six canons, momentoes of the Struggle for Independence. Restaurants, cafés and patisseries line the waterfront and throughout the day until late at night there is an endless toing and froing of people. A short distance from the quayside is the Chatzi-Yanni Mexis mansion in which the museum is housed. Exhibits include heirlooms of the Revolution, archival and folklore material pertaining to the island's past. Other sights worth visiting include the church of All Saints, the church of St. Nicholas on the road to the old harbour, the church of the Dormition of the Virgin. From Dapia one may take a small boat to several of the island's beautiful coves (Aghios Georgios, Aghia Paraskevi, Vrellos) and enjoy the precipitous northwest coast with the tiny islet of **Petrokaravo** or visit the bay of **Aghioi Anargyroi** and the **Bekiri** cave, haven for freedom-fighters during the War of Independence. Last but not least are the scenic bays of **Xokeriza** and **Aghia Marina**. Directly opposite the southeast littoral of Spetses is the dazzling island of **Spetsopoula,** owned by the shipowner Niarchos. Excursions are organised from Spetses to Kosta, Porto Cheli and Kranidi, as well as to Nauplion and archaeological sites in the Argolid.

17. Spetses. The island at the entrance to the Saronic gulf with gentle, picturesque scenery.

18. Spetses. The old harbour.

17

18

CYCLADES

The Cyclades, the pearl of the Aegean, is an archipelago of some 56 islands, large and small, stretching out to the south of Attica and Euboia. Comprising a separate Prefecture, the capital of which is Hermoupolis, Syros they may be divided into four major units; the Western Cyclades (Kea, Kythnos, Siphnos, Seriphos, Kimolos, Melos), the Central (Syros, Paros, Antiparos, Naxos), the North and Northeast (Andros, Tenos, Mykonos, Delos, Rheneia) and the Southern and Southeast (Thera, Amorgos, Anaphi, Pholegandros, Ios, Sikinos and the Lesser Cyclades). Concerning their name, there is a plethora of explanations and traditions. One relates that the islands were named after the nymphs Cyclades, whom Poseidon transformed into rocky islets, another that the name derives from the word *Kyklos* (circle or cycle), since the strong winds force boats to go round in a circle. However, the most popular tradition is that associating them with the sacred isle of Delos, around which they form an imaginary circle. According to geologists, the Cyclades were formed as a result of successive disturbances to the landmass which at one time united Greece and Asia Minor. They acquired their present form as a consequence of earthquakes, volcanic eruptions and tectonic movements of the earth's crust. The majority are mountainous, the ranges being interrupted by small plains, hardly extensive enough for cultivation. Their climate is mild and the cooling effect of the northeast winds in the summer, the *Meltemia* (Etesian winds), ensures good weather throughout the year. The islanders are mainly involved in farming (cereals and the vine) and fishing. There is industrial development on some (Syros, Melos). Marble is quarried on Tenos, Naxos and Paros, while large quantities of pumice and pozzuolana are exported from Santorini.

Finds from excavations (Kimolos, Kephala, Kea, Saliagos) indicate that the islands were already inhabited in the Mesolithic period (7th millennium BC). Towards the end of the 4th millennium BC and throughout the 3rd, a splendid and distinctive civilisation, the Cycladic civilisation, divided into three periods: Early Cycladic 3200 – 2100 BC, Middle Cycladic 2100 – 1550 BC and Late Cycladic 1550 – 1100 BC,

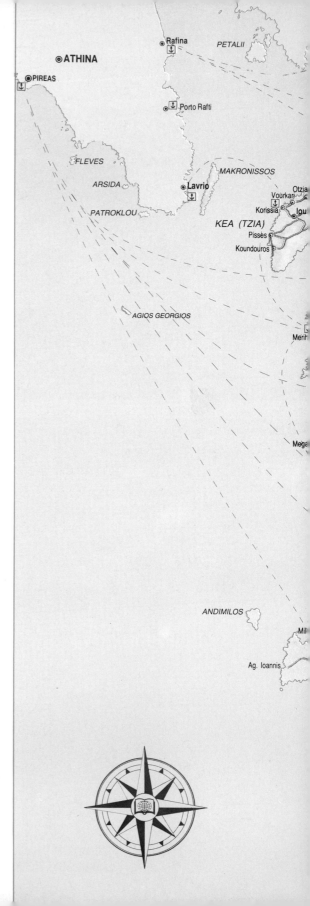

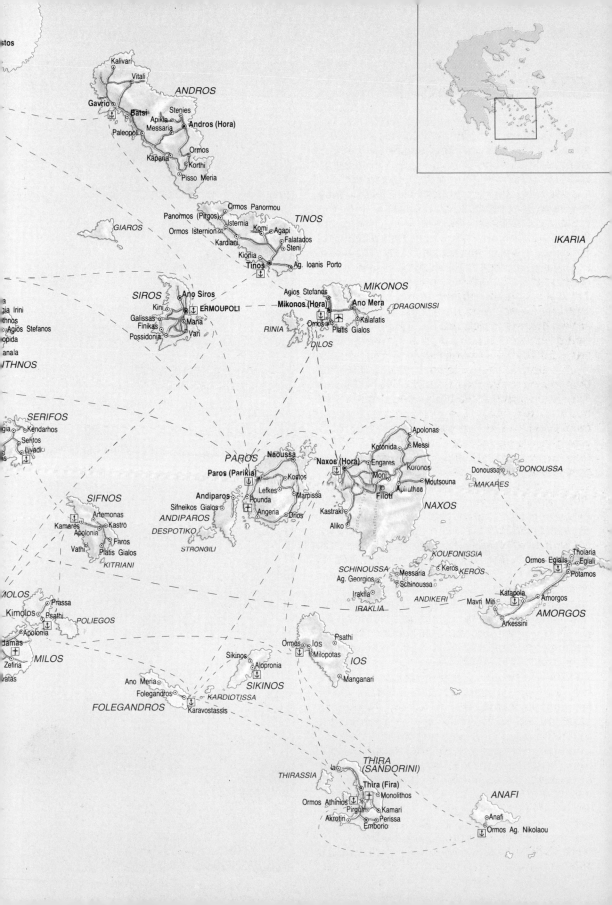

developed here, which produced unrivalled works of art, not least the famous Cycladic figurines. Around 2000 BC the Cyclades were subject to Minoan influences from Crete and the eruption of the Thera volcano (1500 BC) was the death knoll for the Cycladic civilisation and the islands came under Mycenaean domination shortly afterwards. By 1100 BC Ionian colonisers had settled in most of the Cyclades, with the exception of Melos and Thera which were occupied by the Dorians. In historical times their development was virtually independent and they took part in the hostilities between the Greeks and Persians. They were members of the Athenian League, centred on Delos (478 BC) and supported Athens during the Peloponnesian War. In the ensuing centuries they were pawns in the expansionist ambitions of the Macedonians, Egyptian Ptolemies, Rhodians and Romans. In Byzantine times they belonged to the Thema of the Aegean and were the victim of innumerable piratical raids, particularly by Arabs during the 7th, 8th and 9th century. When Constantinople fell to the Franks in 1204, the Cyclades were ceded to the Venetians, comprising the Duchy of Naxos or the Archipelago, which was apportioned into smaller Baronies and Counties assigned to several noble families, such as the Sanudi and Crispi. As a consequence of the long duration of Venetian rule the inhabitants of some islands embraced the Catholic faith. Between 1537 and 1538 the islands were sacked by Khayr ad-Din Barbarossa and by the middle of the 16th century the majority were under Turkish rule, some being granted special priveleges (Naxos, Andros, Tenos inter alia). For a brief interval (1770 – 1774) Russian ships, under the command of admiral Orloff, were anchored on several islands and almost all participated in the 1821 Revolution. The diverse conquerors who passed this way all left their mark, yet the islands still maintained their traditions. Each has its own tale to tell and each has its own, distinctive charm. With their brilliant white houses, narrow cobbled streets, countless churches and chapels, monasteries, castles, windmills and antiquities, they are not only special within the Aegean area, but in the Mediterranean in general.

19-21. Churches in the Cyclades. Churches and chapels abound in the Cycladic islands.
Astonishing architectural creations, almost all are post-16th century.

22. Marble Cycladic figurine, the flautist from Keros. In the Bronze Age a distinctive yet uniform civilisation developed in the Cyclades. Of the artistic creations brought to light in excavations the most impressive and significant are the marble figurines.

23. Large marble Cycladic figurine from Amorgos.

24. Marble figurine of a harpist, from Keros. One of the very few Cycladic figurines of outstanding beauty.

3908

Kea

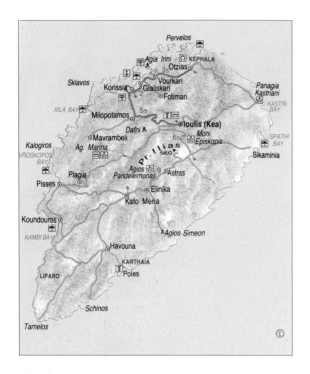

GEOGRAPHY. Kea or Tzia is the northernmost island of the Western Cyclades. It is located between Euboia and Kythnos, almost directly opposite Attica, with Makronisos interposed between them. 131 sq. km. in area, 81 km. of coastline, it is 12 nautical miles from Sounion and has 1,618 inhabitants. The capital is Ioulis (Chora) and its harbour is Korissia (Livadi), from where there is a daily car and passenger ferry service to Lavrion and once a week to Piraeus during the summer season. The only Cycladic island with which there is a link is Kythnos.

A mountainous island, it consists of small valleys leading down to little bays and sandy beaches. Geologically it is the continuation of Sounion. The highest peak is Profitis Ilias (567 m. a.s.l.), almost at the centre of the island. In the northwest part, between the mountainous masses, is the gulf of Aghios Nikolaos, one of the safest natural harbours in the Mediterranean. Very close to Attica and with limited tourist development and road network, it is just the place for a relaxing vacation.

HISTORY. Known in antiquity as "Keios" or "Keio", after the mythical hero Keos, the is-

land's present name, Tzia, is a legacy of the Frankish occupation. Finds from excavations at Kephala testify that the island was inhabited in Neolithic times. Karians, Pelasgians and Lelegians also settled here. In historical times it was colonised by Ionians and consisted of four independent cities —*Ioulis, Karthaia, Poieessa, Koresia*— all of which flourished. The island sired poets (Simonides, Bacchylides), philosophers (Aristion) and athletes, and the four cities minted their own coinage. Kea fought against the Medes during the Persian Wars and afterwards joined the Athenian League. Kea was an ally of Thebes for a brief spell, then passed to the Macedonians, Ptolemies and, eventually, to the Romans, which heralded its decline. In Byzantine times it belonged to the Thema of the Aegean and immediately after the Fall of Constantinople in 1204 it was ceded to the Venetians. In 1537 Kh. Barbarossa plundered Kea and it was easily conquered by the Turks. Between 1770 and 1774 it was taken by the Russian fleet and in 1781 was the base for the sorties of L. Katsonis.

SIGHTS-MONUMENTS. The island's capital, **Ioulis** (Chora) is built amphitheatrically in the hinterland, 6 km. from the harbour, on the site of the ancient city of that name. Its vernacular Cycladic architecture is totally unspoilt, snow-white two-storey houses, narrow cobbled streets and innumerable churches dating from the 17th – 19th century, most with wood carved iconostases and important icons (St. Spyridon, Virgin Rematiani, St. John). From the neighbourhood of Kastro, where remnants of the Venetian castle are preserved, there is a magnificent view over the sea to the mountains of Attica. Engraved on a schistose rock northeast of Chora (approx. 1 km.) is the "Lion of Kea", a colossal lion dated to 600 BC, work of an Ionian sculptor and associated with the island's mythology. In the Archaeological Museum one can see finds from excavations conducted on the island, especially from Aghia Irini. 6 km. southwest of Chora, is the monastery dedicated to **Aghia Marina,** built in the 16th century around a three-storey Hellenistic tower, the ruins of which are still preserved. 2 km. beyond Aghia Marina is **Poises** with its sparse remnants of the once important city of

Poieessa. This richly vegetated region is delightful for swimming, with its tiny bay and sandy beach. The road from here leads to the bay of **Koundouros**, one of the most beautiful on the island, with deep blue waters, many beaches and coves. There are several hotels and in the last few years the area has developed touristically. Proceeding eastwards from Chora, one may visit **Aghia Anna**, formerly a monastery, though nowadays only the church is still in good condition. Southeast of Chora (approximately 12 km.) in an area of particular scenic beauty, difficult of access, is the site of the ancient city of *Karthaia.*

The site of ancient *Koressia* is also the site of the modern town known as Livadi by the locals. Excavations conducted here have brought to light sections of the ancient wall and a cemetery in which the statue of an Archaic kouros of the 6th century BC was discovered, nowadays exhibited in the National Archaeological Museum, Athens. About 2 km. from Koressia is the picturesque bay of **Vourkari**, with the tiny village of that name, a safe anchorage for yachts throughout the year. On the **Aghia Irini** peninsula opposite, excavations carried out by the American School of Classical Studies (under the Direction of the late professor John Caskey) have revealed an important Bronze Age settlement, at its zenith between 2000 and 1400 BC. In addition to the various buildings, many of which are in the sea, significant movable finds have been recovered: vases, domestic objects and Cycladic figurines. After Vourkari is the gulf of **Otzias** from where a road leads to the monastery of the **Virgin Kastriani** (16 km. east of Chora). Within the monastery is the two-storey church of the Virgin, the lower section of which (an 18th century building) is dedicated to the finding of the miraculous icon kept there. On August 15th, the feast of the Virgin, pilgrims flock to the monastery. In addition to the bay of Koundouros and Poises in the south, there are fine beaches at **Koressia, Yaliskari** and **Otzia** which can all be reached by bus or car. For those with a boat there are numerous secluded beaches with sparkling sea. Refuelling stations at Koressia and Bourkari. There are a few hotels and rooms for rent.

25. *Kea. A delightful beach on the southwest coast of the island.*

26. *Modern windmills and country cottages at Koundouros.*

Kythnos

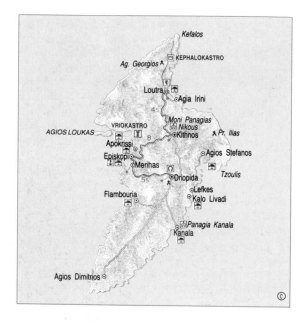

GEOGRAPHY. This island, the second of the Western Cyclades, lies between Kea, Syros and Seriphos. It is 99 sq. km. in area, has 98 km. of coast, 1,502 inhabitants and is 52 nautical miles from Piraeus. Its capital is Kythnos (Chora) or Mesaria. A ferry boat operates between Kythnos and Lavrion, via Kea, as well as Piraeus (more frequent during the summer). The terrain is mountainous (highest peak Profitis Ilias, 368 m. a.s.l.) with small areas of flat land and many coves. The population is engaged exclusively in agriculture and animal husbandry.

The island is particularly well-known for its therapeutic springs (Loutra), on account of which it was known as *Thermia*. With very few tourists and lovely beaches, Kythnos is an ideal spot for those seeking solitude and island life with minimal comforts.

HISTORY. In antiquity the island was known by several names and has been inhabited since Neolithic times, as evident from recent finds from Loutra, dated 7000 – 6500 BC, the earliest proof of human presence in the Cyclades. In Mycenaean times Dryopes lived here and it was they who gave the island its present name. Kythnos played an active role during the Persian Wars, joined the Athenian League, was subject to the Macedonians, Ptolemies and Romans and in Byzantine times

belonged to the Thema of the Aegean. During the Latin occupation it was part of the Duchy of Naxos. In 1337 it was ruled by the Italian Gozzadini family who maintained their preeminence even after the island was pillaged by Barbarossa (1537), up until 1617 when they were ousted by the Turks. During the reign of king Otto it was a place of exile for revolutionaries and political opponents.

SIGHTS-MONUMENTS. The island's capital, **Chora,** stands on a hill in the hinterland and is not visible from the sea. The typically asymmetrical Cycladic houses spread out to right and left of the two parallel main streets. On a nearby spur stands the monastery of the Virgin of Nikos. There are several Postbyzantine churches in Chora (the oldest is the Holy Trinity), built according to Western prototypes since the Catholic faith held sway here for quite some time. The majority have wood carved iconostases (Saviour, Taxiarchs, Christ, St. Savvas, Transfiguration) with important icons in the Veneto-Cretan style, painted by the hagiographer Skordilis.

North of Chora (approx. 1.5 km.) are the remains of a Hellenistic tower.

4 km. south of Chora is **Dryopida**, a characteristic Cycladic village with its snow-white houses built on either side of a dry river bed. In the church of St. Minas there is an intricately carved wooden iconostasis and despotic throne. At the southern edge of the village is the **Katafyki** cave with a wealth of stalagmitic and stalactitic decoration, as yet unexploited.

Southeast of Chora (16 km.) stands the monastery of the **Virgin Kanala**, patroness of the island, whose icon is reputed to have been found in a canal, hence the epithet. On her feast days (15th August and 8th September) pilgrims congregate here in great numbers.

Northeast of Chora (4.5 km.) is **Loutra,** renowned for its medicinal springs. North of Loutra, at **Palaiokastro**, are the remains of the medieval capital of the island with the ruins of its Venetian castle on the hilltop. Parts of the enceinte are preserved but almost nothing has survived of the houses, which numbered more than 1000. Only two of the 100 or so churches are preserved, dating from the 13th and 14th century, that of the Virgin (Our Lady) of Mercy being in better condition.

27. Kythnos. View of the harbour.

On the west side of the island (approx. 8 km. from Chora) is the harbour of **Mericha** and north of this, at **Vriokastro,** are traces of the ancient city. Northwest of Mericha is the islet **Aghios Loukas**, joined to the main island by a narrow spit of sand. South of Mericha, in the locality of **Flamboura,** is the church of the Virgin Flambouriani.

The island's azure waters and numerous sandy beaches are excellent for both swimming and fishing: **Episkopi, Kolona** (only by caique), **Kanala, Flamboura** (by boat), **Aghios Stefanos, Aghia Irini, Kalo Livadi**. These beaches are accessible by bus or on foot, whereas those with a boat may explore all the island's coves, as well as visit neighbouring Tzia. Refuelling station at Mericha. There are a few hotels, rooms and apartments for rent.

Seriphos

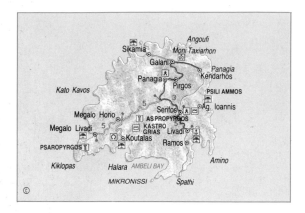

GEOGRAPHY. South of Kythnos, this is the third of the Western Cyclades covering an area of 73 sq. km., with 70 km. of coastline and a population of 1,133. Seriphos is 73 nautical miles from Piraeus, from where there is a daily ferry boat, and is similarly linked with Siphnos, Kimolos and Melos. Its capital is Seriphos (Chora). A mountainous island (highest point Tourlos, 585 m. a.s. l.) with small, fertile plains between the ridges, its coastline is highly indented, the largest bays being that of Livadi in the south and Koutala in the southwest. The population is involved in farming and fishing.

The island has its own specific yet basically Cycladic atmosphere which in recent years has attracted an ever growing number of tourists, even though facilities are somewhat limited.

HISTORY. Mythology tells us that Perseus grew to manhood on Seriphos, arriving here in a bladder, together with his mother Danae, fleeing the wrath of his father Akrisios, king of Argos. It was from Seriphos that he set forth to slay the dreaded Medusa. The island was settled by Ionian colonists in historical times, took part in the Persian Wars and became a member of the Athenian League. During the Roman period it was a place of banishment, in Byzantine times it faded into oblivion and then passed into the hands of the Venetians who apportioned it between several noble families. The Micheli family, which gained predominance, was expelled by the Turks (1537) after Barbarossa sacked the island. Like the rest of the Cyclades, Seriphos was frequently attacked by pirates, was held by the Russians

(1770 – 1774) for a brief interval and took part in the Struggle for Independence.

SIGHTS-MONUMENTS. **Chora**, the main town, is built on a hill overlooking the harbour and presents a truly charming picture when viewed from afar, with its bright white houses, serpentine path wending its way up from the harbour, narrow alleyways with the paving stones outlined in whitewash and ruined Venetian castle. Indeed, it is one of the loveliest Cycladic towns. A small archaeological collection of finds from the region is housed in the Town Hall. There are many Postbyzantine churches, most of which have been renovated (St. Eleftherios, St. Athanasios) and the church of St. Constantine stands inside the castle.

On the other side of the castle are the churches of St. John the Theologian and the Archangels. In the village of **Panaghia** (4 km.), north of Chora, there is a Byzantine church of the Virgin, built in the 10th or 11th century; its feast day is celebrated on August 15th. West of Panaghia is the church of St. Stephen in which traces of Byzantine wall-paintings are preserved.

Close to the village of **Galani** (2 km. northeast) stands the most important monument on the island, the monastery of the Taxiarchs, a fortress-like structure dated to the 17th century. Refurbished 18th century wall-paintings embellish the katholikon. The monastery possesses rare keimelia and valuable books and manuscripts. East of it lies the village of **Kentarchos** and beyond that the region of **Psili Ammos**, suitable for swimming. On the southwest side of the island are the bays of **Livadi** (10 km. from Chora) and **Koutala** (13 km. from Chora) known as Porto Catena in the Middle Ages and the virtually deserted villages of **Koutalas** and **Mega Livadi**. On an eminence above Koutalas is the site known as *Kastro tis Grias,* evidently inhabited at some time since there is a castle there, as well as a few ruined houses, traces of a fortification wall and remnants of a Hellenistic tower popularly known as ***Aspropyrgos***. There is a second Hellenistic tower (***Psaropyrgos***) atop the hill of Kyklopas. West of Koutalas is the homonymous cave, discovered by chance while extracting metal ore, which was a cult place in antiquity; it has not been exploited.

On the southeast side of the island is the harbour, **Livadi,** sheltered from strong winds, a safe haven for all vessels and nowadays a marina for yachts. The island's sandy beaches and crystal clear sea can be reached by caique or on foot and even by vehicle, although the road network is rather rudimentary. Those most easily accessible are **Livadi**, **Koutalas** (by caique from Livadi), **Megalo Livadi**, **Psili Ammos** (by caique), **Ramos** and **Sykamia**. Other coves and beaches can be reached by boat. There is a station for replenishing water supplies at Livadi and all the hotels, rooms and apartments are here, though there are a few rooms for rent in Chora.

28. Seriphos. Chora as seen from the harbour.

29. Seriphos has lovely sandy beaches and clear water.

Siphnos

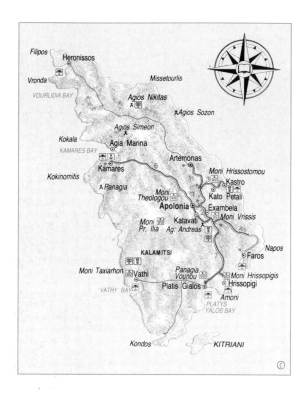

GEOGRAPHY. The fourth isle of the Western Cyclades lies between Seriphos, Kimolos and Antiparos. Seriphos is 74 sq. km. in area, has 70 km. of coastline and is 76 nautical miles from Piraeus. There is a car and passenger ferry from Piraeus every day, as well as connections with Seriphos, Kimolos and Melos, while during the summer there is a local service with Paros. The island's capital is Apollonia and its population is 2,027. A mountainous island (highest peak Profitis Ilias, 680 m. a.s.l.) intersected by small, fertile plains in the bays and along the coast. It also has considerable mineral wealth (schistose rocks, marble, granite and limestone). With its shining white houses, countless churches and lovely landscape, Siphnos is ideal for those seeking a quiet, island atmosphere, as well as for those wishing to combine relaxation with sophistication and company. The island is quite well equipped to cater for tourists and there are regular communications.

HISTORY. In ancient times Siphnos was extremely wealthy on account of its gold, copper and silver mines. It was first inhabited by Kar-

ians and Phoenicians who called it *Akys* or *Meropia*. Later it was called *Minoa* by the Minoans who settled there. In historical times it was colonised by Ionians and experienced a splendid floruit, as exemplified by the Siphnian Treasury, votive to the god Apollo in his sanctuary at Delphi. Prehistoric remains have been located at Kalamitsi, Aghios Andreas and Aghios Nikitas. Siphnos took part in the Persian Wars and afterwards joined the Athenian League. In Hellenistic and Roman times it followed the same fate as the other Cyclades and in the Byzantine period belonged to the Thema of the Aegean. Between 1207 and 1269 it was subject to the Venetian Duchy of Naxos. It was pillaged by Barbarossa in 1537 but only capitulated to the Turks in 1617, until which date the Gozzadini overlords managed to maintain their dominance. Siphnos played an active role in the 1821 Revolution and was liberated at the same time as the rest of the Cyclades.

SIGHTS-MONUMENTS. **Apollonia**, the island's capital, is built in its hinterland, spreading amphitheatrically over three hills. Its narrow streets with whitewashed paving stones are flanked by two-storeyed, brilliant white Cycladic houses, mansions of old families and churches (Virgin Ouranophora, Saviour, St. Sozon). North of Apollonia is the private convent of the *Theologian tou Moungou*. In town there is a folklore collection. 1.5 km. northeast, at a higher level, is picturesque **Artemonas** with its windmills on the crest of the hill and a stunning view. North of Artemonas is the Hellenistic tower of *Kastanas*. A pathway leads from Artemonas, through the olive groves and vineyards, to Kastro (there is also a metalled road from Apollonia, which is less picturesque). **Kastro**, built on a sheer cliff on the east side of the island overlooking the sea, has been inhabited since prehistoric times. Excavations have brought to light some finds from the Early Bronze Age, but mainly of the Geometric, Archaic and Classical eras. This was the island's capital until 1836 when it was transferred to Apollonia. Traces of the ancient acropolis on the northwest slope of the hill

30. Siphnos. Chora and Katavati as seen from Kato Petali.

31-32. Siphnos. Dazzling white houses and numerous churches typify this island.

33. Siphnos. Seaside settlement.

31

32

have been revealed in excavations conducted by the British School of Archaeology, as well as the foundations of houses dating to the 8th and 7th century BC. The castle we see today was thus arranged in the 14th century and is architecturally similar to those on Kimolos, Antiparos, Sikinos and Pholegandros, where the houses are built one joined to the other, forming the external enceinte, and parallel with these is a second, internal row of houses. Several of the many churches within the castle have survived (St. Eleousa, Dormition, St. Catherine, St. Demetrius, Forty Saints). Housed in the old Catholic church of St. Anthony of Padua is a small archaeological collection. At **Seralia**, southeast of Kastro, remains of the medieval harbour installations are preserved.

A short distance to the southeast of Apollonia are the villages of **Exambela** (2 km.), birthplace of the poet Aristomenis Provelengios (further south is the 16th century Vrysi monastery), **Kato Petali**, (with the nearby monastery of Chrysostom, built in 1550) and **Katavati** (3 km.). A path leads from here to the hill of **Aghios Andreas,** on which stands a church of that name, built in 1890. Prehistoric finds discovered in this region confirm its continuous habitation from Mycenaean till Hellenistic times. There are quaint little villages at **Platys Yalos** (10 km. south of Chora) and at **Vathy** (where there are also potters' workshops). Northeast of Platys Yalos is a ruined Hellenistic tower and, on an eminence above, the monastery of the **Virgin of the Mountain**. On a spit in the gulf of **Faros** stands the 17th century monastery of the **Virgin Chrysopigi**, protectress of the island. The **monastery of the Taxiarchs** is situated above Vathy and that of **Prophet Elijah** in the island's interior is the most important Byzantine monument on Siphnos, dating back to the 8th century, according to tradition, and with a 12th century marble iconostasis in its katholikon.

At **Kamares**, the island's port, there are potters' workshops. From here one can take a boat trip to the bays of Vathy, Platys Yalos and Faros with their shallow, sparkling waters and sandy shores. There are other beaches suitable for swimming at **Kamares**, **Chrysopigi**, **Seralia** below Kastro and **Chersonisos**, which is a long way off and can be reached by caique. There is a refuelling station for boats at Kamares. Accommodation is available in hotels, of which there are several, pensions and rented rooms.

Melos

GEOGRAPHY. Melos differs from the other isles of the Western Cyclades on account of its volcanic geomorphology, to which it owes its mineral resources. Surface area 151 sq. km., length of coast 126 km., distance from Piraeus 86 nautical miles. There are both car and passenger ferries from Piraeus, connections with Siphnos, Seriphos and Kimolos, via the route Piraeus-Kavala, with Pholegandros, Anaphi, Santorini, Aghios Nikolaos and Siteia in Crete, the Dodecanese and the islands of the east and north Aegean (once a week throughout the year). There is a local link with Kimolos and, during the summer, with Siphnos. Last but not least, there are flights from Athens. The island's capital is Melos (Plaka) and its population of 4,554 is engaged in agriculture, fishing and trade. The climate is mild, vegetation quite rich, the landscape lovely and there are plenty of sandy beaches beside its clear sea. There are good tourist facilities capable of providing services for many holidaymakers, attracted by its scenery, places of interest and the quiet island life of its attractive villages.

HISTORY. Melos holds an outstanding place in the history of the Aegean area in general. Inhabited since prehistoric times, it attained pre-eminence during the period of the Cycladic civilisation. Tools and artefacts of Melian obsidian have been found not only in the Cyclades but also in Crete, indicating the island's advanced development. Around the middle of the 2nd millennium BC it came within the Minoan sphere of influence and not long afterwards Mycenaeans settled here, to be followed by Dorian colonists in around 1000 B.C. Melos fought in the Persian Wars but because of its insistence on neutrality during the Peloponnesian War the Athenians launched two punitive campaigns against it, laying waste the land, decimating the male population and putting the women and children in bondage. Ten years elapsed before the island was resettled. In Hellenistic times it belonged to the Macedonians, heralding a new era of prosperity, based on the export of its mineral wealth. This acme is verified by such artistic creations as the Aphrodite (Venus) of Melos and the statue of Poseidon. There followed the Roman occupation and then the Byzantine era when it was harassed by pirates. At about this time (circa 800 AD) the area of Kastro was inhabited, being rebuilt later by the Venetians, who governed Melos under the Franks. It was sacked by Barbarossa in 1537 and later subjugated by the Turks. Throughout the Turkish occupation its harbour was a refuge for corsairs. Melos played an active role in the Struggle for Independence and was liberated along with the rest of the Cyclades. In 1853 Sfakiotes from Crete settled here, establishing its present port, Adamas.

SIGHTS-MONUMENTS. Melos' unusual shape is a consequence of volcanic activity in the depths of the harbour at **Adamas**. This is one of the largest natural harbours in the Mediterranean and the small town on its creek with its snow-white houses and cobbled streets is a hub of tourism and commerce. The important church of the Holy Trinity with its valuable icons is located here. **Plaka**, the island's main town, stands on a hill above the harbour (4.5 km.), its characteristic Cycladic houses commanding a unique view of the Aegean. It is dominated by the mass of its castle, to which the cobbled streets lead up beneath archways. The churches of the Virgin Thalassitria and St. Eleousa are preserved. Housed in the local Museum are notable finds from Neolithic times to the present, outstanding among which are the Cycladic figurines, obsidian tools and artefacts. The Folk Museum is housed in a 19th century building, along with

34

a creditable library. From the top of the castle one can survey the villages of **Trypiti**, **Triovasalos** and **Pera Triovasalos**. 2 km. south of Plaka is **Klima,** site of the ancient city of Melos in historical times, where sections of the fortification wall (6th – 5th century BC) have been revealed in excavation, as well as the auditorium of the theatre near **Treis Ekklesies**. Here too there are remains of an Early Christian baptistry and a three-aisled basilica, near which the site of the ancient stadium has been located. It was in this area that the statue of the Venus of Melos (now in the Louvre) was recovered in 1820. 7th century BC pottery has also been found here, as well as a number of so-called Melian vases with polychrome representations in the Orientalising style. In 1840 the famous **Katakomves** (catacombs) were uncovered at Klima, counterparts of

34. View of Melos, one of the loveliest of the Cyclades.

those in Rome and the only monuments of that kind. They consist of a system of underground passages 180 m. long and divided into three unequal sectors. Dated to the 3rd and 4th century AD, they were a place of asylum for the first Christians and also the place where they buried their dead. Indeed some 2000 bodies were laid to rest in graves along the passages and recesses. It is not possible to visit the catacombs. 12 km. east of Plaka is the village of **Apollonia** or **Pollonia** with its lovely seashore. Some 3 – 4 km. before this village is the prehistoric city of *Phylakopi* where excavations have brought to light three successive levels dated, on the basis of the finds, to the Early Cycladic (City I) Middle Cycladic (City

35

36

II) and Mycenaean (City III) period, the latter with its palace and fortified enclosure. Finds from this general area (mainly pottery and obsidian) have considerably augmented our knowledge of the Early Cycladic civilisation. Beneath the ancient city are the three *Papafranga caves,* formerly a pirates' lair. Southeast of Adamas (8 km.) is the village of **Zefyria** on the desolate site of Palaiochora which was abandoned at the end of the 18th century. To the north of the village is the ruined church of Christ, as well as the deserted, fortress-like monastery of the Virgin Kastriani. The churches of the Virgin Portiani (in which sections of wall-paintings are preserved) and St. Charalambos are of 17th century date. Among the island's Byzantine monuments is the church of the virgin at **Kipos** (5th century), while one of the oldest monasteries is that of St. Marina at **Chalakas**. The beach at **Chivadolimni** (8 km. from Adamas) is perhaps the most beautiful on the island. There are holiday villages at **Palaiochori** and **Emboreio**. All the beaches around the bay of Melos are delightful, as are those at **Apollonia**, **Provatas** and **Mandrakia**. There are therapeutic springs at Adamas, in the gulf of **Provatas** and at **Alyki**. On the southwest side of the island, below the monastery of St. John, is the *Smaragdenia* cave (Emerald cave) or *Sykia*, where the sunbeams filter through part of the roof, creating emerald reflections in the calm waters of the grotto. In the cliffs further south (3 miles) are the caves known as *Thalassina Meteora* or *Kleftiko* from which pirates launched their raids.

Fringing the north coast of the island are diverse rocky islets of volcanic origin (Akrathi, Arouda, Erimomilos), while in the vicinity of Pollonia there are the **Glaronisia**, one of nature's rarest and most impressive creations. They are formed of symmetrical, hexagonal columns of basalt, vertically or obliquely aligned and up to 20 m. high. To sail between them in a boat or caïque is a truly memorable experience. For those with a boat there are several other wonderful beaches (Chivadolimni, Emboreio, Provatas) and nearby islets and there is a refuelling station for yachts at Adamas. Visitors may choose accommodation in hotels, rooms or furnished apartments.

35. *Partial view of Plaka, the pretty capital of Melos.*

36. *Another view of Melos.*

Kimolos

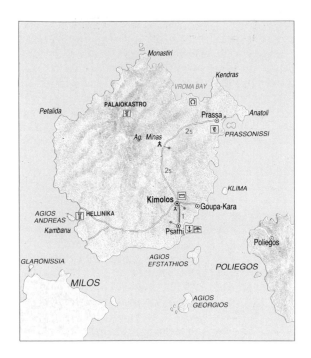

GEOGRAPHY. Southwest of Siphnos and very near Melos lies the island of Kimolos. 36 sq. km. in area, with 38 km. of coast line, it is 86 nautical miles from Piraeus and has 786 inhabitants. Its capital is Kimolos. The boat link with Piraeus is via Seriphos, Siphnos, Melos, with which islands there is also a local connection by caique. A predominantly mountainous island (highest point Palaiokastro, 397 m. a.s.l.) it is mainly known for its chalk (kimolia) which is used in porcelain. There has been no touristic development on Kimolos, which is an ideal place for holidays far away from the hustle and bustle of urban life and close to nature.

HISTORY. According to mythological tradition the island was named after its founder, Kimolos, and its history has always been intimately linked with that of neighbouring Melos, on which it was always dependent, even during Frankish times when it was called *Arzentiera*. After the marauding incursion of Barbarossa (1537) it passed into Turkish hands and was a haven for pirates.

SIGHTS-MONUMENTS. 2 km. north of the harbour (**Psathi**) is the island's capital, **Kimolos** (Chora) with its typical Cycladic houses clustered around the nucleus of the castle or Kastro, exactly like the houses around the castle on Siphnos. The castle consists of two concentric baileys formed by two contiguous rows of houses: Mesa (middle) Kastro, built in the 13th and 14th century, and Exo (outer) Kastro, a mid-17th century structure. Of the numerous churches, those of Christ (1592) and the Evangelistria (1608) are the oldest, while that of St. Chrysostom is particularly important. There is a small archaeological collection in the local Museum of Chora and another, mainly of sherds and pottery, in the Afentakeion Foundation. Opposite the coast, in the locality of **Ellinika**, 4 km. southwest of Chora, is the islet of **Aghios Andreas** or **Daskaleio** where foundations of houses, towers and other remnants of the ancient city of Kimolos are preserved, for this islet was originally joined to the island. It was cut off as a result of an earthquake and is now linked by a shallow channel. There was an extensive cemetery at Ellinika, while at **Limni-Varvarakaina** there is a cave in which there are graves (nowadays rifled), very like the catacombs on Melos. At **Palaiokastro** remains of the fortification wall are still visible, as well as vestiges of a small, round tower which the locals call *Portara*.

The sea and shores of Kimolos are truly lovely and can be reached by caique or on foot: **Psathi**, **Prasa** (with its sulphurous medicinal springs), **Alyki**, **Bonatsa**, **Ellinika**. The only accommodation available is in rented rooms.

37. Chora Kimolos, as seen from the harbour.

37

Syros

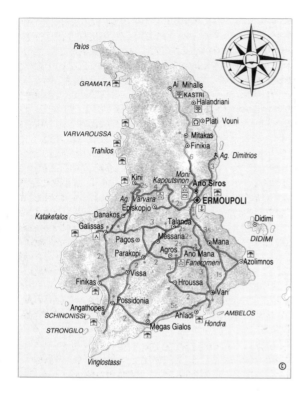

HISTORY. Excavations have verified the island's habitation since Neolithic times. The prehistoric acropolis of Kastri and the site of Chalandriani have both yielded finds of the Early Cycladic civilisation (2700 – 2200 BC). Phoenicians were settled here, the name of the village Phoinikas being a legacy of their presence. In historical times Syros was colonised by Ionians and had two large cities, one of which stood on the site of Hermoupolis. During the Persian Wars it initially sided with the Medes, though later joined the Athenian League. In Hellenistic times it was under the aegis of Macedonia and the Egyptian Ptolemies. In contrast with the other islands, Syros experienced an acme in Roman times, which, however, was eclipsed in Byzantine times. In 1207 it was a Venetian possession under the jurisdiction of the Duchy of Naxos. Then it was that the fortified town of Ano Syros was built on the hill to the west of the harbour. It was taken by the Turks in 1537. Many Catholics from the surrounding islands sought refuge on Syros which, with the support of Venice and the interest shown by the king of

GEOGRAPHY. In the centre of the Cyclades, between Kythnos, Tenos, Rheneia and Mykonos, Syros or Syra is 84 sq. km. in area, has 87 km. of coastline and is 83 nautical miles from Piraeus. There are daily passenger and car ferries from Piraeus, linking Syros with the other Cycladic islands, with Herakleion in Crete, Ikaria, Samos and Fournoi. A car ferry service from Rafina links Syros with Andros and Tenos. Hermoupolis, the island's main town, is also capital of the prefecture of the Cyclades, their administrative and commercial centre with a population of 19,668.

Syros is a mountainous island (highest point Pyrgos, 431 m. a.s.l.) particularly in the north, whereas in the south it is flat with small, fertile plains. As a consequence of this alternating terrain the coast is indented with small coves, headlands and two large bays: Phoinika on the west side and Hermoupolis on the east, with lovely beaches between, popular with visitors. The island retains much of its former grandeur and because of its facilities for tourists, natural beauty, historical and archeological monuments, one is assured of a pleasant stay.

France, developed into a bastion of the Latin faith. Shortly before the 1821 Revolution Syros enjoyed considerable prosperity and its harbour was a hive of commercial activity. Fugitives from persecution by the Turks sought asylum here and in 1822 refugees from Psara, Chios and Smyrna built Hermoupolis between Ano Syros and the waterfront. For almost half a century Syros flourished as a commercial, nautical and cultural centre. The development of Piraeus as the foremost port of Greece signalled its decline, but even today its population is largely involved in entrepreneurial and maritime activities.

SIGHTS-MONUMENTS. As one sails into the island's harbour, **Hermoupolis**, the view of the town is truly splendid, with its impressive mansions. Neoclassical buildings, houses with pronounced folk architectural elements extend upwards from the quayside to the brow of the hill. Of the public buildings the Town Hall in Miaoulis Square (designed by Ziller), built between 1876 and 1881, the commemorative statue of Miaoulis, the Municipal Theatre "Apollo", small-scale copy of La Scala in Milan, are of interest. Throughout the day Miaoulis Square with its elegant palm trees throngs with life, while in the late afternoon its

cafés are a favourite meeting place. Churches of note include that of the Transfiguration (the cathedral), the Dormition, St. Demetrius (3 km. out of town), St. Barbara, St. Nicholas and the Three Hierarchs. The seafarers' quarter, Vaporia, has narrow streets bordered by Neoclassical mansions. The Archaeological Museum houses significant finds and the public library has a rich selection of volumes old and new. The medieval town of Ano Syros, built in Venetian times, stands on the hill of San Giorgio. Its steep, stepped streets endow it with a special charm and at its pinnacle stands the Catholic church of San Giorgio, which acquired its present aspect in 1843, replacing a smaller, medieval chapel, now incorporated within its interior, which stood on the site of a 12th century Byzantine church. East of the church of San Giorgio is the Bishop's residence and nearby the Capuchin monastery and the Jesuit monastery. There are over 50 Catholic churches on Syros, both in Hermoupolis and other villages.

On the northeast side of the island (approx. 12 km. from Hermoupolis) is the site of **Cha-**

38. Syros. Hermoupolis. On the hilltop, left, the Catholic church of St. George, on the right the Orthodox church of the Resurrection.

38

39

40

landriani, dug by the Greek archaeologist Christos Tsountas who brought to light an important prehistoric cemetery (500 graves). The copious finds from here greatly enriched our knowledge of the Early Cycladic civilisation, particularly the early years of its floruit (2700 – 2200 BC). Other prehistoric cemeteries have been located on Syros (Pidna, Aghios Loukas). Northwest of Chalandriani, on the hill of Kastri, early and more recent excavators have brought to light a fortified settlement, one of the earliest in the Cyclades. From the rich finds, dating to the second half of the 3rd millennium BC, contact with Asia Minor can be inferred, According to tradition, at **Platy Vouni**, near Chalandriani, is the cave of the historian and philosopher Pherekides, pupil of Pittakos and teacher of Pythagoras, who hailed from Syros.

The southern part of the island is the most fertile and densely populated. Greenery abounds in the richly planted gardens of the old summer houses built by sailors and merchants from Hermoupolis. 2.5 km. from Hermoupolis is **Talanta** with its church of St. John the Theologian. To the southeast, in the area of **Ano Manna**, is the Phaneromeni monastery. **Vari**, the most beautiful holiday spot, is 9 km. from town and has a sandy beach and clear blue sea. In the bay of **Phoinikas** (12 km. from town) is **Poseidonia** (Della Grazia) one of the loveliest areas on the island, rivalled perhaps by **Parakopi** (4 km. further north). The sea and sand at **Angathopes** is irresistable, while at **Kini** on the west side (9 km. from Hermoupolis) one is assured of an enjoyable vacation. The beaches at **Galissa**, **Megas Yalos** and **Grammata** are also delightful, while one can swim at **Kymata** and **Aghios Nikolaos** right beside Hermoupolis. There is no problem in reaching any of the beaches and there is regular public transport. Caiques make trips from Kini or Hermoupolis to the more remote beaches (Varvarousa, Grammata) and it is easier to get to those on the northeast and northwest coast by boat, since access by road is rather difficult. Refuelling station at Hermoupolis. Accommodation is available in lots of hotels, pensions, furnished rooms or flats and even Neoclassical villas (Poseidonia, Manna).

39. The hill of St. George and Ano Syros.

40. Partial view of the harbour with the church of St. Nicholas.

41. Fishermen on Syros.

41

Paros-Antiparos

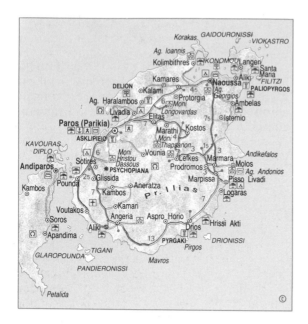

GEOGRAPHY. The third largest island in the Cyclades (after Naxos and Andros), Paros is 195 sq. km. in area, has 118 km. of coast and is 95 nautical miles from Piraeus. There are daily car and passenger ferries from Piraeus and a link with Rafina (daily during the summer, three times a week in winter). There is also a connection with Syros, Naxos, Ios and Santorini. In the summertime there are links with the Lesser Cyclades, Amorgos, Anaphi, Sikinos, Pholegandros, the Dodecanese and Herakleion in Crete. One route also goes to Samos and Ikaria. There are local services to Naxos, Ios, Santorini, Mykonos and Siphnos, as well as frequent sailings to and from Antiparos each day. There are daily flights from Athens and in the summer an air link with Rhodes and Herakleion (not very frequent). The island's capital is Paros (Paroikia) with a population of 7,881.

Because the mountainous masses are concentrated in the centre and southeastern part of the island (highest peak Profitis Ilias, 771 m. a.s.l.), there are several flat areas for cultivation and the beaches are easy to reach. There are two natural gulfs, Naoussa in the north and Paroikia on the west side. The mild climate, sandy beaches, picturesque villages with their attractive Cycladic architecture, lovely countryside and well-appointed tourist facilities entice a large number of visitors,

sometimes "swamping" the island. For those wanting to spend a cosmopolitan vacation Paros is perfect, while for those seeking solitude and serenity there are still many parts of the island of great natural beauty and "far from the madding crowd" of tourists.

HISTORY. Paros has been inhabited since prehistoric times when the Early Cycladic civilisation attained its apogee (3200 – 2100 BC). There was a Late Bronze Age installation on the summit of the hill at Paroikia and, as finds from here indicate, the island was also in contact with Mainland Greece. There followed a period of desolation and the island was resettled at the end of the Mycenaean age, though only sparsely. Minoans, Arcadians, Achaeans all settled on Paros and in around 1000 BC it was colonised by Ionians. In historical times, from the 8th century BC until the Persian Wars, the island experienced a sustained floruit; it was engaged in trading transactions with Miletus in Asia Minor and founded a colony on Thassos. This major acme was due to the quarrying of marble, used in the construction of many ancient temples and the creation of numerous works of art. During the 6th and 5th century BC there was a school of sculpting on Paros (Skopas, Agorakritos) and art and letters flourished. Paros was the home of the 7th century lyric poet Archilochos. The island sided with the Medes during the Persian Wars but later became a member of the Athenian League. It subsequently belonged to the Macedonians and then the Romans. Little is known of its course in the Byzantine period except for snippets of information on piratical raids. In 1207 it was captured by the Venetians and ceded to the Duchy of Naxos until 1389. It was then governed by a succession of families (Crispi, Sommaripa) until it was pillaged by Barbarossa in 1537 and subjugated by the Turks. Between 1770 and 1774 it was the headquarters of the Russian fleet under Orloff and it played an active role in the 1821 Revolution.

SIGHTS-MONUMENTS. **Paroikia**, the island's capital, lies on the west coast and is also its main port. It occupies the same site as the ancient city and its oldest quarter, more or less at the centre of the town, is clustered around the

42. Paros. Windmills at the harbour.

43. Partial view of Paroikia, the beach at Kato Yalos and Kastro hill.

42

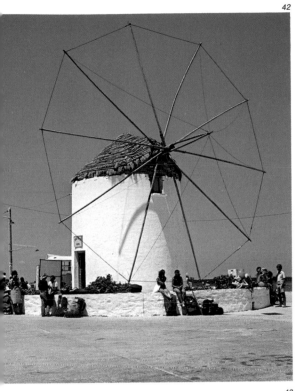

43

hill of Kastro on the southwest side of the harbour. It is a typical Cycladic town with paved streets, archways ("volta"), dazzling white two-storey houses interspersed with churches and windmills. A road leads from the harbour to the market place ("agora"), at the heart of the town, where all manner of wares may be purchased. The castle or Kastro stands on the highest point of the town, southwest of the harbour. It was built on the site of the ancient acropolis and much of the building material comes from ancient buildings, since column drums and fragments of marble are nowadays visible in the restored sector of the castle. Excavations conducted here have brought to light the ruins of an Archaic temple of Demeter (adjacent to the present church of St. Constantine). There are very few extant remains of the Venetian castle on the east and southeast flank (parts of the wall and a tower). The Byzantine church of St. Constantine is outstanding not only on account of its unique architecture but because of its gilded wood carved iconostasis. In various parts of the town there are handsome mansions belonging to eminent island families, some even with their coat of arms incorporated over the lintel. There are also many tiny churches with wood carved iconostases. However, the most important church of all is that of the Virgin Katapoliani (or Ekatontapyliani) on the northern outskirts of Paroikia. One of the oldest Early Christian basilicae in Greece, it was founded, tradition relates, by either St. Helen or St. Constantine. In the course of the study and restoration of this monument it became apparent that this large church dedicated to the Virgin (feast day August 15th) was built at the end of the 4th century. To right and left are small side chapels and to the south a Baptistry. During the reign of Justinian (6th century) additions were made to the church and it thus acquired the form we see today. There is a Byzantine Museum in one of the buildings in its precinct. The modern building a short distance from the church is the Archaeological Museum, in which are housed finds from the Neolithic to the Roman era. Noteworthy exhibits include vases, sculptures (Skopas' Nike) and a section of the Parian Chronicle (dated to Hellenistic times), found in 1627 built into the enceinte of the castle, on which events in the island's history from 2000 – 264/63 BC are recorded in chronological order. Ancient sanctuaries have been discovered at Delion (sanctuary of Apollo) to the north of the bay, near

44

45

the cave of Archilochos, on the Kounados hill (sanctuary of Aphrodite and Eileithyia) on the northwest side of the town, while in the southwest are ruins of an Asklepieion.

10 km. northeast of Paroikia is the gulf of Naoussa, the largest on the island. On the way to Naoussa, about 1 km. outside Paroikia, in the locality known as **Treis Ekklesies,** there are vestiges of an Early Christian basilica and three Byzantine churches, further on is the **Longovardas monastery** (6 km. from Paroikia), founded in 1638, which has a significant library and icon-painting atelier. **Naoussa**, with its pristine white houses, Postbyzantine churches (St. Athanasios, St. John the Theologian, the Saviour etc.), its monastery (St. George) and the little harbour with the Venetian castle is one of the most beautiful parts of Paros. From here one can visit the villages on the east and south side of the island (there is another road from Paroikia to these villages) **Marmara**, **Marpissa,** with its ruined Venetian castle on top of Kefalos hill and the monastery of St. Anthony, **Piso Livadi** and **Drios**, **Kostos** and **Lefkes**, with its 17th century church of the Holy Trinity. A short way beyond Lefkes is the **convent of Thapsana** with its miraculous icon of the Virgin Myrtidiotissa. In the locality of **Marathi** (4 km. from Paroikia) there is an ancient marble quarry. 6 km. from Paroikia is the region of **Psychopiana** with its verdant vegetation, running water and myriads of butterflies. Not far off is the nunnery of Christ of the Wood (tou Dasous), repository of the shroud of St. Arsenios. This is a convenient place for visiting villages on the south side of the island (**Alyki**, **Angairia**, where the airport is located), or to proceed to **Pounta** from where boats leave for Antiparos. Paros has a large number of beaches, ideal for swimming, fishing and sea sports. At Paroikia: **Livadia**, **Krios**, **Aghios Phokas**; at Naoussa (west side): **Mikro** and **Megalo Piperi**, **Limnes** and **Kolymbithres**, with its spectacular rock formations, reminiscent of sculptures; on the east side: **Aghioi Anargyroi**, **Xifara**, **Langeri**, **Alyki**, **Santa Maria**, **Ambelas**. All are easily accessible on foot or by bus and car, as well as by small craft which make regular trips, leaving from Paroikia for Krios and Livadia, and from Naoussa for Kolymbithres, Langeri, Santa Maria. There are

44-45. Quaint streets in Chora.

46. The little harbour at Naoussa and part of the village, as seen from above.

stretches of sand at **Logaras**, **Piso Livadi**, **Drios** and **Alyki**. Those with a boat may investigate other beaches, as well as the offshore islets. Refuelling stations at Paroikia and Naoussa. Paros has numerous hotels, pensions, furnished apartments and rooms available for a pleasant stay.

Antiparos

GEOGRAPHY. West of Paros is Antiparos, the largest of the islands lying along that littoral (Despotikon, Kavouras, Diplo, Saliagos, Strongylo). Area 35 sq. km., length of coast 57 km., population 635. Very close to Paros, there are local caiques from both Paroikia and Pounta, the nearest point on Paros. With its sandy beaches and sparkling clear water the island attracts an ever increasing number of tourists.

HISTORY. In ancient times it was known as *Oliaros*. Excavations carried out by the British School of Archaeology on the adjacent islet of Saliagos testify that there was a Neolithic settlement here, one of the earliest in the Cyclades (4500 – 3500 BC). An Early Cycladic settlement has been found on the nowadays uninhabited islet of Despotikon.

SIGHTS-MONUMENTS. The island's capital, **Antiparos**, is built around the original nucleus of the medieval castle, erected by the Venetians and very similar to that of Kimolos, where the outermost row of houses actually comprises the enceinte. On the hill of **Aghios Ioannis**, on the west side of the island, is the famous Antiparos Cave with its rich stalagmite and stalactite decoration and the tiny chapel of St. John Spiliotis at its entrance. The enormous stalagmite known as the Altar Table was thus named because on Christmas Day 1673 the French ambassador de Nointel celebrated midnight mass there, as we are informed by a commemorative inscription on its base. The sea around the island is shallow and there are many lovely beaches where one can swim - **Molos**, **Sifnaikos Yalos**, **Diapori**, **Soros** -while the surrounding islets are ideal for fishing. Visitors may stay in hotels on the waterfront or rented rooms in the village.

47. Naoussa, as seen from Kolymbithres.

48. Paroikia, the main shopping street.

49. Naoussa, inside the Venetian fortress.

Naxos

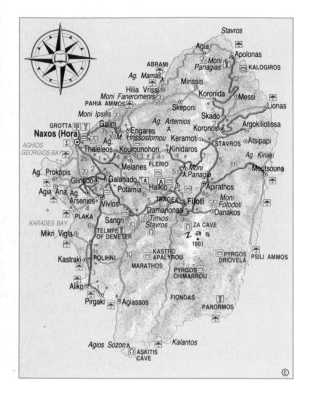

GEOGRAPHY. Naxos, in the midst of Mykonos, Amorgos and Paros, is not only the largest island in the Cyclades but also the most fertile. 428 sq. km. in area. 148 km. of coast, 103 nautical miles from Piraeus. There are car and passenger ferry links with Piraeus, as well as Paros, Ios and Santorini. Regular communications with Syros, Sikinos, Amorgos, Anaphi, Pholegandros and Herakleion (Crete) (less frequent during the winter). Car ferries from Rafina link the island with Paros, Syros, Tenos and Amorgos (infrequent). There is also a local boat service operating between Mykonos, Ios, Santorini, Siphnos and Seriphos and even with Amorgos, Schinousa, Herakleia, Kouphonisia and Donousa. Excursions by caique to Paros are also organised. The island's capital, Naxos (Chora) has a population of 14,037. Though a mountainous island (highest peak Za, 1004 m. a.s.l., the highest summit in the Cyclades), there are extensive tracts of flat land since the mountainous massifs are concentrated in the eastern and southern part of the island, which is also the most sparsely populated. In addition to its agricultural pro-

duce, Naxos has considerable mineral wealth (marble, granite, emery). Its green landscape, numerous sandy beaches, picturesque villages and abundance of archaeological and historic monuments attract many visitors, particularly those to whom an enjoyable vacation includes hikes and rambles. Whereas tourist facilities are good in Chora, they are somewhat rudimentary in the hinterland, as is the road network.

HISTORY. Tradition relates that Naxos was first settled by Thracians, bringing with them their cult of Dionysos. They were succeeded by Karians and Ionians. From the plethora and wealth of finds from excavations (Grotta), Naxos was evidently the centre of the Cycladic civilisation (3200 – 2100 BC), it was inhabited in Mycenaean times (Aplomata) and during the period of Ionian colonisation (circa 1000 BC) it experienced yet another floruit, culminating in the 7th and 6th century BC. It fought against the Persians in the Persian Wars, became a member of the Athenian League and subsequently passed to the Macedonians, Egyptian Ptolemies, Rhodians and, finally, the Romans. Raids by pirates were so frequent in Byzantine times that the inhabitants withdrew to its interior for protection and built reconnaissance towers from which they repelled the attackers. In 1207 Marcos Sanudos captured the island, establishing it as seat of the Duchy of Naxos and the Archipelago. In 1537 it was laid waste by Barbarossa, from 1566-67 it belonged to Joseph Naze and, eventually, capitulated to the Turks. It was liberated along with the rest of the Cyclades.

SIGHTS-MONUMENTS. Chora, the main town, is built on the west side of the island and is one of the most beautiful Cycladic towns, including monuments from all eras. On a tiny islet at the entrance to the harbour stands a large gateway (pyle) known as "Portara", which belonged to the incomplete Archaic temple of Apollo (6th century BC), purported to be Ariadne's palace in popular tradition. In Byzantine times a three-aisled basilica was erected here, which was destroyed by Turkish invaders in 1344 and was never rebuilt. The dominant feature of Chora, with its steep streets and old houses (sometimes three-

50. Naxos. Portara.

51. Partial view of Chora.

50

storeyed), is the Venetian castle, built in 1207 by Marcos Sanudos. The Catholic burghers lived inside the castle, whereas the Orthodox Greeks lived outside in Bourgos. There was also a Jewish quarter. Sections of the outer bailey of the Venetian castle are preserved, three gateways and seven towers. Within its confines there is an Ursuline convent, a Capuchin monastery, the Archaeological Museum (with important finds of the Cycladic period, sculptures and kouroi), the Byzantine and Folk Museum in a restored tower and, in the centre, the Catholic cathedral with the insignia of the Frankish families of the island above its entrance. Nearby is the nowadays ruined palace of the Sanudo family with their coat-of-arms. In addition to the old mansions in Chora, there are many notable Byzantine and Postbyzantine churches; the cathedral (Metropolis, 18th century), Virgin Chrysopolitissa (one of the oldest on the island), Prophet Elijah (with two important icons by the 16th century hagiographer Angelos). At Grotta: St. George (circa 1200) and close to Palatia St. Anthony of the Catholics (15th century). Excavations at Grotta have brought to light an installation from the early phase of the Cycladic civilisation with a wealth of finds, as at Aplomata (where there was continuous occupation right into the Geometric period – 8th century BC and there are even finds of 4th century date). This evidence, in conjunction with finds from elsewhere on the island, indicates that Naxos was one of the centres of the Cycladic civilisation. 3 km. from Chora is the monastery of **St. John Chrysostom**. Chora is a good base for visiting other villages on the island, seeing its lovely countryside, Venetian towers and churches. At **Angidia** (2 km. from Chora) there are remnants of an Archaic sanctuary and the twin (Catholic and Orthodox) church of St. Artemios. The Venetian tower of Belonia at **Calanado** was the summer retreat of the Catholic bishop in days gone by. Further south is the **monastery of the Holy Cross,** also known as Bazaios' tower. This area, called *Tragaia* in antiquity, is one of the most fertile on the island, dotted with charming houses, churches and towers.

At **Chalki** (Chalkeion) there are the important churches of the Virgin Protothroni (10th/12th century), St. George Diasoritis (11th cen-

51

tury), with significant wall-paintings and, to the east, the Venetian tower of the Barozzi, property of the Gratsias family. Other noteworthy churches are the Virgin Damniotissa (at **Kaloxylo**) and St. Nicholas at **Akadimoi,** where the Makropolitis tower also stands. At **Moni** (4 km. northeast of Chalki) stands the Byzantine church of the Virgin Drosiani (6th century), the oldest on the island. North of Chalki are the churches of St. Isidoros, the Virgin Rachidiotissa and the ruins of the Catholic monastery of St. Francis. West of Chalki are the ruins of the Venetian Ano Kastro (upper castle) (circa 1250). There are ruined Venetian towers at **Potamia,** as well as the church of St. Mamas (9th Century). The road from Chalki leads to the village of **Filoti** with its church of the Virgin (Dormition). On one of the peaks of mount Za, southwest of Filoti, is the *Za* cave or cave of the *Bacchae*, an ancient cult centre where, legend has it, Zeus was born. 7 km. east of Filoti is the village of **Danakos** and 4.5 km. northeast is the lovely village of **Apeirathos** with its markedly Venetian aspect in the architecture of the houses and the towers of the Sommaripa, Crispo and Sfortza-Kastri. In the local museum there is a significant collection of finds from the area, mainly of the Early Cycladic period. A short distance from the village are the churches of the Theologian (14th century), St. Kyriaki (9th century) and the Virgin (13th century).

There are equally charming villages to the southwest of Chora, with windmills and places of interest. At **Glinado** there is the church of St. George, while west of **Tripodes** is the church of St. Matthew and the ruined tower (Palaiopyrgos) of Plaka. Further south, near the coast, is **Polichni,** where there are traces of a prehistoric installation, as well as of a Venetian tower. The towers of Sammaripa, Della Rocca, Palaiologos and Barozzi at **Sangri,** the Byzantine churches of the Sts. Anargyroi, St. John on the site of the ancient sanctuary of Demeter and Persephone, St. Eleftherios, the Virgin Kaloritissa in the east and St. Nicholas in the south (10th/13th century), the Virgin Arkouliotissa and Sts. Akindynos and George all merit attention. South of Sangri is the ruined medieval *Apalyros* castle. Southeast is the impressive *Cheimarros tower,* which can be reached from Filoti. At Korfari ton Amygdalion in the gulf of Panormos, on the southeast coast, remnants of a fortified prehistoric settlement (2400 – 2300 BC) have been found.

In the village of *Galini* on the east side of the island, between Chora and Engares, is the Ypsili monastery, a fortified tower built by Iakovos Kokkos in 1600. There is a preserved Venetian tower at **Kourounochori,** from where the road leads south to *Kinidaros,* where there was a temple of Artemis. North of the village, at **Florio,** there is a half-finished Archaic kouros (6th century BC). One reaches the northeast side of the island via the road from Apeirathos, visiting the villages of **Koronos, Skado, Komiaki** and **Apollonas,** where there is a colossal, unfinished statue of a kouros in the form of Apollo (7th century BC) "in situ" on the ground. At Kalogeros, even further south, there is a ruined medieval fortress.

The best beaches are on the west side of the island: **Aghios Prokopis, Mikri Vigla, Kastraki, Alykos, Pyrgaki, Ayassos** with fine golden sand. Those on the east side **Apollonas, Psili Ammos** and **Panormos** and in the north **Pacheia Ammos, Chilia Vrysi** and **Abrami,** only accessible by private car or boat, are suitable for swimming and fishing. There are buses from Chora to all the beaches; the road to Panormos is unmetalled. Accommodation is available in several hotels, pensions, rented rooms and apartments. If one has a boat there are any number of small coves to discover. In the island's interior it is also possible to shoot birds and small game (northeast and southwest side) in season.

52. Naxos. Transport by boat.

53. Another view of Chora with the castle.

52

53

Andros

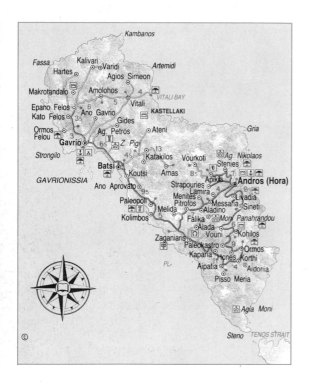

GEOGRAPHY. Andros is the northernmost island in the Cyclades, the second largest and the closest to Euboia, which is only 7 nautical miles away (Cape Kafirea or Cavo d'Oro). 380 sq. km. in area, 177 km. of coastline, distance from Rafina 36 nautical miles. There are car and passenger ferries from Rafina which also link the island with Tenos and Mykonos, as well as Paros, and Naxos (more frequent during the summer). The island's capital, Andros, has a population of 9,020. Its terrain is mountainous (highest point 994 m. a.s.l.), dissected by ravines and three lush, verdant valleys with running water. The coast is likewise precipitous and there are sandy beaches only in the south. As of old most of the inhabitants are seafarers. On account of its extraordinary scenery, therapeutic springs, picturesque villages and historic monuments, the island is gaining in popularity, despite the locals' objection to tourism.

HISTORY. Little is known about the island's remote past. It was colonised by Ionians in historical times and was closely associated with Athens and Euboia. Its acme lasted from the 7th to the 4th century BC, particularly in art and literature. Andros sided with the Medes during the Persian Wars, for which action the Athenians imposed a punitive tax. A member of the Athenian League, it supported Sparta in the Peloponnesian War, afterwards passing into Macedonian hands and, later, to the Romans who ceded it to Attalos of Pergamon. The floruit enjoyed in Byzantine times, despite persistent piratical attacks, was due to the thriving silk industry. In 1207 it was taken by the Venetians, belonging to the Duchy of Naxos, and was ceded to Marinos Dandolos. At that time towers and castles were erected all over the island to ward off marauding pirates. It was sacked in 1537 by Barbarossa and captured by the Turks in 1566. The insurgence against the Turks in 1821 was led by Kairis.

SIGHTS-MONUMENTS. The island's capital, **Andros** (Chora), is built on the southeast side on the same site as the medieval town. In appearance it is typically Cycladic with steep, narrow streets, pristine white houses, archways and churches. At Mesa Kastro, built by the Venetians on the tiny peninsula on the outskirts of Chora, parts of the ramparts, tower and vaulted stone bridge over the moat, uniting it with Kato Kastro, can still be seen today. Entry to Mesa Kastro was through a main gateway (oxoporta) and smaller, secondary gateways (paraportia). Sections of the walls and traces of the buildings have survived from the Kato Kastro. In Chora itself the churchs of the Virgin Palatiani and the Virgin Hodegitria are worth visiting, as is the Maritime Museum, the Archaeological Museum, with rich finds of all eras, and the Art Gallery with works by the sculptor Tobros.

To the south of Chora are the villages of **Lamyra**, **Strapouries** and **Ypsila** with their gardens and greenery, as well as **Menites**, one of the loveliest on the island with ruined towers and the church of the Madonna of Koumoulos. Further south is **Mesaria**, centre of the island in the 18th and 19th century, with the Kairis family tower and church of the Taxiarchs, built in the reign of Manuel Comnenus (1143 – 1180), according to an inscription, and with an 18th century marble iconostasis. The churches of Archangel Michael at **Melida** and the Dormition at **Mesathouri** are contemporary with the church of the Taxiarchs, while the

54

monastery of Panachrantos at **Fallika** was founded in 961 by Nicephorus Phocas, after the liberation of Crete. 9 km. southeast of Chora is the village of **Livadia** with its Frankish church, in olden days the Catholic cathedral. At **Apoikia** (northwest of Chora) are the Sariza springs and to the north the monastery of St. Nicholas (18th century). **Stenies,** another very attractive village to the north of Apoikia, has many handsome houses, mostly belonging to sea captains and sailors. One of the most beautiful regions of the island extends from just south of Chora as far as Korthi and includes several charming villages and Venetian towers. The church of the Virgin Phaneromeni at **Kochylos** merits a visit and the castle to the north, built in the early years of Venetian occupation, is variously known as *Apano Kastro, Palaiokastro* or *tis Grias to Kastro.* On the southernmost tip of the west coast, at **Zagora**, excavations have brought to light finds of the Geometric era (8th century BC), indicating that the region was also at its zenith during the 7th century. At **Palaiopolis**, on the west coast of the island, are the ruins of the ancient capital of Andros and its acropolis, which survived into Byzantine times. **Batsi** (27 km. northwest

54. Andros. Partial view of Chora.

of Chora), to the north of Palaiochora is extremely popular with tourists. **Aprovato,** north of Batsi, has a ruined tower and monastery of the Lifegiving Source (Zoodochos Pege), patron of the island. A road leads from Batsi to the village of **Katakoilos** and from there to the mountain village of **Arnas**, set in the midst of woodland. On the west side of the island is its main port, **Gavrion** (34 km. from Chora). On the north side of Andros, just beyond the village of **Aghios Petros** is **Kastellaki**, with a ruined tower. Further north, at **Makrotalanto**, the ruins of yet another medieval garrison are preserved. North of here are the villages of **Kalyvari** and **Varidi** and on the hill above them the remains of a fortress known as *Vriokastro*. Notable churches in the **Fellos** region (3.5 km. north of Gavrion) are those of St. Charalambos and the Transfiguration. The beaches in both bays at Chora, **Nimborio** and **Paraporti** are fine for swimming and sea sports, as are those at **Korthio**, **Batsi**, **Gavrion** and **Vitali**. For those with boats, water is available at Batsi and water and fuel at Chora. There are several hotels and furnished flats to let.

Tenos

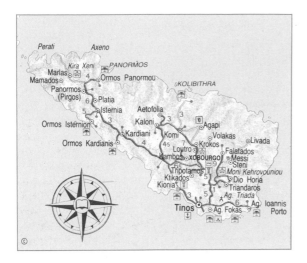

GEOGRAPHY. Tenos, the Holy island of the Virgin, lies between Andros (700 m.), Mykonos (8 nautical miles) and northeast of Syros (13 nautical miles). It is the fourth·largest of the Cyclades, after Naxos, Andros and Paros, covering an area of 194 sq. km., with 106 km. of coast and 85 nautical miles from Piraeus. Its population is 7,730. There are daily car and passenger ferries from Piraeus and Rafina (62 nautical miles), as well as links with Andros, Mykonos, Paros, Ios and Santorini. The island's capital and harbour, Tenos, is a convenient centre for visiting the other villages on the island, large and small. Tenos is essentially mountainous (highest peak Tsikinas, 713 m. a.s.l.) with a few small, fertile valleys. Its coast, mainly steep in the east, follows the configuration of the land, forming small bays, the largest and most sheltered of which is the gulf of Panormos on its northeast side. Tenos has its own, distinctive Cycladic charm: lush, verdant vegetation, small villages with snow-white houses, ornate dovecotes and numerous tiny chapels. There is limited touristic development and Tenos is just right for quiet holidays.

HISTORY. In antiquity the island was called *Ophiousa.* We have very little information about Tenos in prehistoric times though excavations (Vryokastro) have shown that it was inhabited in the Bronze Age, during the period of the Cycladic civilisation. Throughout antiquity, as indeed today, it was famed for its marble and there is a tradition of stone-carving. In the 8th and 7th century BC it was under the domination of Eretria. During the Persian Wars it was captured by the Medes, liberated after the battle of Marathon and took part in the naval battle of Salamis. It achieved its zenith in the 3rd century BC, while in the 2nd it was a naval station of the Rhodians. Tenos was taken by the Romans in 88 BC and decimated by Mithridates. During the Byzantine period it faded into obscurity and with the Fall of Constantinople to the Franks it, like the rest of the Cyclades, came under the control of Venice, which ceded it to the Ghisi family. The Venetians built a fortress on the pinnacle of a steep cliff on its south coast. Within its walls the Venetian nobles resided, while outside, at Exoburgo, the peasants dwelt. During the Venetian occupation many of the islanders adopted the Catholic faith. In 1538 it was pillaged by Barbarossa but did not fall to the Turks until 1715. Between 1770 and 1774 it was under Orloff. Many Greek refugees from Psara and Chios fled to Tenos during the Revolution of 1821. In 1822 the miraculous icon of the Virgin was discovered. It was in the harbour of Tenos that

the Greek warship "Elli" was torpedoed by the Italians in 1940.

SIGHTS-MONUMENTS.

Tenos, the island's capital, stands on its south side. It developed after the Venetians´ retreat in 1715 and is a typical island town with whitewashed houses and narrow streets. The most important monument there, and indeed on the entire island, is the church of the Virgin, built in 1823 following the discovery of her icon. It is an imposing edifice of white marble and has several ancillary buildings. The Museum of Tenian Artists and Modern Greek Painters is well worth a visit, with works by contemporary Greek artists, while in the Art Gallery there is a collection of reproductions of works by Renaissance painters. There is a rich library in the monastery and sacristy with vestments and ecclesiastical plate. Exhibited in the Archaeological Museum are finds from sites all over the island. East of the town of Tenos is the monastery of the Holy Trinity (1610) where there is a small collection of local folk art, and even further east is the Venetian harbour of Aghios Ioannis (Ai Yannis sto Porto). In the environs of the town and in the villages there is a proliferation of dovecotes; elaborately embellished, they constitute one of the distinctive features of the island. 5 km. northeast of Tenos is **Triantaros**, a picturesque village with a church of the Taxiarchs. Slightly to the north is *Dyo Choria* (two villages) built on a richly wooded hillside. From here one has a view of the nearby convent of *Kechrovouniou,* dedicated to the Dormition of the Virgin, where there is the cell of Hosia Pelagia, the nun who dreamt of the finding of the icon of the Virgin Evangelistria. There is a little chapel consecrated to her memory, as well as several other smaller churches and handicraft workshops. 2 km. northeast are the villages of **Mesi** and **Steni**. In the immediate vicinity is the monastery of St. Anthony with its magnificent Byzantine iconostasis. From Steni one can proceed to the villages of **Myrsini** and **Falatados**. Remains of the Venetian castle and medieval town are preserved 3 km. from Steni, at Xobourgo. In addition to the Venetian ramparts and ruined castle, some ancient Greek remains can be discerned (8th/7th century BC) in the area between *Xobourgo* and *Xynara*. The Ursuline convent at **Loutra** was renowned for its school. The next village, **Komi**, is one of the largest on Tenos and has many authentic

55. Tenos. The town and harbour as seen from the sea.

55

56

57

Tenian houses in good condition. A minor road leads to **Kolymbithra**, one of the most delightful beaches on the island's east side. From Xobourgo one can also visit **Kampos**, and further northwards one passes through the villages of **Tarabados** with its ornate dovecotes and **Kardiani** with its quaint houses and little churches. Immediately after Kardiani is the village of **Ysternia**, where many modern artists live, and northwest of here is one of the oldest churches on Tenos, that of St. Athanasios (1453) and the monastery of the Virgin Katapoliani (1786). The largest and perhaps loveliest village on the island is **Pyrgos**, (Panormos) with a long tradition in stone-carving and painting, birthplace of many Greek artists. There is a museum of works by Yannoulis Chalepas in his family home and there are ateliers of sculpting, painting and wood-carving. The houses in Pyrgos are characterised by their ornate exteriors particularly of carved marble. There are also elaborately decorated fountains and several interesting churches, of St. Eleousa and of the Presentation of the Virgin. About 3 km. distant from Pyrgos is the picturesque bay of **Panormos** which is quickly growing into a holiday resort. 5km. northwest of Pyrgos, at **Marlas** is the nowadays abandoned monastery of Hosia Xeni.

Northwest of the town of Tenos is **Kionia** (3 km.), in an attractive setting with a unique view of the open sea. Excavations have brought to light ruins of the 3rd century BC temple, initially for the worship of Poseidon and later of Amphitrite, one of the major cult centres in the Cyclades in antiquity.

Several of Tenos' shores are ideal for swimming and fishing, as well as sea sports. The beaches at **Aghios Phokas**, **Kionia**, **Ai Yannis sto Porto**, **Kolymbithra**, the bay of **Kardiani** and **Ysternia** are particularly beautiful, and further north is the bay of **Panormos**. All are accessible by car. One can shoot birds and small game in the island's mountainous hinterland. For those with a boat there are plenty of beaches to explore. Refuelling stations in the harbour.

56. The pretty villages of Tenos have quaint houses and churches.

57. Ktikados, a particularly beautiful village on the southwest coast.

58. Tenos. The church of the Virgin.

59. Mass in the the church of the Virgin, Tenos.

Mykonos

GEOGRAPHY. Despite its sophisticated ambience and thousands of visitors, Mykonos, between Tenos and Naxos, is still one of the most beautiful isles of the Cyclades. 85 sq. km. in area, with 81 km. of coastline, there is a regular boat service to and from Piraeus (110 nautical miles), as well as Rafina (71 nautical miles). Flights to the island are equally frequent and during the summer months there are planes to Rhodes, Herakleion in Crete and Santorini. Car and passenger ferries from Piraeus link Mykonos with Syros, Tenos, Paros, Ios, Santorini, Naxos (less often). Once a week there is a ferry from Rafina via Andros, Tenos and Syros. Finally, small local craft make excursions to Paros, Ios and Santorini (only during the summer) and Tenos. Mykonos has a population of 5,530. Renowned for its lovely beaches and distinctly Cycladic atmosphere, Mykonos attracts a host of visitors, arriving here by all possible means, including cruise liners.

HISTORY. Information about Mykonos' past is scant, for the island was not particularly important in antiquity. It was colonised by Ionians in historical times and, judging from its meagre participation in the Athenian League, apparently remained impoverished. The ancient geographer Skylakas reports the existence of two cities on Mykonos: one on the west side, close to the present town, the other in the north, at Paliokastro. In the time of the Ptolemies the island experienced something of a floruit, as also under Roman rule, though this waned in the Byzantine era. Along with Tenos it was ceded to the Ghisi family between 1207 and 1390, from which date it was directly dependent on Venice. In 1537 it was laid waste by Barbarossa and then conquered by the Turks. Thence forth the islanders turned to piracy. One of the major events in its history was the setting up of the "Community of Mykonians" in 1615. By the end of the 18th century Mykonos had achieved an economic acme, assembling a mercantile fleet which was later to play a supportive role in the Struggle for Independence in 1821. One of the outstanding personalities of that time was the Mykonian Mando Mavrogennis. From the late 1950s onwards there has been sustained touristic development leading to a new period of economic prosperity.

SIGHTS-MONUMENTS. The most important monument in the island's capital, **Mykonos** (Chora), built on its west side, is the church of the Virgin Paraportiani, outstanding among the 400 or so churches throughout the island, according to local tradition. It is located in the quarter of Kastro and its architecture, a combination of Byzantine, folk and Western elements, is unique. The quarter of Kastro is situated on an elevated area and it was here that the Venetians built their castle, only vestiges of which are nowadays visible. On the south side, beneath Kastro, is "Venice", an enclave of quaint old houses actually built in the water, their wooden balconies and doors giving the captains who lived here in days of old direct access to the sea. In one of the squares not far from here the cathedral (metropolis) stands, as well as an old Catholic church. On the ridge nearby there is a row of windmills, standing sentinel. This seems to have been the site of the ancient city. Objects displayed in the Archaeological Museum, at the northeast edge of the town, mainly comprise finds from Rheneia: sculpture, vases and figurines, while in the Folk Museum in Kastro, there is a collection of furniture, icons, sculpture and folk musical instruments. In addition to the many volumes in the Municipal Library there is a col-

60. Mykonos. Chora and the harbour.

61

62

lection of Hellenistic coins and recent seals. The Nautical Museum, recently established, is also of interest.

Chora, with its narrow, winding streets, archways, dazzling white houses and distinctive architecture is a veritable labyrinth, with a harmony and equilibrium which set it apart from other Cycladic towns. The island's villages have their own "couleur local", dominated by stark white volumes, grey rocks and paucity of vegetation. 1 km. south of the town, at **Lino**, are the ruins of a tower known as "Portes" by the locals. In the same area, on the north side of **Platys Yalos**, is the subterranean cistern known as Yannaros' Well (Pighadi tou Yannarou). In the region of **Ano Mera** (6 km. from the town) stands the monastery of Tourliani, founded, so tradition relates, by two Parian monks in 1542 on the site of an earlier church. It acquired its present aspect in 1767. The elaborately decorated, Western-style belltower adds a distinctive touch to the monastery's exterior. Further north, at **Palaiokastro**, there are remains of a fortification and the convent of Palaiokastro, a 17th century building. A pathway leads up to a knoll behind, on which there are remnants of an enceinte. From the remains of buildings and other finds of the Archaic and Classical period it is surmised that the hill was settled in antiquity. There is a small church in the centre. In this general area (Panormos bay) there are other prehistoric remains and at its western edge, in the locality of Mavri Spilia, an albeit limited number of Neolithic finds have been recovered. From Ano Mera one can easily reach **Kalafatis** (12 km. from Chora) one of the most beautiful beaches on the island. There are seaside villages at **Tourlos**, **Aghios Stefanos** (3.4 km. north of Chora), **Ornos** and **Platys Yalos** (south). Beaches in the south of the island paricularly good for swimming and sea sports are **Psarou**, **Aghia Anna**, **Paradise** and **Super Paradise** (for nudists) and **Elia**. All can be reached by bus or caique from Chora or Platys Yalos. There are plenty of hotels, rooms and furnished flats to cater for the needs of the many visitors.

61. *Picturesque corner at the water's edge.*

62. *In the quaint, unspoilt villages of Mykonos the locals still engage in traditional tasks.*

63. *"Venice", Mykonos.*

64. *Another view of the harbour.*

63

64

Delos

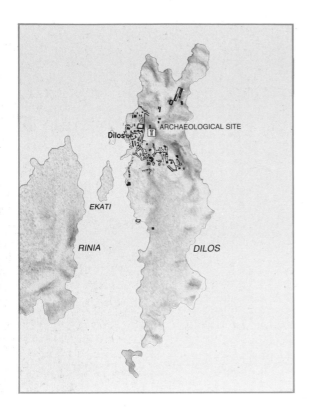

In ancient times a sacred isle, birthplace of Apollo, Delos now attracts myriads of visitors, all coming to marvel at its monuments. Now-adays uninhabited and very close to Mykonos (3.5 nautical miles from its westernmost head-land) there is a daily boat service with it. In the summer caiques making excursions from other Cycladic islands also call here. A small canal separates it from the island of Rheneia.

Delos was known as **Ortygia** in antiquity and, according to myth, Leto sought refuge here, escaping the wrath of Hera, and gave birth to Apollo and Artemis. Archaeological evidence attests that the island was inhabited as early as 3000 B.C. In Mycenaean times a settlement existed on the west side where there was also a shrine to a female deity. It seems that the Ionian colonisers who arrived in around 1000 BC introduced the cult of Apol-lo, god of light and music. From the 9th cen-tury BC Delos became the centre (political and religious) of an Amphictyony of Ionians living in the Aegean islands, under the hegemony of Naxos. In the 6th century BC the Athenians joined this Amphictyony, on the pretext of

their Ionian provenance. After the end of the Persian Wars (478 BC) Delos became the cen-tre of the Athenian/Delian League and it was here that the representatives of the League's members met annually to confer. The com-mon treasury of their contributions was also kept here until 454 BC when it was transferred to Athens. In 426 BC the island was cleansed or purified, the bones of the dead removed from their graves and deposited on the neigh-bouring island of Rheneia. Thence forth it was forbidden to give birth or die on Delos. When the successors of Alexander the Great came into the ascendancy Athenian influence on the island was displaced and it became independ-ent, the centre of diverse alliances under the Macedonians, Egyptians and Rhodians. In 166 BC the Roman Senate passed a decree placing Delos once again under the aegis of Athens. In 88 BC it was laid waste by Mithridates, its monuments destroyed and its population of some 20,000 souls decimated. Close on its heels, in 69 BC, came a new disaster from which the island never recovered, remaining deserted, a haven for corsairs. In 1872 the French Archaeological School began system-atic excavations there, which still continue today.

Delos is a vast archaeological site extending from its west side, which was the sacred har-bour in ancient times. On the northwest side are the **Propylaia** and Agora of the Competali-asts or **Hermaists**, founded in the 2nd century BC and used by Roman merchants and freed slaves. Immediately beyond is the **Sacred Way** with bases for "ex votos". To the west stood the large Stoa of Philip, built in around 210 BC and opposite this is the so-called **South Stoa** (3rd century BC) and **South Agora** or **Agora of the Delians**. The **Sanctuary of Apollo** was lo-cated northeast of the Stoa of Philip, consist-ing of three temples dedicated to the god, of which the foundations of the third, the "temple of the Athenians", are nowadays visible. A lit-tle before the temple of Apollo stood the **Oikos of the Naxians** (6th century BC) and the **Stoa of the Naxians** (mid–6th century BC), to the north the **Horn Altar** (Keratinos) and northeast the **temple of Artemis,** built in the 2nd century

65-66. Delos. The Sanctuary and the Archaic lions:

65

66

BC upon the ruins of a previous temple of the 7th century BC. On the north side of the temple of Apollo were the so-called **Treasuries** and east of these the **Prytaneion** (mid–5th century BC). Southeast of this was the **altar of Zeus Soter,** protector of seafarers and, on the north side the **temple of Dionysos** (early 3rd century BC) and the Stoa reputedly founded by Antigonos Gonatas at the end of the 3rd century BC. To the west were diverse buildings, the **Ekklesiasterion** where the Boule of the Deme of the Delians met and the **Thesmophoreion**, a 5th century edifice associated with the cult of Demeter. Situated on the north side of the sanctuary, in the quarter of the lake, was the **Agora of Theophrastus,** the **Sanctuary of the Twelve Gods of Olympus**, the **Temple of Leto** and the **Agora of the Italians**. A road led from the temple of Leto and north of the Sacred Lake to the famous Avenue of the Lions, votive of the Naxians in the 7th century BC. Only five of the original seven lions are still extant. At a slightly lower level lay the **Sacred Lake** on which the swans of Apollo swam in antiquity and which was filled in with earth following an outbreak of malaria in 1926. Northwest of the Avenue of the Lions was the **Koine of the Poseidonists** of Beirut, centre of merchants who worshipped Poseidon, two palaestrae, the **sanctuary of Archegetes**, the **Gymnasium** and the **Stadium. The quarter of the Theatre**, to the south of the Sanctuary was the major residential area and the houses of the Hellenistic and Roman periods were decorated with mosaics. From here one can easily reach the museum in which finds from the excavations on the island are housed. To the east of the Theatre quarter are remnants of various structures, while a road leads to the eminence of Kynthos, on the summit of which Zeus and Athena were worshipped. Northwest of the House of the Masks are remnants of the ancient **Theatre** (17 to 26 tiers of seats), which had a capacity of 5,500 spectators and was built in the 2nd century BC.

67. Mosaic floor from the House of Masks.

68. Mosaic floor with representation of a Panathenaic amphora from the House of the Trident.

69. Mosaic floor from the House of Masks. Dionysos is shown mounted on a panther, crowned with a wreath of vine leaves.

70. Mosaic floor from the House of Dolphins.

Ios

GEOGRAPHY. To the south of Naxos, between Sikinos and Thera, Ios (Nios) is 108 sq. km. in area, has 81 km. of coast and is 107 nautical miles from Piraeus. Its capital is Ios (Chora) with a population of 1,451. There are car and passenger ferry links with Piraeus and the islands of Paros, Naxos, Santorini, Sikinos and Pholegandros, Siphnos, Syros, Anaphi, Herakleion in Crete. During the summer there are regular connections by local craft with Santorini, Paros, Naxos, Mykonos and Tenos and daily trips to Sikinos and Pholegandros. A mountainous island (highest peak Pyrgos. 732 m. a.s.l.) it has no cultivable tracts of land and its coast consists of dozens of tiny bays and three larger ones: Aghia Theodoti in the east, Kalamos in the southwest and Mylopotamos in the west. Its wonderful sandy beaches, crystal clear sea and serene landscape with olive groves and vineyards attract hordes of tourists in quest of tranquility and communion with nature.

HISTORY. Mythology relates that the island was first settled by Phoenicians. It is also claimed to be the last resting place of Homer. In historical times it was colonised by Ionians, became a member of the Athenian League and later passed into the hands of the Egyptian Ptolemies. During the Roman period it was a place of exile and in Byzantine times faded into oblivion. From 1207 onwards it belonged to the Duchy of Naxos, was a perpetual victim of piratical attacks and in 1537 was captured by the Turks. It continued to be a refuge for corsairs. Ios participated in the 1821 Struggle for Independence.

SIGHTS-MONUMENTS. **Ios**, the island's capital is located in the centre of the west side, overlooking the harbour. It is built on the site of the ancient city and is dominated by the mass of its medieval castle, built in the 14th century on the same spot as the ancient acropolis. Remnants from ancient structures have been located also in Psathi.

Chora is a typical Cycladic town with dazzling white houses, narrow streets and many churches, outstanding among which are those of St. Catherine, erected on the site of the ancient temple of Apollo, the Forerunner, and Sts. Anargyroi. The northern outskirts of Chora are delimited by a series of windmills and from this ridge one has an unimpeded view in all directions: the gulf of Kalamos to the east, the gulf of Aghia Theodoti to the south and the ruins of a medieval castle at **Palaiokastro**. At **Plakoto**, on the north coast of the island, is "Homer's Tomb" and the ruins of a Hellenistic tower known as *Psaropyrgos*. Special attention should be paid to the numerous chapels on the island which, according to local tradition, exceed 300.

The bays and beaches of Ios —**Aghia Theodoti**, **Psathi**, **Kalamos**, **Manganari**, **Mylopotas**, **Ormos**— are ideal for swimming and fishing and are easily reached by caique. For those with a private boat there are numerous secluded bays but there is no refuelling station on the island. There are plenty of hotels and furnished rooms to cater for the needs of the many visitors.

71. Picturesque windmill on Ios.

72. Old men in traditional Cycladic costume walk up a lane in Chora.

73. Ios. View of Chora with its characteristic windmills.

71

72

73

Pholegandros

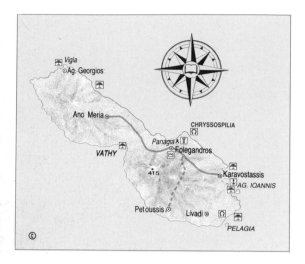

GEOGRAPHY. Between Sikinos (5 nautical miles) and Melos (15 nautical miles), Pholegandros has a surface area of 32 sq. km., 40 km. of coastline and is 105 nautical miles from Piraeus. Its capital is Pholegandros (Chora) with 567 inhabitants, mainly concentrated there but also in a few scattered hamlets. In the summer there is a daily link with Piraeus and regular connections with Paros, Naxos, Sikinos, Ios and Santorini and, less frequently, with Syros, Siphnos, Seriphos, Delos, Herakleion in Crete, the Dodecanese, Chios, Samos, Mytilene, Ikaria, Lemnos and Kavala. Local craft make trips to Sikinos and Ios during the summer season. A mountainous island (highest peak Aghios Eleftherios, 415 m. a.s.l.) with little provision for tourists, it is an ideal place for a restful vacation.

HISTORY. Karians are mentioned as the island's first settlers. They were succeeded by Phoenicians and then Cretans. In historical times it was colonised by Dorians, became a member of the Athenian League and under Roman rule was a place of exile. From 1207 till 1607 it was governed by the Gozzadini family, then it was captured by the Turks. It was pillaged by pirates many times.

SIGHTS-MONUMENTS. **Chora** stands in an elevated position (200 m. a.s.l.) above the harbour and consists of the quaint old quarter around Kastro, the castle built by Marco Sanudo in 1212 which is architecturally very simi-

lar to those of Siphnos and Kimolos in which the external row of houses comprises the outer wall. Two of the entrances to the castle are preserved and three little churches. The more recent sector of the village is equally picturesque with its dazzling white houses, narrow streets and courtyards. On the northeast side of Chora, at **Palaiokastro** are remnants of fortifications and ruins of the ancient city. The church of the Virgin is actually built on part of the city wall. Further south is the *Chrysospilia,* a cave with stalagmites and stalactites, evidently used as a cult centre in antiquity but as yet unexplored. In the region of *Ano Meria,* on the northeast side of the island, there are traces of a small fortress at "Kastelli". Southwest of Ano Meria is the small bay of Aghios Georgios with a lovely beach. There are numerous tiny churches all over Pholegandros, most of them for private worship.

One can swim at **Karavostasis**, the island's harbour and in *Aghios Georgios* bay below Ano Meria, which one can reach in the local bus. Accommodation is available in rented rooms.

74. Pholegandros. An alleyway in Chora with its unspoilt Cycladic architecture, quaint byeways, pristine white houses, stairways and wooden balconies, contrasting sharply with the grey rocks on which it is built.

75-76. Two views of the harbour.

74

75

76

Sikinos

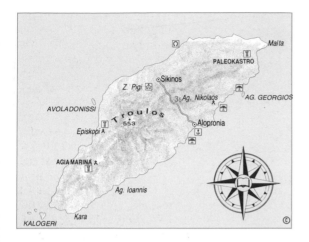

GEOGRAPHY. Very close to Ios (10 nautical miles) and Pholegandros, Sikinos is 41 sq. sm. in area, has 41 km. of coastline and is 120 nautical miles from Piraeus. During the summer there is a regular boat service with Piraeus, as well as with the islands of Pholegandros, Ios, Santorini, Paros, Naxos, Syros, Anaphi, Kimolos, Melos, while in the wintertime connections are maintained with Syros, Paros, Naxos, Ios, Pholegandros, Santorini and Anaphi. The island's capital is Sikinos (Chora) with a population of just 290, living in Chora and around the harbour. A mountainous island (highest peak Troullos, 600 m. a.s.l.) with tiny plains and a rocky coast, it has remained off the tourist track and is therefore an ideal spot for peaceful holidays on quiet beaches by the clear sea, but with somewhat spartan living conditions.

HISTORY. The island was known as *Oinoe* in antiquity and, from the archaeological data, was evidently inhabited some time during the Mycenaean period. Both Ionian and Dorian colonisers reached Sikinos and it was later under the domination of the Macedonians, Egyptian Ptolemies and the Romans, for whom it was a place of banishment. In 1207 it was annexed to the Duchy of Naxos and ruled by the Da Coronia and Gozzadini families. It fell to the Turks in the 17th century and was pillaged by pirates in 1774.

SIGHTS-MONUMENTS. North of the harbour, **Alopronoia** or **Ano Pronoia** (3.5 km.) is **Chora** with its bright white two-storey houses, narrow alleys and impressive mansions in the quarter of Kastro, though virtually nothing has remained of the actual castle. A short distance from Chora is the ruined monastery of the Life-giving Source, with its homonymous church in the Byzantine order. Southwest of Chora, at **Episkopi**, are the ruins of a Heroon (according to most recent research) of Roman times and on exactly this spot the church dedicated to the Dormition was built. Further south, at **Aghia Marina**, are ruins and foundations of buildings of the ancient city. At **Palaiokastro** on the northeast side of the island there are vestiges of the fortifications and traces of buildings. From here there is a magnificent view towards Ios.

Tourist facilities on Sikinos are absolutely minimal, the road network poor and access to the shore difficult. However, there are some beautiful beaches which can be reached by boat: **Aghios Georgios**, **Dialiskari**, **Aghios Panteleimon**, suitable for swimming and fishing. Visitors may stay in rented rooms.

77. Sikinos. Looking down on the flat roofs.

77

Anaphi

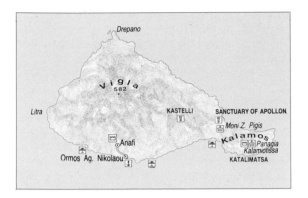

GEOGRAPHY. Anaphi is the southeastern-most island of the Cyclades, isolated from the rest of the archipelago, its nearest neighbour being Thera (12 nautical miles away). 38 sq. km. in area, with 32 km. of coastline, it is 272 nautical miles from Piraeus. In the summer there is a regular boat service from Piraeus, once a week in winter. Again in the summer there is a link with Ios and Santorini and, less frequently, with Syros, Paros, Naxos, Sikinos, Pholegandros. Once a week there is a connection with Crete, the Dodecanese, the isles of the north and east Aegean and Kavala when the boat on the route Piraeus -Kavala calls in. Its capital is Anaphi (Chora) with a population of 292. Its terrain is mountainous (highest peak Vigla, 584 m. a.s.l.) and there are no tracts of cultivated land. Virgin soil as far as tourism is concerned, Anaphi is fine for those wanting to withdraw from the world and get back to nature.

HISTORY. Mythology relates that the island was named by the Argonauts for whom Apollo caused it to appear, to rescue them from a storm. Phoenicians are mentioned as its first inhabitants, succeeded by Dorians who colonised it in historical times. In the following centuries its fate was the same as that of the other Cyclades and in 1207 it was annexed to the Duchy of Naxos, under which jurisdiction it remained until 1537 when, following its sacking by hayr ad Din Barbarossa, it was captured by the Turks.

SIGHTS-MONUMENTS. **Anaphi** (Chora or Chorio, as it is called by the locals), is built more or less in the centre of the island, its bright white, single-storey houses with white-washed courtyards and steep, narrow streets arranged amphitheatrically around a hill some 300 m. high. At the top are the remains of the ancient city -graves, foundations of buildings and sections of the rampart. Nothing has survived of its sanctuaries (Apollo Pythios, Artemis Soteira, temples of Sarapis and Isis). Close to the chapel of the Virgin are parts of a sarcophagus. At **Katalimatsa** (southeast of Chora) there are other ruins, while at the southeastern edge of the island there was a sanctuary of Apollo in ancient times, founded by the Argonauts. Upon its ruins the monastery of the Virgin Kalamiotissa was built on the summit of the rugged mount Kalamos. Only the church has survived —renovated after the 1956 earthquake— in which the icon of the Virgin is kept. In addition to the monastery there are vestiges of buildings and ruins of the fortifications of the Venetian castle, perhaps that referred to in Venetian documents as Kastro Gibitroli. The Kalamos region is particularly steep, as is the rocky north coast in general, whereas, by contrast, the southern shores are sandy. All the beaches can be reached by caique and are fine for swimming and fishing. There are rooms to let in Chora and at the harbour (Aghios Nikolaos).

78. Anaphi. Typical corner in Chora.

78

Amorgos

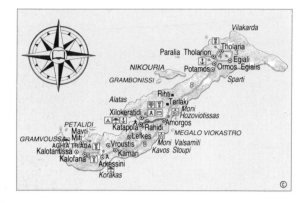

GEOGRAPHY. Amorgos is the easternmost island of the Cyclades, lying between Naxos, the Lesser Cyclades and Astypalaia. 121 sq. km. in area, 112 km. of coastline, it is 240 nautical miles from Piraeus. Both the island's ports are linked with Piraeus, five days a week during the summer (Katapola) and three times a week throughout the year (Aigiali). During the summer season there is also a boat from Rafina to Katapola once a week. The island's capital is Amorgos (Chora) with a population of 1,718. The terrain is mountainous (highest peak Krikelon, 821 m. a.s.l.) and is bisected by a mountainous ridge which effectively divides the island into two sections, east and west, with fertile valleys in between and flat, fertile strips around the two bays (Katapola and Aigiali). The authentic Cycladic atmosphere, beautiful beaches and relaxed rhythm of life in its small villages are idyllic conditions for those seeking a quiet vacation without particular comforts, since there are few facilities for tourists and the road network is undeveloped.

HISTORY. Data from excavations conducted on the island demonstrate not only that it was settled in prehistoric times, but that it experienced a significant floruit during the period of the Cycladic civilisation. Apart from pottery, weapons and tools, a series of figurines has been discovered (nowadays in the National Archaeological Museum, Athens) of exceptionally harmonious proportions and large size. In historical times three cities existed on the island - Aigiale on its northeast side, Arkesine (present-day Kastri) in the west, which were founded by Ionian colonisers from Naxos, and Minoa (near Katapola), settled by

Samian colonisers during the 7th century BC. Commerce and seafaring brought prosperity to the island and art and letters flourished. The lyric poet Simonides lived here around the middle of the 7th century BC. A member of the Athenian League, Amorgos passed to the Ptolemies of Egypt in Hellenistic times, later to the Romans, while in the Byzantine period it was part of the Thema of the Aegean. From 1207 onwards it belonged to the Duchy of Naxos and after its sacking by Barbarossa in 1537 was captured by the Turks. Throughout its history the island was plagued by piratical incursions.

SIGHTS-MONUMENTS. **Chora**, the island's capital, northeast of its harbour, *Katapola,* is a picturesque village with steep, narrow streets, windmills, brilliant white houses and remnants of the Venetian castle (sections of the enceinte, battlements and ruined buildings) built in the 13th century. A small archaeological collection of finds from all over the island is housed in an 18th century mansion in town. Northeast of Chora, perched on a precipitous cliff 300 m. a.s.l. is the **Chozoviotissa monastery,** a multi-storey building, according to one tradition founded in the 11th century by the emperor Alexios Comnenus, and to another by monks from Palestine. The monastery is dedicated to the Virgin (Feast of the Presentation, 21st November) and in it are housed valuable manuscripts and icons. About 15 km. northeast of Chora is **Aigiali**, reached by boat from Katapola. There is a road from Chora to Aigiali and though less comfortable it gives one the opportunity of seeing the island's landscape (remember to take a supply of water). At *Terlaki* and *Richti* there are ruins of Hellenistic towers. The gulf of Aigiali with its three white hamlets —**Potamos, Langada, Tholaria**— is one of the loveliest regions on the island. Only a few remnants of ancient Aigiale have survived —ruins of the Archaic and Classical fortification wall on the eminence Vigla where the ancient acropolis was. A pathway leads from Langada to the abandoned monastery of St. John the Theologian with its lovely wall-paintings. The island's main port, **Katapola**, on its west side comprises three settlements— **Katapola, Rachidi** and **Xylokeratidi**. During the 19th century it was a thriving port

and anchorage for ships, since it is sheltered from prevailing winds. Northwest of the harbour is the site of ancient *Minoa,* of which only scant vestiges are preserved. In the environs of the church of the Virgin Katapoliani, built on the site of an Early Christian basilica, stood the temple of Apollo Pythios. On the southeast side of the island is another deserted monastery, of **St. George Balsamites**, founded in 1631. Nowadays only the homonymous church is preserved. West of it there was a water mill and above this are traces of a Venetian tower. A path leads from this point to *Marmara* where there is a ruined Cyclopean wall and the foundations of buildings. On the southeast side, beyond the villages of **Vroutsi** and **Kamari**, where there is a Byzantine church of St. Nicholas, is the site of ancient *Arkesine.* Remains of the fortifications of the ancient city are preserved, the most important on the entire island. The acropolis was located on a low eminence where the church of the Virgin Kastriani stands today. Foundations of houses can also be discerned on the hill, dating from the Classical to the Roman period, while the site was occupied even in prehistoric times, as evident from pot sherds. Remains of the Venetian fortification are also preserved. North of Arkesine and close to the church of the Holy Trinity, stands the Hellenistic tower popularly known as *Pyrgos tou Choriou.* In the area of **Kalofana** there are ruins of three similar towers.

The island has several beautiful beaches suitable for both swimming and fishing. Apart from those at **Katapola**, the other beaches are only accessible by caique: **Arkesine, Kalotaritisa, Faros, Aghia Anna, Paradeisia.** Those visitors with their own boat may explore other coves and even nearby offshore islets, **Anydros**, **Kynouros** and **Nikouria**. Accommodation is available in furnished rooms and apartments in Chora, Aigiali and Katapola and there is hotel at Aigiali.

79. *Amorgos. View of Chora from the castle.*

80. *The Chozoviotissa Monastery.*

Lesser Cyclades

This is the name given to a group of tiny inhabited and uninhabited islands lying south of Naxos, between Ios and Amorgos: *Herakeleia, Schoinousa, Kouphonisia, Keros, Antikeros, Aghios Ioannis, Dryma, Makaries* and *Daskaleio* and *Donousa* (east of Naxos). There is a twice weekly boat service from Piraeus via Amorgos. Isolated islands with somewhat primitive facilities, they are only suitable for those intrepid travellers wishing to return to nature. Finds from excavations indicate that most of these islands were inhabited in prehistoric times.

On **Herakleia** there are traces of a Cycladic settlement and a ruined medieval fortress. Remains of Hellenistic and Roman installations can be seen on **Ano** and **Kato Kouphonisia**.

Excavations on **Keros** have brought to light a significant Early Cycladic settlement and very important finds of that era, among the most splendid from the whole of the Cyclades. These include the two marble figurines of musicians (Harpist and Flautist), nowadays in the National Archaeological Museum in Athens.

On **Donousa** too a prehistoric settlement has been revealed, as well as remnants of a fortified installation of Geometric times.

Apart from their unspoilt environment these islands have sparkling seas, lovely beaches and are wonderful for swimming and fishing. There are no refuelling stations and only limited accommodation in rented rooms.

81-85. Fishing is almost the sole occupation of the islanders on the smaller Cyclades. Characteristic moments in the fishermen's life with its many joys and great anxiety.

83

84

85

Thera

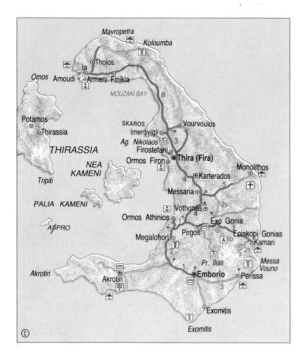

GEOGRAPHY. Thera or Santorini is quite unlike the other Cycladic islands on account of its geomorphology, resulting from the activity of its now dormant volcano. The present configuration of the island is due to the sinking of the caldera and it is surrounded by two other islands, Therasia and Aspronisi. Thera is on the southernmost fringe of the Cyclades, between Ios and Anaphi. It is 76 sq. km. in area, has 69 km. of coastline and is about 200 nautical miles from Piraeus. There is a daily boat service from Piraeus and with the rest of the Cyclades, daily during the summer. The boat on the Piraeus-Kavala route also goes via Santorini, linking it with Crete, the Dodecanese and the islands of the east and north Aegean, while in the summer there is a local connection with Ios, Paros, Naxos and Mykonos. There are also flights to Mykonos, Rhodes and Herakleion Crete. The island's capital is Phira, its main port is Athinios and its population is 7,083.

Most of the island's terrain is covered by deposits of volcanic material, its west coast is sheer cliffs, while its east side is an extensive, fertile plain. In the interior of the island is the mountainous mass of Profitis Ilias (565 m. a.s.l.).

Santorini's unusual landscape, impressive architecture, wealth of monuments and overall fascination attract visitors in their thousands, especially during the summer months. They arrive by all possible means, including cruise liners and its albeit well-developed tourist facilities are often insufficient to cope with them all. However, despite this deluge of tourists the island's picturesque aspect remains unspoilt and one can just as easily spend a quiet holiday as a cosmopolitan one.

HISTORY. In antiquity the island was known as *Strongyle* (perhaps because of its shape); it is also referred to as *Kalliste* (the most fair) and, historians tell us, was settled by Phoenicians. Excavations have shown that the island was inhabited in prehistoric times, during the Early Cycladic period (3200 – 2000 BC), and the dig at Akrotiri (Sp. Marinatos – continued by Christos Doumas) indicate that the island reached its apogee during the ensuing period (2000 – 1550 BC), which was cut short by the eruption of the volcano in 1500 BC. Finds from the area of Monolithos suggest that the island was reinhabited from at least the 13th century BC. Around 1000 BC Dorian colonisers arrived here, led by Theras, after whom it was named. In historical times its capital was on Mesa Vouno and contacts were established with Cyprus, Crete, Melos, Paros, Rhodes, as well as Attica, Corinth and Asia Minor. Therans founded the colony of Cyrene and in the 6th century BC minted their own coinage. In the following years it remained affianced to Sparta, but in 426 BC became a member of the Athenian League. On account of its strategic position it was used as base by the Egyptian Ptolemies in Hellenistic times and an anchorage for ships was established in the harbour of Elefsis. The island's decline commenced in Roman times, though in the Byzantine period its political and military siginificance was exploited once more. From 1207 onwards it belonged to the Duchy of Naxos and was governed by several noble families —Barozzi, Crispo, Pisani. Though well fortified —castles and garrisons— the island was the victim of numerous piratical attacks, culminating in that of Barbarossa in 1537. It was ceded to Joseph Naze until 1579 and then taken by the Turks.

86. Phira. View of the centre of the village.

87

88

The Latin occupation not only influenced the political and economic organisation of the island but also the religious, since many Therans were converted to Catholicism. During the 19th century there was a flourishing economy based on shipping and Thera's contribution of vessels to the 1821 Struggle for Independence was superceded only by Hydra and Spetses.

SIGHTS-MONUMENTS. Phira, the main town, is built amphitheatrically on the west side, atop the rim of the sunken caldera. A serpentine path of broad steps unites it with the harbour *(Ormos Phiron)* —much quicker ascent is assured in the recently built funicular railway— from which there is an astonishing view of the bay and the sheer cliffs. The architecture of the houses is unique; small, blinding white, with vaulted roofs and tiny windows. In and amongst stand grander mansions with courtyards. A little way beyond the Archaeological Museum is the Dominican convent, incorporating a cultural centre and school of carpet-making. Adjacent to it is the Catholic cathedral; the Orthodox metropolis is on the south side of town. North of Phira, at **Merovigli**, once the home of aristocratic families, the remains of many impressive bourgeois mansions can be seen and the convent of St. Nicholas (founded in 1674). At its western extremity is **Skaros**, site of the medieval capital which endured until the early 17th century, from which time it was gradually abandoned. In 1811 the capital was finally transferred to Phira. From the harbour of Phira one can take a caique trip to the volcano, **Nea Kameni**, with its cinderous rocks and sulphurous vapours and warm gases issuing from fissures. There are thermal springs on neighbouring **Palaia Kameni**.

On the south side of the island, close to the present village of **Akrotiri**, is the prehistoric city, revealed in excavations begun by the late Professor Sp. Marinatos in 1967 and continued by Professor Chr. Doumas.

The entire city with houses, streets, squares and workshops was destroyed by the volcanic eruption of 1500 BC and remained buried beneath the mantle of pumice and ash. Of the many finds recovered —pottery, stone tools and vessels, minor objects, bronze tools and vessels— the wall-paintings are outstanding, their subjects and style testifying to the society's high level of artistic and cultural achievement. Many of the finds from Akrotiri are exhi-

89

bited in a special gallery in the National Archaeological Museum, Athens. The excavation, with its building complexes, is open to the public. 1.5 km. away from the site is the present village, which the Venetians called "La Ponte". In addition to the remains of its once mighty castle, there are the churches of the Presentation of Christ (Hypapante) and the Holy Trinity. East of Akrotiri is **Emboreion** (9 km. south east of Phira) where there was another sturdy castle in medieval times, remnants of which still stand on a low knoll. The **Goulas** on the northern outskirts of the village is a square tower built during the Turkish occupation to protect the property belonging to the Patmos monastery of St. John. From here one reaches the beach of **Perissa**. A pathway leads from here to the region of **Mesa Vouno**, site of ancient Thera, which can also be approached from Kamari, as well as from Pyrgos. Excavations carried out by Hiller von Goetringen uncovered the agora, temene, temples, theatre, gymnasium, public edifices and private residences, that is the remains of the city which was the island's capital in the 8th century BC and continued in use until at least the 1st century BC. Notable finds from here include an intact Archaic clay figurine and pottery. The churches of St. Stephen, built on the ruins of an Early Christian basilica, and the Annunciation are also inside the archaeological site. At the base of Mesa Vouno is the 19th century monastery of Perissa. About 4 km. south of Phira is the village of **Mesaria** with several old mansions, and slightly further south is **Vothonos** with its quaint houses and churches, of the Virgin in Trypa, actually set in the rock, and St. Anne. To the southeast is **Exo Gonia** and then **Mesa Gonia** with the Byzantine church of Episkopi, dated to the 11th century, in which there are valuable icons and significant wall-paintings. 1.5 km. to the west is the village of **Pyrgos**, its picturesque houses built amphitheatrically on the hill slopes. In the Middle Ages the village was fortified with a castle of the same type as on Siphnos and Kimolos, where the outermost row of houses comprised the enceinte and with a garrison at its summit —Kastelli— which is still in rather good condition. The 10th century Byzantine

87. *Mending nets beside the sea.*

88. *Traditional ascent from the harbour.*

89. *Oia, as seen from Ammoudi.*

church of Theotokaki stands here. From Pyrgos one can continue one's ascent to the monastery of Prophet Elijah, an 18th century building housing sacred keimelia, a small folklore museum and an icon-painting atelier. A bend in the main road brings one to **Megalochori** where there are ruins of a small 3rd century BC temple and the churches of the Presentation of the Virgin, Sts. Anargyroi and St. Nicholas Marmaritis. Southeast of Phira (7 km.) is the quiet little village of **Monolithos**. On the northwest side of the island (10 km. from Phira) is the traditional village of **Oia** which is particularly well preserved, its pristine white houses and brightly coloured vaults, courtyards and mansions endowing it with a special beauty. East of Oia (1.5 km.) is yet another unspoilt village, **Phoinikia**.

Most of Thera's beaches (many with black sand and pebbles) are concentrated on its east side and are particularly good for swimming. Good beaches on the north coast are those near **Oia**, **Armeni**, **Ammoudi** and **Baxedes**. There is a refuelling station for boats at Athinios. There are plenty of hotels, pensions, furnished rooms and apartments, as well as all manner of places of entertainment. The most popular beach is **Kamari**. Directly opposite Oia is the little island of **Therasia** (4 nautical miles from Phira) to which caiques make regular trips. A winding, stepped path leads up to the village with its lilliputian houses. There are a few rooms to let.

90
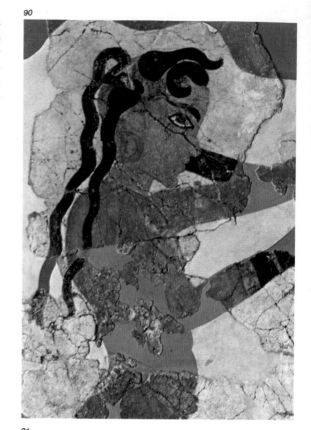

91

90. Detail from the wall-painting of the "Boxing Children". The themes and style of the wall-paintings found in the prehistoric city at Akrotiri, Thera bespeak the island's high level of cultural and artistic achievement in those days.

91. Detail from the "Spring fresco". Without doubt the most wonderful of all the wall-paintings, its subject is the rebirth of nature.

92. The Fisherman. One of the best-preserved wall-paintings with a markedly naturalistic tendency.

92

Euboia

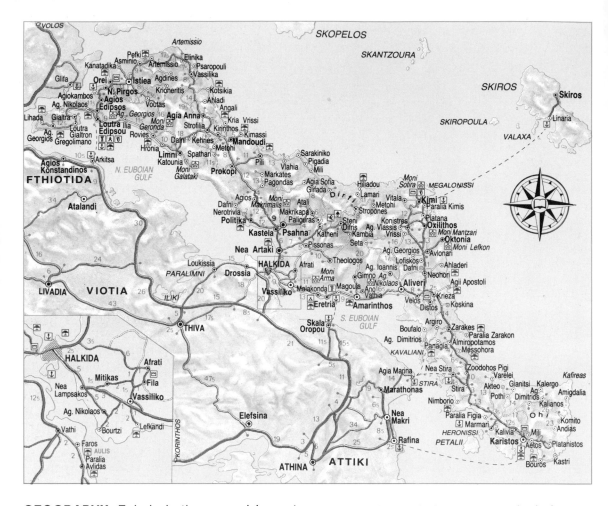

GEOGRAPHY. Euboia is the second largest island in Greece and the seventh largest in the Mediterranean. Lying opposite the northeast coast of Attica and the east coast of Boiotia, it extends along their entire length. Its terrain is virtually identical with that of the mainland, being mountainous, intersected by fertile plains and valleys along the coast. There is dense afforestation and an abundance of timber and other tree products, as well as rich arable farming, stock raising and poultry-rearing. The climate is mild and the sea sparkling clean in both the north and south Euboian gulf, due to the currents in the Euripos straits. Close to Athens, with a lovely verdant environment, sandy beaches, many places of interest and developed tourist facilities, Euboia is ideal for all manner of vacations.

Throughout the island there are extant re-minders of its turbulent past, particularly towers, Byzantine churches and medieval fortresses. The road network on Euboia is extensive and one can nowadays visit many parts previously difficult of access. The island's capital is Chalkida, 88 km. from Athens. Euboia is 3,654 sq. km. in area, has 678 km. of coast and 185,626 inhabitants. The centre of the island is occupied by the mountainous massif of Dirfys (1745 m. a.s.l.) and there are other, lower peaks. One can reach Euboia by road, railway (as far as Chalkida) and car or passenger ferry from Oropos to Eretria, from Rafina to Nea Styra, Marmari, Karystos, from Arkitsa to Aidipsos, from Volos to Orei and from Glyfa to Aghiokampos. There are also car ferries between Kymi and Skyros (Daily), Skopelos and Halonnisos (more frequent in the summer), Skiathos, Aghios Efstratios, Lemnos and Kavala (once a week) and even with Volos (twice weekly during the summer and once in the winter) and Trikeri. Apart from the numerous hotels and rooms to let there are many restaurants, tavernas, and grill houses. One can also engage in such sports as swimming, tennis, water-skiing, fishing, hunting and mountaineering.

HISTORY. In ancient times the island was called *Makrys, Makre* or *Doliche* and it has been inhabited since late Neolithic times. In its central and western part there was a high incidence of settlements, particularly in the Early Bronze Age (2600 – 2000 BC) when trade links were developed with the Cyclades. In Mycenaean times (1600 – 1200 BC) the island was densely populated and participated in the Trojan War, sending 40 ships. In the course of displacements and migrations of populations within the helladic area (1200 – 1000 BC), Thessalians, Dryopes and Dorians came to Euboia. The island attained its zenith during the 8th century BC. when its two major cities, Chalkida and Eretria, founded colonies in both western Greece, southern Italy and Sicily. These two cities were not long in coming into conflict over rights to the "Plain of Lilantion", which extends between them, traversed by the river Lilas and even today the most fertile part of Euboia. After a dispute with Athens, Euboia was forced to submit to Athenian lotholders between 506 and 411 BC. The large city of Eretria was pillaged and destroyed during the Persian wars, at the end of which the island came under Athenian domination. It was a member of the Athenian League (378 BC), belonged to the Macedonians for a brief interval and was taken by the Romans in 194 BC. In 1204, as a Byzantine province, it fell to the Franks who divided it into three ridings. The many towers and fortresses scattered throughout the island date from those days. From 1366 onwards it was in Venetian hands and known as Negreponte, a name originally applied only to the Euripos strait but quickly assumed by the whole island. It was taken by the Turks in 1470, under whose domination it remained until 1829, the year of its liberation.

The island is divided into three large geographical units, Central, Northern and Southern Euboia.

Central Euboia

SIGHTS-MONUMENTS. The island's capital,

Chalkida (pop. 44,867) is located on the west side of Central Euboia. A modern town with high rise buildings, plenty of hotels, restaurants, tavernas and patisseries, it is built beside the Euripos strait, well-known for its marked tides. Nowadays a movable bridge connects Chalkida with the opposite shore. Even in antiquity there was a movable wooden bridge (441 BC on this spot, facilitating the passage of ships sailing north-south, and vice versa, through the gulf of Euboia to avoid the open sea. The site of the ancient city is to the east of the present town. Almost nothing has survived of the agora, houses and other buildings mentioned by ancient authors. The city was first inhabited in Neolithic times and achieved its acme in the 8th century BC, when it founded colonies in the Chalkidiki peninsula, South Italy and Sicily. In the protracted dispute with Eretria for control of the fertile Lilantion plain it became subject to Athens in 506 BC, entailing compulsory acceptance of 4000 Athenian lot-holders as landlords. In the battle of Salamis (480 BC), Euboia fought alongside the Athenians and joined the Second Athenian League (378 – 377 BC), it belonged to the Macedonians for a short time and in 196 BC was taken by the Romans. During the Frankish occupation it constituted one of the three Baronies of Euboia. It fell to the Turks in 1470, from whom it was liberated in the 1821 Revolution. Hardly anything has survived of the medieval and Turkish buildings which once stood in Chalkida. Remnants of the Turkish garrison are preserved on top of the hill, which had even been fortified in the 4th century BC. In the quarter of the Kastro (castle) an early Christian church of St. Paraskevi has survived, originally the nave of the church of the Perivleptos, altered by the Venetians and converted into a mosque by the Turks, it was dedicated to St. Paraskevi in 1833. The town has a Folk Museum, Art Gallery and Archaeological Museum, housing important finds from excavations on the island, including the outstanding sculptures from the pediment of the temple of Apollo Daphniphoros at Eretria.

Chalkida is a convenient starting place for trips to other scenically beautiful parts of mountainous Central Euboia. **Kathenoi** (23 km.) with its Byzantine chapel (12th century) of the Presentation of the Saviour. **Steni Dirfys** (33 km.), set in the midst of woodland on the slopes of mount Dirfys, a summer and winter resort with picturesque springs, is a conglom-

93. Aerial view of Chalkida. The bridge across the Euripos strait where the tide ebbs and flows every 6 or 7 hours.

erate of three settlements; **Ano Steni**, **Kato Steni** and **Pyrgo Skouteri**. **Stropones** (10 km. northeast of Steni and 48 km. from Chalkida) is a mountain village with a Byzantine church of the Dormition of the Virgin. Southeast of Chalkida (8 km.) is another lovely village, **Vasiliko**, with ruins of a Frankish tower, along with two hamlets, *Lefkandi,* where excavations have brought to light settlements from prehistoric till Geometric.times, and **Kampos**.

Even further south of Chalkida (22 km.) is **Eretria**, a focus of routes to many parts of Euboia and the Sporades. The city was built in the 8th century BC, the time of its economic and artistic floruit, and was one of the most important on the island. Between the 8th and 6th century BC Eretrian vases were famous throughout Greece. In 490 BC it was destroyed by the Persians. However, it was not slow in recovering its strength and took part in the naval battle of Salamis, sending 7 triremes. A member of the Athenian League, in 446 BC it was forced to sanction the allocation of its land to Athenian citizens. In 411 BC it fought against Athens as an ally of Sparta, but in 377 BC it joined the Second Athenian League. Throughout the 4th, 3rd and 2nd century BC a large part of central and southern Euboia was under its control. In 198 BC it was sacked by the Romans and in 87 BC was destroyed yet again and remained desolate until 1824 when refugees from the decimation of Psara were resettled here and it was appropriately named *Nea Psara*. The ruins of the ancient city are very close to the present town: sections of the fortification wall of the Classical period, remnants of the 4th century BC theatre, as well as of the sanctuary of Dionysos, the palaistra and the gymnasium are preserved. On the top of the acropolis are the remains of the large sanctuary of Apollo Daphnephoros (6th century BC). In the local museum one can see finds from Eretria and Lefkandi.

The sandy beaches on the coast of Eretria and the modern hotel complexes make it an attractive holiday resort.

East of Eretria (9 km.) is **Amarynthos**, an attractive country town which has developed into a tourist centre in recent years. There was a sanctuary here in antiquity where Artemis Amarysia was worshipped and in whose honour the Amarysian games were held. From Amarynthos one can easily visit the mountain villages of **Kallithea** and **Gymno** (6 km.) or take a trip to **Aliveri** (25 km.), a seaside town known as *Tamynai* in ancient times when a sanctuary of Apollo existed there, in whose honour games were held. Other interesting features in the town include some old houses, a Venetian tower and Byzantine church of the Dormition of the Virgin, a four-columned nave dated to 1310/1311 with relief decorations from an Early Christian basilica on its exterior (5th century).

Just beyond Aliveri the road forks - the left branch leads to Avlonari and the right to Kymi. **Avlonari** is a quaint, traditional mountain village (44 km. from Eretria) with stone-built houses with tiled roofs and wrought-iron balustrades. There is a Byzantine church of St. Demetrius (11th century) and a medieval tower. In the direction of Kymi there are another two villages, typical of the region, **Ochthonia** (9km. from Avlonari), with traces of the medieval garrison, and **Oxylithos**, with Byzantine churches dedicated to the Dormition of the Virgin, St. Nicholas and St. Anne, as well as the Mantzaris monastery, the katholikon of which dates to the 11th century. It is possible to travel along the coast from Oxyithos to Kymi (one can also follow another route from Avlonari, which leads directly to Kymi).

Kymi is set in a green, wooded area (44 km. from Eretria) overlooking the sea. It is a town with a rich history, being one of the most important Euboian cities in antiquity (in the 8th century BC it participated in the founding of colonies in southern Italy), as well as in recent times (its fleet played an active role in the 1821 Revolution). Nowadays it is famed for its therapeutic spring of Choneftikon. The church of the Virgin Liaoutsanissa and the monastery of the Transfiguration of the Saviour, above which stands a preserved medieval fortress, are worth visiting. Swimming and fishing along the coast between Ochthonia and Kymi is excellent.

South Euboia

SIGHTS-MONUMENTS. On the road from Aliveri to Karystos one passes through the following villages: **Lepoura**, **Krieza** (7 km.), the remains of the ancient city of the Dryopes, **Dysto**, **Styra** (73 km. from Eretria) with the nearby Cyclopean structures known locally as

94. View of the modern town of Eretria.

95. The archaeological site of Eretria. The West Gate, palace complex and theatre can be seen.

"Drakospita" (Dragon lairs), **Nea Styra**, which is developing as a tourist centre thanks to ease of access and communication with Athens. **Marmari** (97 km. from Eretria) takes its name from the coloured marble of the region, much sought after since antiquity. The islets opposite, **Petalioi**, of which Tragonisi, Xeronisi and Megalonisos are uninhabited, are a popular summer resort.

Karystos (102 km. from Eretria) encircles the shores of the homonymous gulf and attracts a host of tourists due to its frequent connections with Athens, via Rafina. Ruins of the ancient city, renowned in antiquity —as today— for its marble, are preserved in the locality of **Palaiochora**, along with those of the medieval **Castel Rosso**. The modern town was planned and designed by the Bavarian architect Bierbach in 1841, on the orders of king Otto, which, is why it was also known as *Othonoupolis* until 1862 when it reverted to its ancient name. Sights of interest there include a Venetian castle, the ruins of a Byzantine castle, the suburbs with their 18th century buildings, the cathedral (metropolis), small local museum and, of course, the densely wooded glades with brooks and springs. From Karystos one can easily visit villages in the mountains, as well as those of the Cava d'Oro (Cape Kafireas), the most notable being **Platanistos**.

North Euboia

SIGHTS-MONUMENTS. Modern country towns, verdant villages and seaside resorts comprise Northern Euboia. 16 km. north of Chalkida is **Psachna** with its nearby convent of the Virgin Makrymalli and St. John Kalyvitis. Not far away is another town, **Politika,** set in the midst of rich woodland in which stands the convent of the Virgin Perivleptos with its 12th century katholikon, decorated with wall-paintings of Turkish times. **Prokopi** (52 km. from Chalkida) is a small village created in 1925 by refugees from Asia Minor and in its church of St. John the Russian, the saint's relic is preserved. Other features of interest in the area include the enormous plane tree (27 m. in diameter) in the neighbouring village of **Mantoudi** (4 km.).

One of the most picturesque villages is **Limni** (87 km. from Chalkida) on the site of ancient *Elymnion*, where the green of the pine trees merges with the azure of the sea. From here one may visit other villages: **Rovies, Agh-**

ia Anna (75 km. from Chalkida) with a vista of the Aegean, **Strofylia** and the coastal ones of **Angali, Vasiliki** (96 km. from Chalkida) and **Ellinika** (103 km. from Chalkida), just north of which is **Cape Artemision**. At this point a famous naval battle was fought during the Persian Wars (480 BC) and it was here too that the wonderful bronze statue of Poseidon was recovered from the depths of the sea.

The largest town in the area (NE Euboia) is **Istiaia** with many market gardens and vineyards, for which it was also renowned in antiquity, when it acquired the epithet "Polystaphylle" (many grapes). One can visit the small archaeological collection housed in the town hall and the church of St. Nicholas. **Oreioi,** the port of Istiaia (6 km. to the west) is a lovely village which has been inhabited without interruption since Early Helladic times and is now a thriving tourist centre. On the two low eminences on the outskirts of the town are the ruins of the two acropoles and of the Frankish castle. There is a small archaeological collection in the office of the community and a 4th century BC marble bull which was recovered from the depths of the sea. Of the numerous charming seaside villages we mention **Pefki**, **Aghiokampos** and **Lichada**, each surrounded by pine forest, extending down to the water's edge. Other villages on the plain include **Neos Pyrgos** (2 km. from Oreoi); **Aghios** (6 km. west) and **Aidipsos** (149 km. from Chalkida) which is a well-known spa. The curative properties of the waters there have been known since ancient times and are mentioned by such authors as Herodotus, Aristotle, Aristophanes and Strabo. In Roman times the emperors Augustus and Hadrian visited the springs, as well as the general Sulla, who sought a cure for his gout and built a bathhouse (Thermae), of which only scant traces have survived. Nowadays there are several hydrotherapy centres at the spa, as well as hotels and pensions where visitors may stay. There are frequent communications with Arkitsa. 10 km. from Aidipsos is a pleasant area of woodland and to the east of this the village of **Profitis Ilias**, with the convent of St. George in the vicinity, as well as the villages of **Yaltra**, **Loutra Yaltron** and **Aghios Georgios**.

96. Karystos. The beach and part of the Venetian fortress.

97. Limni, one of the most picturesque regions of northern Euboia.

96

97

SPORADES

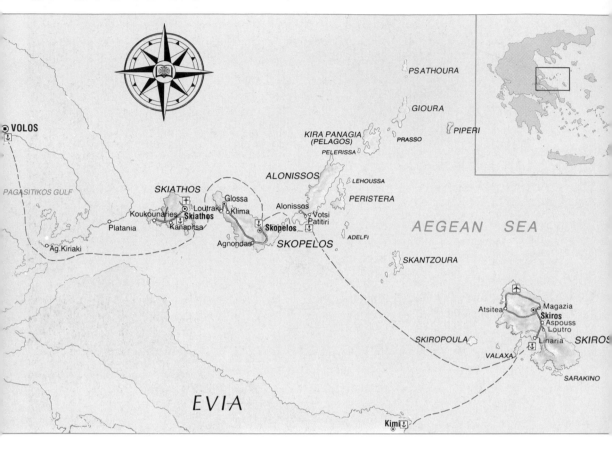

The labels on the map:

PSATHOURA

GIOURA

KIRA PANAGIA
(PELAGOS)
PELERISSA
PRASSO
PIPERI

VOLOS

ALONISSOS
LEHOUSSA
PERISTERA

PAGASITIKOS GULF

SKIATHOS
Glossa
Klima
Alonissos
Votsi
Patitiri

Koukounaries Skiathos
Loutraki
Platania
Kanapitsa
Agnondas
Skopelos
SKOPELOS
ADELFI

AEGEAN SEA

Ag.Kiriaki

SKANTZOURA

Atsitea
Magazia
Skiros
Aspouss
Loutro
Linaria
SKIROS

SKIROPOULA
VALAXA

SARAKINO

EVIA

Kimi

98. Skiathos, the lovely beach at Lalaria.

The archipelago of the Sporades, to the north-east of Euboia and south of the Magnesia peninsula, comprises four main islands —Skiathos, Skyros, Skopelos and Halonnisos— plus a number of rocky islets, the majority of which are ideal for hunting and fishing.

Administratively all the islands belong to Magnesia, except Skyros which belongs to Euboia.

These islands, with their more or less common history, countless coves, verdant landscape and charm of their natural environment are becoming increasingly popular with tourists. The holidaymaker is assured of spending the kind of vacation most suited to him, since each island has its own special atmosphere. Picturesque bays, villages with traditional architecture, churches, castles and monasteries await exploration.

Skiathos has a particularly cosmopolitan ambience, Skyros a distinctive landscape and rich folk culture, Skopelos is outstanding for its churches and monasteries and Halonnisos for its scenery.

It is easy to reach these islands, for there are airports on Skiathos and Skyros and car and passenger ferries from Aghios Konstantinos, Volos and Kymi.

Skiathos

GEOGRAPHY. Situated opposite Pelion and north of Euboia, Skiathos is 43 nautical miles from Volos, 44 from Aghios Konstantinos and 57 from Kymi. Surface area 48 sq. km., length of coastline 44 km. and population 4,127. There is a daily car ferry service from Aghios Konstantinos and a twice weekly link with Kymi during the summer, once during the win-

ter. In the summertime there are frequent connections with Skopelos and Halonnisos and once a week with Mytilene, Limnos, Aghios Efstratios, Samothrace, Kavala and Alexandroupolis. Excursion craft also sail to Skopelos and Halonnisos, as well as Pefki and Oreoi in Euboia, while there is a link with Trikeri all year round. There is a daily flight to and from Athens. The island, with its many lovely beaches, unusual and diverse landscape, is one of the most cosmopolitan in Greece. Though tourists flock here in great numbers, it maintains its distinctive picturesqueness and there are still places suitable for quiet, restful holidays.

HISTORY. The island's strategic position was decisive for its fate in antiquity. During Xerxes' campaign three Greek triremes were anchored here, ready to confront the Persian fleet. Skiathos was colonised by Ionians and later by Chalkidians; it became a member of the Athenian League (477 BC) and for a short period belonged to the Macedonians, later to the Romans and then reverted to the Athenians (199 – 221 AD). Under the Latins it became a

possession of the Ghisi family (1207 – 1454). In 1537 it was sacked by Barbarossa and was captured by the Turks in the following year. During the Revolution the ships of Skiathos played their part and the island was liberated in 1823. In 1829 the fortified Kastro was abandoned and its inhabitants settled in the present town, on the site of the ancient city. In 1851 the great Greek novelist Alexandros Papadiamantis, the "saint" of Greek letters, was born here in a house close to the harbour, now a museum in his memory. Another famous short-story writer, Alexandros Moraitidis, also hailed from Skiathos.

SIGHTS-MONUMENTS. The island's capital and main harbour, **Skiathos,** presents a gay and colourful picture, with its bright white houses with tiled roofs, narrow streets, flower-filled courtyards and balconies, not to mention its churches. One of the most charming quarters is Bourtzi, where the Ghisi jamily built a mighty fortress in 1270. From here there is a magnificent view, as also from the church of St. Nicholas, to the east of Chora. The church of the Virgin Limnia is perched to the west. In addition to Papadiamantis' house, one can also visit the shipyards (tarsanades) where fishing boats (trechandiria) and caiques are made. Apart from the main town there are

two small holiday resorts (Kanapista, Koukounaries).

In the northern part of the island is the old fortified capital of **Kastro**, best reached by boat. The islanders settled there for greater security during Turkish times and quit it in 1829 when they established the present capital. During World War II Kastro provided a haven for the Allied Forces en route for Egypt, nowadays it is virtually in ruins. Of the original 30 churches only 3 have survived, including the old cathedral church of Christ (metropolis). Beneath the castle two precipitous rocks, the **Kastronisia**, stand sentinel.

Of the island's monasteries that of the Evangelistria nestles in the foothills of the highest peak, Karaflitzanaka (436 m. a.s.l.). The monastery was built in the 18th century and in its katholikon there is a wood-carved iconostasis and exceptional wall-paintings. Its library houses some important manuscripts. The monastery of St. Charalambos (north side of the island), to which Alexandros Moraitidis withdrew towards the end of his life, also dates from the 18th century. Nowadays it is deserted, as is the monastery of the Virgin of Kechria

99. View of Chora, Skiathos, a particularly charming picture with its stark white houses.

99

(northwest side) of which only the katholikon with its wood-carved iconostasis, old icons and traces of wall-paintings, has survived. On the west coast of the islands, above the lovely beach of **Troulos,** stands the monastery of the Virgin Kounistra, built in 1727, which attracts a host of pilgrims on account of its miraculous icon of the Virgin.

The island has any number of delightful coves and beaches, excellent for swimming and sea sports and carefree holidays. Particularly good bathing at: **Bourtzi, Plakes, Kochyli,Megali Ammos** (7 km. from Chora), **Kanapitsa** (6 km. from Chora). Beaches on both the west and east side are: **Xanemo, Megas Yalos, Elia, Aselinos,** while the beaches at **Troullos** and **Banana** are preferred by nudists. One can get to the coast by bus, which departs from the harbour and goes as far as Koukounaras, or by caique, which regularly sail out of the harbour on trips to all the beaches and neighbouring islets.

One may make an excursion by caique to **Lalaria,** one of the most beautiful coves in Greece, also known as *Trypia Petra,* due to the fantastic rock formations caused by wind erosion. Quite close is the *Galazia Spilia* (Blue Grotto) where the sun is mirrored in the calm waters, filling the cave with its reflections. Without doubt the most beautiful beach on Skiathos is **Koukounaries,** (12 km. west of Chora) renowned not only for its sea, but also its unique landscape where the waves lap at the edge of the pine forest. A boat is a definite advantage for getting to know the island. Refuelling facilities in the harbour. Visitors may stay in hotels, pensions, furnished rooms or apartments.

100. A view of Chora.

101. Beautiful beaches and verdant landscape are the main features of the island.

102-103. Koukounaries. The most beautiful beach on Skiathos, renowned for its unique environment.

Skopelos

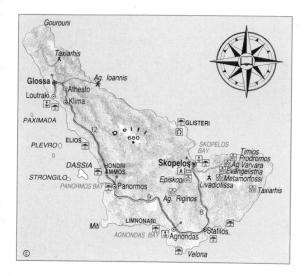

GEOGRAPHY. Located between Skiathos and Halonnisos, Skopelos covers an area of 96 sq. km. It is 41 nautical miles from Euboia, 60 from Aghios Konstantinos and 60 from Volos. Its coastline is 67 km. There are daily connections from both its harbours —Skopelos and Glossa— with Aghios Konstantinos, Kymi and Volos. The island has a population of 4,451 and its capital is Skopelos (Chora).

The terrain mainly comprises fertile plains and there are only a few mountainous parts (highest peak Delphi, 662 m. a.s.l.) on this exceptionally beautiful island. Its folk architecture, numerous churches and verdant landscape attract a host of tourists who can choose between a cosmopolitan vacation or a quiet stay.

HISTORY. The island was known as *Peparithos* in antiquity and its present name first appeared in Hellenistic times (2nd century BC). According to mythological tradition, the island's first inhabitants were Cretans, who came here led by Staphylos, son of Dionysos and Ariadne, and his brother Peparithos, landing in the bay still known as Staphylos today.

Archaeological evidence indicates that the island was inhabited in Mycenaean times (1600 – 1100 BC), while in the Archaic period (700 – 500 BC) it was colonised by Chalkidans. A member of the Athenian League, it passed under Macedonian rule (340 – 168 BC) and then returned to the Athenians. In Byzantine times it was a place of exile and during the Latin occupation belonged to the noble Venetian family of Ghisi. In 1538 it was sacked by Haradin Barbarossa and remained under Turkish rule until the 1821 Revolution, in which its fleet played an active role.

SIGHTS-MONUMENTS. The main village, **Skopelos** (Chora), is located on its southeast side and is characterised by its picturesque two-and three-storeyed houses with grey roofs and brightly coloured doors and windows. At the top of Chora is the quarter of Kastro where remnants of the 13th century Venetian castle, built by the Ghisi family upon the ruins of the ancient citadel, are preserved. As one wanders along the quaint alleys with their brilliant white houses and flower-filled balconies, climbing up its steps and steep streets, Chora casts its spell. One can also visit its many churches with their fascinating icons and wall-paintings. Particularly note-worthy are the churches of the Virgin, St Nicholas and the Evangelistria, which date to the 17th and 18th century. Others of interest are: St. Athanasios tou Kastrou (11th century), with important wall-paintings, the Holy Apostles and the church of Christ with its gilded, wood carved iconostasis with valuable icons. Close to the town there are several monasteries: that of the Evangelistria stands about 4 km. northeast of the harbour in a delightful setting. It dates to the beginning of the 18th century and has a gilded wood-carved iconostasis with significant icons in its katholikon. Not far away is the monastery of the Virtuous Forerunner, which was renovated in 1721. It too has a notable, gilded iconostasis, valuable icons and floor paved with coloured flagstones. Next to the monastery is the church of All Saints which is adjacent to yet another monastery, St. Barbara, built in 1648 and enclosed by a high precinct wall. A path leads from here to the monastery of the Transfiguration, built in 1600 in the midst of lush vegetation. Another important monastery is that of the Virgin Livadiotissa, a 17th century building, and there are others dedicated to Prophet Elijah, St. Constantine, St. George, St. Paraskevi, St. Efstathios and St. Nicholas. South of the town is the now abandoned monastery of St. Reginos, patron of the island, martyred here in 362 AD. Last but

not least, one should also visit the local potter's workshop in Chora and the ovens for drying plums to make prunes, the island's chief product.

From the harbour one can make trips to the lovely bays on the south side of the islands: **Staphylos** (6 km. from Chora), **Agnontas** (4 km., the boat docks here when weather conditions are bad), **Panormos** (16 km. from Chora with the islet of Daseia opposite), **Klima** (25 km. north of Chora), Glossa and Loutraki with their lovely, sandy beaches surrounded by unspoiled greenery. At Staphylos, where the island's founding settler lies buried, rich grave goods were recovered from his tomb. Nearby is the beautiful beach of **Velani**. 30 km. northwest of Chora is **Glossa**, built in a wooded upland area overlooking the open sea. Here one may admire the two-storey houses with their wooden balconies, as one wends one's way through its narrow alleys, and in late afternoon the womenfolk sit outside on the kerb, clad in their traditional costume. A path leads east from Glossa to the **chapel of St. John**, with its unique vista of the sea, and north to the chapel of the **Taxiarch** with its distinctive Byzantine masonry. This whole area is marvellous for rambling through. Some 2 km. south is **Loutraki**, harbour of Glossa and the second port on the island, which developed as a village after 1935 when the village of **Atheato**, to the east of Glossa, was destroyed by a major earthquake. The beaches by the harbour are fine for swimming, as are those on the south and west side, reached by bus or car. One may go to **Kastri**, **Limnonari**, **Panormos** by caique, as well as **Staphylos** and **Velani** (nudist beach). It is possible to make excursions from Skopelos to neighbouring islands, to **Glysteri** with the Trypiti cave and for those with their own craft there are any number of otherwise inaccessible coves and beaches to be discovered. Refuelling stations at Skopelos and Loutraki. Accommodation is available in hotels, pensions and rented rooms.

104. Skopelos. View of Chora.

105. Stafylos, one of the loveliest bays on Skopelos.

Halonnisos

GEOGRAPHY. North of Euboia lies Halonnisos, the least frequented of the Sporades. Port and capital of the island is Patitiri, 35 nautical miles from Euboia and 68 from Volos. Surface area 64 sq. km., 64 km. of coast, population 1,528. There are passenger and car ferries from Aghios Konstantinos, Volos and Kymi, as well as daily services to Skopelos and Skiathos –more often during the summer– by regular boat or caique excursions in the summer. One can also visit the north and east shores of the island by caique, as well as seaside villages for tourists, though touristic development is rather rudimentary, as is the network of roads. Halonnisos is fine for those wishing to spend a quiet holiday exploring and enjoying the countryside.

HISTORY. In antiquity the island was known as *Ikos* and was first inhabited in prehistoric times. The name *Chelidromia* or *Diadromia* later prevailed, and even today it is referred to as *Liodromia* sometimes. Traces of the ancient city are preserved on the southeast side of the island, at *Kokkinokastro*. Halonnisos was a bone of contention between Philip of Macedon and the Athenians who maintained a naval base there. Like the other islands it was

fated to suffer the plunderous attacks of Haradin Barbarossa (1538) and the Turks. In 1965 extensive damage was caused by an earthquake and the islanders abandoned the old capital, Halonnisos (5 km. west of the present one) and resettled nearer the sea. Only a handful of inhabitants have remained, but one can still see the ruined Venetian castle.

SIGHTS-MONUMENTS. Apart from **Patitiri**, other settlements on the island, mainly tourist installations, include **Votsi**, **Marbouda**, **Steni Vala** with beautiful beaches and tourist facilities. The beach at Kokkinokastro is particularly lovely, about half an hour's sail by caique, and on the islet opposite stone tools and animal bones of the Middle Palaeolithic era (100,000 – 33,000 BC) have been discovered, the earliest Palaeolithic remains in the entire Aegean. It is possible to visit the entire coast by small boat, as well as the off-shore islets. There are refuelling stations at Patitiri and Votsi. Hotels and pensions are few and there are also rooms to let.

Halonnisos is surrounded by a host of tiny islands with delightful beaches, just right for swimming and fishing. The nearest of these is **Peristera**, with only a couple of families and northeast of it is the uninhabited islet of **Lechousa**. There are two rocky islets to the southeast (**Mikro** and **Megalo Adelphi**) and **Skantzoura**, the ancient *Skandyle* or *Skandeira*. To the northeast is the island of *Kyra Panaghia* with its homonymous monastery, metochion of the Athos monastery of the Great Lavra. Northeast of the island is **Youra**, with its indigenous wild goats, very similar to the Cretan ibex, while on its south coast there are caves with stalagmites and stalactites. East of Voura is another island, **Piperi** and further north **Psathoura**, where remains of the ancient city may be discerned submerged beneath the sea, a consequence of the splitting of the island into Psathoura and Psatharopoula in the 1965 earthquake. Only the lighthouse attendants live here. The caves are a haven for seals.

106. Halonnisos. Typical view of the island.

107. The lovely beach at Votsi.

106

107

Skyros

GEOGRAPHY. Only 24 nautical miles from Euboia, Skyros has an area of 209 sq. km., 130 km. of coast and a population of 2,757. The island's capital is Skyros (Chora) and its harbour Linaria. There is an air link with Athens and daily boat services from Kymi; via Kymi there are connections with the other islands, Skiathos, Skopelos and Halonnisos. The island is divided into two sectors: the northern —densely populated and very green— and the southern —rocky and virtually inaccessible (highest point Kochylos, 814 m. a.s.l.), which are joined by a narrow isthmus.

Not only one of the loveliest isles of the Sporades, but of the Aegean in general, Skyros is distinguished for its vernacular architecture, rich folk heritage and diversity of landscape, ranging from sandy beaches, sheer cliffs, picturesque little bays, caves with deep blue water, abundant greenery and historic localities.

HISTORY. Skyros gained historic renown as the refuge of the hero of the Trojan war, Achilles, whose mother Thetis hid him there in the guise of a maiden, among the daughters of king Likomides, in order to evade recruitment in the Trojan campaign. Theseus, king of Athens, is also reputed to have died on Skyros. The island has been inhabited since the Neolithic period (5000 BC), as attested by

finds from Kastro. This was always the site of the island's fortified acropolis and the present capital has been built around it. In historical times the Athenian general Kimon was lord of the island and installed colonists here. From 469–340 BC its territory was apportioned among Athenian lot-holders. Until 196 BC it belonged to the Macedonians, then to the Athenians, who donated it to the Romans. In Byzantine times it was a place of exile, while under Latin rule it belonged to the Ghisi family. In 1453 it was captured by the Venetians who held it until 1537 when, following the pillaging of Barbarossa, it was taken by the Turks. Skyros was liberated, along with the other Sporades, in 1829.

SIGHTS-MONUMENTS. Its capital, **Skyros** (Chora), is situated on the east side, 11 km. from the port of **Linaria**. Built amphitheatrically on the hill slopes and crowned by the castle and church of St. George, it creates a unique impression when first espied from afar, with its stark white cuboid houses. A steep, wide street leads up through the centre of Chora to the north, where there is a square overlooking the open sea and in which stands the portrait statue of the poet and philhellene Rupert Brooke, whose grave is at **Treis Boukes** in the south of the island.

Continuing upwards along this same street, one arrives at the castle, east, passing interesting churches, such as Archontopanaghia and the Virgin of Koutsos on the way.

The castle is built on the same spot as the ancient citadel, remnants of the fortifications of which are preserved, as well as ancient, Byzantine and Venetian architectural remains. Actually atop the castle stands the historic church of St. George, katholikon of the homonymous monastery, founded by the emperor Nicephoros Phocas in 963, a metochion of the Athos monastery of the Great Lavra. The monastery was renovated several times in the course of its history, due to damage suffered from time to time. Nowadays the gilded, wood carved iconostasis in the church has been refurbished and its significant wall-paintings restored and conserved.

There are also two museums in Chora: the Archaeological, with very important finds from excavations on the island, and some folk art

108

items too, and the Faltaits Museum, which is housed in their family mansion and includes objects of Skyrian popular art, both past and present. The houses of Skyros are themselves veritable museums with their wood-carved decoration, wooden furniture, pottery, hand-woven fabrics and embroideries. Many old men still wear the traditional male costume with its peculiar footwear, the trochadia, and during carnival season one can see many such costumes, as well as the elaborately embellished female attire, for the Skyrians celebrate carnival in their own traditional way. There is a wood-carving workshop in Chora where traditional hand-carved Skyros furniture and decorations are fashioned, while at **Magazia**, on the seashore beneath Chora, there are potters' workshops.

In the south of the island some 100 of the formerly 3,000 strong population of indigenous ponies live.

From Linaria one can take a bus or drive a car to the west and northwest coast of the island **Pefkos**, **Atsitsa**, **Acherounas**, Kalamitsa, **Aghios Petros,** or sail in a caique to the southern shore (**Treis Boukes**) and southeast where there are caves inhabited by seals. For those with a boat there are innumerable deserted beaches with crystal clear sea and caverns. There are refuelling stations at Linaria and Pefko. Visitors may stay in an hotel or rented room, both of which are available in Chora.

109

108. Magazia, the beach below Chora.

109. Skyros. View of Chora looking down from the castle with the monastery. The peculiar architecture of Chora with its bright white cuboid houses and narrow, stepped alleys, is especially charming to behold and impresses the visitor.

ISLANDS OF THE NORTH AEGEAN

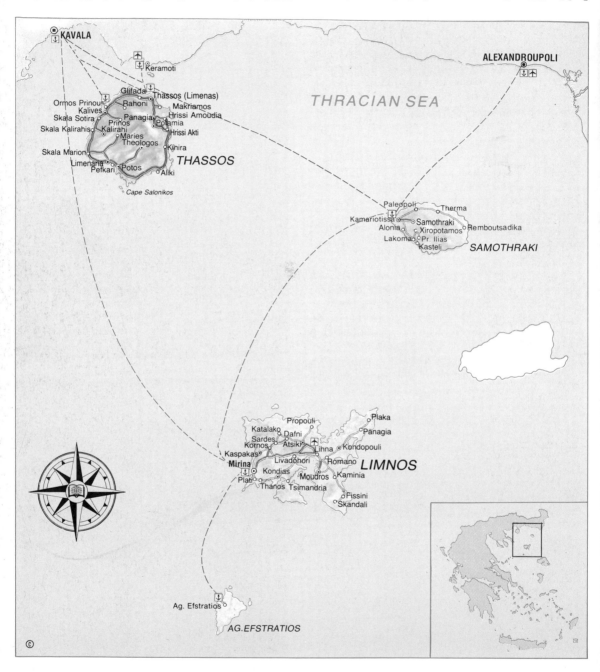

KAVALA

Keramoti

THRACIAN SEA

ALEXANDROUPOLI

Glifada
Thassos (Limenas)
Ormos Prinou
Kalives
Rahoni
Makriamos
Skala Sotira
Panagia
Hrissi Amoudia
Skala Kalirahis
Prinos
Potamia
Maries
Kalirahi
Hrissi Akti
Theologos
Kinira
Skala Marion
THASSOS
Limenaria
Pefkari
Potos
Aliki

Cape Salonikos

Paleopoli
Therma
Kamariotissa
Samothraki
Alonia
Xiropotamos
Remboutsadika
Lakoma
Pr. Ilias
Kasteli
SAMOTHRAKI

Propouli
Plaka
Katalako
Dafni
Panagia
Sardes
Atsiki
Kornos
Lihna
Kondopouli
Kaspakas
Mirina
Livadohori
Romano
LIMNOS
Kondias
Plati
Moudros
Kaminia
Thanos
Tsimandria
Fissini
Skandali

Ag. Efstratios

AG. EFSTRATIOS

In the northernmost reaches of the Aegean lie the islands of Lemnos, Thasos and Samothrace. Lemnos belongs to the Prefecture of Lesbos, Samothrace to that of Evros and Thasos to that of Kavala. All have a long and illustrious past, lush vegetation cover and unique scenic beauty. Lemnos with its many antiquities, and indolent way of life attracts an ever increasing number of visitors. Thasos with its verdant, unusual landscape is first and foremost a tourist island. Samothrace with its traditional villages and numerous monuments still remains off the tourist track, being just the place for quiet holidays.

110. *The Victory of Samothrace, votive of the Rhodians in the sanctuary of the Cabeiroi to commemorate their victory over Antiochos in 190 BC. One of the masterpieces of ancient Greek art, it is nowadays housed in the Louvre.*

110

Thasos

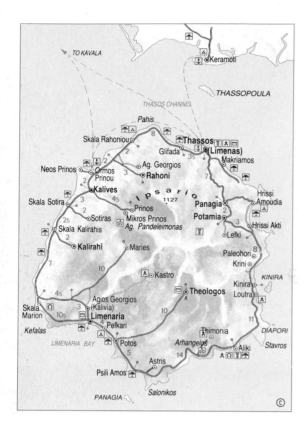

GEOGRAPHY. Very close to Kavala, Thasos is one of the most popular tourist islands in Greece. Its lovely, green landscape, clean sea, outstanding beaches and many places of interest attract a host of visitors. Even so, there are still parts of it unspoilt by the throng where those who wish can enjoy the peaceful countryside. Thasos is 379 sq. km. in area, has 95 km. of coastline, lies 16 nautical miles southeast of Kavala and is 3 nautical miles from Keramoti. The population is 13,111. There are daily car and passenger ferries from Kavala to both Limenas and Prinos, as well as frequent connections between Keramoti and Limenas. The mountainous terrain (highest peak Psario, 1127 m. a.s.l.) not only influences its natural vegetation but also the morphology of its coastline, which is gentle on the west and north side, on its east shore there are sandy beaches with trees growing down to the water's edge, while in the south there are precipitous cliffs and tiny coves. The island is surrounded by several tiny islets, particularly near its four major bays, Limenas, Potamia,

Koinyra and Potos. In the north is Thasopoula, to the east Krambousa and the islet of Koinyra and, in the south, that of Panaghia. The island's fifteen or so hamlets and villages, new and old, are located between the mountains and the coast and most of the more recent settlements have grown up around the anchorages of the old.

HISTORY. Finds from excavations demonstrate that Thasos was inhabited in prehistoric times (3500 – 2600 BC). In antiquity it was known as *Odonis* or *Idonis* and was apparently settled by Thracian tribes initially. The Phoenicians arrived later and, at the beginning of the 7th century BC, colonisers came from Paros. After an arduous struggle they eventually expelled the Thracians and were thus able to exploit the island's rich mineral resources (gold, marble) unhindered, soon extending their influence to the littoral of the mainland. By the 6th century BC Thasos was at its zenith —economic and cultural— and in about 525 BC it minted its own silver coin which enjoyed a wide circulation up until the end of the Persian Wars. It was at this time that the city was fortified and the island's system of defensive towers organised, traces of which still survive. During the 5th century BC Thasos lost its independent status, being subject in succession to the Persians, Athenians and Spartans. In 477 BC it became a member of the Athenian League and in around 340 BC belonged to the Macedonians. It was conquered by the Romans in 168 BC. Pirates were a constant menace throughout the Byzantine era and in 1204 Thasos was captured by the Franks who held it until 1259, when it was retaken by the Byzantines. This was a troubled phase in its history with countless incursions by pirates and alien occupations, the last one by the Gatelouzoi, to whom it was ceded in 1416. The Turkish conquest (1457) signalled a period of decline and between 1770 – 1774 there was a brief period of Russian domination. Thasos played an active role in the 1821 Struggle for Independence though was not liberated until 1912 and incorporated in the Greek state the following year.

111. Thasos. A characteristic corner of the island.

SIGHTS-MONUMENTS. Thasos (Limenas), the island's capital, is built on the same site as the ancient city founded by Parian colonisers in the 7th century BC. Excavations conducted by the French Archaeological School have revealed several buildings, many of which are quite well-preserved. The Dionysion (Archaic period) was located overlooking the present harbour, which served as a naval station in ancient times, while above the commercial harbour stood the sanctuary of Poseidon (Posideion). The sea wall with its two gates is still preserved, as well as the ancient theatre, near one of the gates. Originally built in the 5th century BC, it acquired its present aspect in Roman times. Remnants of one of the quarters (North Quarter), inhabited without interruption from the 8th – 3rd century BC, are preserved, while on the promontory of Evraiokastro there are traces of an Archaic sanctuary (6th century BC). An Early Christian basilica was evidently constructed on the same site (6th century). On the eminence occupied by the ancient acropolis, southeast of the theatre, is the medieval citadel which was repaired and altered by the Byzantines, Venetians and Genoese in turn. At the base of the hill is the best-preserved section of the fortification wall with bastions and gateways: Silenus Gate, Herakles and Dionysos Gate, Zeus and Hera Gate and, a short distance away, the sanctuary of Herakles, Caracalla's Arch —to the north—(3rd century AD) and the Roman odeum. The ancient agora, focus of city life, extended from the naval harbour to the foot of the acropolis and was surrounded by sanctuaries. West of the main square of the agora are the remains of a 6th century Early Christian basilica. Finds from these exavations, representative of all forms of ancient Greek art and dating from the Archaic period (7th century BC) up until the 4th century AD, are exhibited in the Archaeological Museum at Limenas. The town is a convenient departure point for trips to the rest of the island, since the metalled road circumventing it commences here. On the east side is the village of **Panaghia** (7 km. from Limenas). Its port, **Skala Panaghias** *(Chrysi Ammos)* is one of the beauty spots of Thasos. 2 km. south of Panaghia is the village of **Potamia** with its church of St. Demetrius (1845). At **Skala Potamias** (its port), site of the ancient city of *Ainyra,* there is a shipwright's yard belonging to a monastery (1892), the chapel of St. Nicholas and, on the islet of Krambousa at the entrance to the bay, a de-

fensive tower. At **Palaiochori** (11 km.) south of Potamia, galleries of an ancient gold mine are preserved. The region of **Koinyra,** extending southwards, has a richly wooded coastline. In ancient times there was a flourishing settlement here which survived into the Byzantine era. Remnants of Byzantine baths have been located at **Loutra,** as well as the remains of an Early Christian basilica. Beyond Loutra are the villages of the south side of the island. At **Alyki** there are vestiges of an ancient sanctuary (two temples and two cult caves) and two Early Christian basilicae built on the site of the Roman cemetery, attesting the continuous occupation of the area from the arrival of the Parian colonists until Postbyzantine times. There was an important quarry here, in use from the 6th century BC till the 6th century AD. Just beyond Alyki is **Thymonia,** where there are ruins of a Byzantine basilica and two Hellenistic towers. Perched atop the sheer cliffs which plunge into the sea is the monastery of the Archangel Michael, patron saint of the is-

land. At **Astris** there are remains of ancient towers and a 4th century BC potter's workshop. The lovely cove of **Psili Ammos,** close at hand, as well as the beaches in the bays of **Potos** and **Limenaria**.

Theologos (55 km. southwest of Limenas) is also one of the prettiest villages on Thasos with its old houses, ruined medieval tower and Postbyzantine churches (St. Demetrius, with its intricately carved wooden iconostastis, St. Paraskevi), Macedonian-style houses and the now-ruined mansion of the member of the Philiki Etaireia, Chatziyorgis.

In the nowadays abandoned village of **Kastro,** the oldest on the island, there are traces of the Byzantine fortress, churches and mansions. A short distance away is **Limenaria,** one of the seaside tourist villages, and the headland of Kefala which divides the west from the north side of the island, which is tranquil and verdant. The harbours (**Skales**) of the mountain villages of Kallirachi, Maries, Sotiras are here. Further north (20 km. southwest of Li-

112. The wonderful beaches of Thasos where the woodland meets the golden sand.

menas) is **(Neos) Prinos** which has recently gained fame due to the discovery of underwater oil sources in the vicinity. It is the port of the typical mountain villages of Mikros and Megalos Prinos.

The shores of Thasos are particularly lovely, with the pine trees growing down to the water's edge, and the crystal clear sea is ideal for swimming and fishing: **Limenas, Chrysi Ammoudia, Chrysi Akti, Alyki, Arsanas** and **Livadi, Psili Ammos, Potos, Limenaria** and **Prinos.** All beaches can be reached by public transport or private car and those with a boat may also visit the nearby islands. Refuelling stations at Limenas and Potos. One can even enjoy mountaineering and hunting in the island's interior. Thasos has more than adequate facilities for tourists, including hotels, pensions and rooms to let.

Samothrace

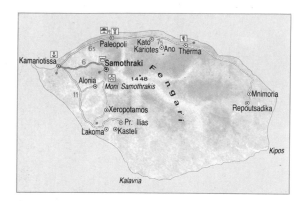

GEOGRAPHY. Samothrace is located in the northeast Aegean, opposite Alexandroupolis, from which it is just 29 nautical miles distant. It belongs to the Prefecture of Evros and covers an area of 178 sq, km., has 58 km. of coastline and a population of 2,871. There is a local boat service from Alexandroupolis and, once a week, a connection with Kavala and Lemnos. A mountainous island (highest peak Fengari, 1648 m. a.s.l.) with dense vegetation cover and numerous monuments, it is still relatively untouched by tourism and may be recommended for quiet holidays. In addition to its capital, Samothrace, there are other villages on the island: Kamariotissa, Palaiopolis, Xiropotamos, Therma, Profitis Ilias and Lakoma.

HISTORY. Samothrace was first inhabited in the Neolithic era. In around 1000 BC Thracian colonisers came here, intermarrying with the indigenous population. The island's present capital, **Samothrace** *(Chora)*, is located on its west coast. A traditional town, it is dominated by the massive medieval castle. At **Palaiopolis,** on the north side of the island, there are traces of the ancient city, built in around 700 BC close to the sanctuary of the Cabeiroi (Great gods). The sanctuary, which attained its zenith in Hellenistic times, was never totally destroyed and has been excavated by the American School of Classical Studies. Various sections of the Cyclopean wall, palace (6th century BC edifice), theatre, propylon and the foundations of diverse buildings of the sanctuary (temples, "ex votos", votive of Philip II and Alexander IV etc.) have been revealed. One may also visit the ancient cemetery (7th century BC – 2nd century AD) and remnants of

medieval towers (15th century) nearby. Among the diverse finds displayed in its small Archaeological Museum is a plaster cast of the famous statue of the Winged Victory, discovered at Palaiopoli and nowadays housed in the Louvre, Paris. At **Therma** (13 km. from the harbour), where there is a therapeutic spring, one may enjoy the unique vista of the coast opposite, as well as the islands of Thasos and Lemnos. There are excursions by local boats to the southern shores (Ammos) of Samothrace with their dense vegetation, streams and brooks. There is little provision for tourists (just one hotel and a few rooms to let) and a very rudimentary network of roads.

113. Samothrace. View of Chora.

114. Samothrace has a gentle landscape and lovely coastline, ideal for quiet holidays.

115. Samothrace. Restored columns in the sanctuary of the Great Gods.

14

15

Lemnos

GEOGRAPHY. Southwest of Samothrace lies Lemnos, one of the loveliest isles of the Aegean. 476 sq. km. in area, 259 km. of coastline, 15,721 inhabitants. There are car and passenger ferries from Piraeus, Kavala, Kymi Euboia, Aghios Konstantinos, as well as a link with Lesbos and, via the route Kavala - Piraeus, with the islands of the east Aegean, the Dodecanese, Cyclades and Crete. A regular local service operates between Lemnos and Aghios Efstratios. There is a daily flight from Athens, Thessaloniki and Mytilene. Lemnos has a gentle landscape, wide tracts of flat land (highest point Skopia, 470 m. a.s.l.), clear sea and beautiful beaches. Even though hoards of tourists descend on it, it has lost none of its distinctive charm.

HISTORY. According to Homer the island was first settled by Sindians of Thracian provenance. Hephaistos was worshipped here. Indeed, the island's largest city was called Hephaisteia. In antiquity the island was known as *Aithalia* and played an important role at all times due to its strategic position (24 miles from the Dardanelle straits). Excavations conducted by the Italian Archaeological School have shown that Lemnos has been inhabited since Neolithic times. During the Bronze Age a splendid civilisation developed here (Poliochni), closely affined to that of Troy, finds from which are exhibited in the National Archaeological Museum, Athens and in the local museum at Myrina. In the 5th century BC Lemnos was laid waste by the Athenian ge-

neral Miltiades, then subjugated by the Persians. In 478 BC it joined the Athenian League. Its land was apportioned among Athenian lotholders who dedicated the famous bronze statue of Athena Lemnia, work of Pheidias, on the Acropolis. Lemnos remained dependent on Athens throughout antiquity except for brief intervals when it belonged to the Macedonians (307 – 202 BC) and the Romans (202 – 166 BC). In the Byzantine era it was included in the Thema of the Aegean and was a fief of a Venetian family until 1269, when it was expelled by the emperor Michael Palaeologus. In the ensuing centuries the island was a bone of contention between the Venetians and the Turks; the latter eventually captured it and held it until 1912 when it was liberated and incorporated into the Greek state.

SIGHTS-MONUMENTS. Myrina (Kastro), the island's main town and harbour, is a mixture of old and new buildings. It has retained its ancient name, taken from one of the Amazons. Very little has remained of its ancient city, one of the largest on the island: traces of the fortification wall, houses and streets are nowadays discernible. A large number of clay figurines have been recovered in excavations and from their inscriptions it is deduced that a sanctuary of Artemis existed here. From Myrina one can visit other villages on the island both inland and coastal. At **Kornos** (7.5 km. northeast of Myrina) there are churches of the Dormition of the Virgin and St. Andrew. In the region of **Kotsinas** (3 km. northeast) are ruins of a Venetian castle and, just beyond, are the ancient sites of Hephaisteia and Kabeirio. *Hephaisteia* (nowadays **Palaiopoli**), inhabited since prehistoric times, was one of the island's most important cities in the 5th century BC, when it was captured by Miltiades and subsequently made a member of the Athenian League. Excavations have brought to light houses, a sanctuary (destroyed in the 6th century BC), an extensive cemetery (8th – 6th century BC) and a theatre of the Roman period. The rich finds (figurines, weapons, pottery) bear witness to the city's floruit and its contacts with Attica, Corinth and Macedonia. Athena was worshipped in this region and there was a sanctuary in her honour at Kome, to the north of Hephaisteia. At **Chloi**, 3km. north of Hephais-

116-117. Two views of Myrina, capital and main harbour of Limnos.

teia, is the sanctuary of the Cabeiroi, discovered in 1937. This sanctuary is older than that on Samothrace and a large stoa, Telesterion and countless inscriptions, furnishing a wealth of information concerning the sanctuary and important cities on the island, have been revealed. Near the village of **Kaminia** (35 km. east of Myrina), in the bay of Vroskopos, the prehistoric city of *Poliochni* has been uncovered, which achieved its acme between 2700 – 2200 BC and continued to be occupied until around 1600 BC. Finds from here (mainly pottery and jewellery) comprise not only evidence of the cultural apogee but also of the close links maintained with Troy. Four successive well-stratified phases of occupation have been revealed, including foundations of large houses, walls and public buildings, the most splendid examples of which date to the fourth phase.

The island's picturesque villages, **Moudros, Kontopouli, Livadochori**, can be visited by car, as can the lovely beaches in the vicinity of Myrina and at **Platys, Thanos, Skandali, Kaminia**, all of which are accessible by caique and are ideal for fishing and swimming. For those with a boat there are any number of delightful little bays awaiting discovery. Refuelling stations at Myrina and Moudros. The only hotels of Lemnos are at Myrina but there are rooms and apartments for rent both there and elsewhere (Kontias, Moudros).

Aghios Efstratios

This tiny, islolated island between Lesbos, Skyros and Lemnos, to which it belongs administratively, is 43 sq. km. in area, has 30 km. of coastline, a population of 296 and is only 16 nautical miles from Lemnos. Well-known as a place of exile, Aghios Efstratios has, apart from its harbour, just one village on its northeast side and several lovely, clean beaches. There is a boat connection either from Aghios Konstantinos and Kymi (once a week), or from Kavala (three times a week). Twice a week there is a link with Lemnos and Alexandroupolis, Samothrace, Mytilene (once a week). Its picturesque bays, chapels and caves, the few ancient ruins and tomb of St. Efstratios (9th century) are the only places of interest.

ISLANDS OF THE EAST AEGEAN

At the easternmost edge of the Aegean are the islands of Lesbos, Chios, Samos, Ikaria, Psara, Oinouses and Fournoi, comprising a separate entity known as the islands of the East Aegean. On account of their geographical position, in close proximity to the Asia Minor littoral, these islands have always held a special place in the Hellenic world, forming a bridge between West and East. The three large islands —Lesbos, Chios, and Samos— were destined to play a leading role, while information about the others is scant.

Palaeontological finds from the islands of Samos and Chios have confirmed that in the distant past these were joined to the coast of Asia Minor opposite.

Settled since Neolithic times (5000 – 3000 BC), it was during the ensuing Bronze Age that the islands achieved an acme. Around the end of the 2nd millennium BC the inhabitants of Chios and Samos were known as Ionians, while those of Lesbos as Aiolians. At the time of great upheavals and population movements in the helladic area, around 1100 BC, Ionian colonisers from central Greece settled on Chios and Samos and Dorians on Lesbos. From the end of the 8th up until the 5th century BC the islands enjoyed great economic prosperity, commercial success and cultural pre-eminence, as attested by finds from excavations. Major cities were created and the arts and letters flourished.

Poetry, especially epic (particularly on Chios which was considered to be the homeland of Homer) and lyric, prominent representatives being Sappho and Alkaios, was at its zenith. The islands also sired eminent philosophers, such as Pittakos and Pythagoras. The islanders were able merchants and established trading stations throughout the Mediterranean and even on the shores of the Black Sea. During the Persian Wars the islands were dominated by the Medes and once over they joined the Athenian League in 477 BC, of which they were members for some 40 years. The years between 440 and 404 BC were turbulent and the islands were at the centre of the conflict between Athens and Sparta. In the ensuing century (3rd - 2nd BC) they passed into the sphere of Macedonia, then the Egyptian Ptolemies, the Seleucians and, in 196 BC the Romans, against whom they allied with Mithridates of Pergamon in 88 BC. The period from the 1st to the 3rd century AD was one of autonomy. In the middle of the 3rd century St. Isidore was martyred on Chios, while Samos was virtually deserted as a consequence of the incursion of the Herulae. In Byzantine times they formed part of the Province of the Islands and in 1124 they came under the suzereinty of Venice. Thence forth their history is more or less common. Chios belonged to the Genoese Giustiniani family from 1346 until 1566, when it was captured by the Turks. In 1822 it was destroyed by the Turks and in 1861 was the victim of a catastrophic earthquake. In 1355 Lesbos passed into the hands of the Gatelousi family, to whom it belonged until 1462, when it was sacked by the Turks, while Samos, which also belonged to the Genoese, was raided several times, being taken by the Turks in 1475. The islands were liberated in 1912 and incorporated within the Greek state. With the disastrous débacle of the Asia Minor Campaign in 1922, thousands of refugees flocked there.

Nowadays each island has its own distinctive personality and recollections of the past. The wealth of monuments, picturesque scenery and enchanting natural environment, as well as the ease of access and communications, guarantee their popularity with vistors.

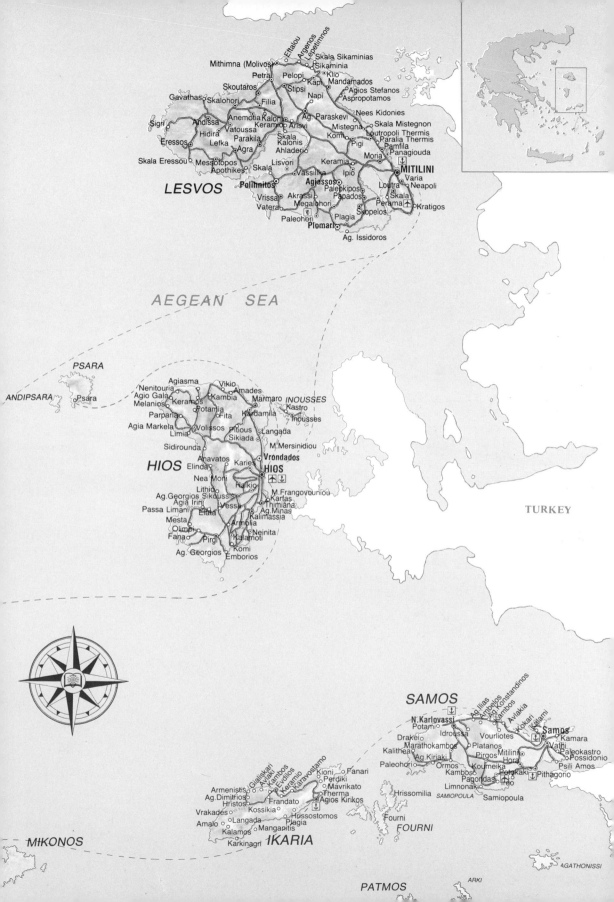

118-120. Pictures from Samos. Samos, the birthplace of Pythagoras, is one of the loveliest isles of the east Aegean with golden sands and gentle landscape.

120

Lesbos

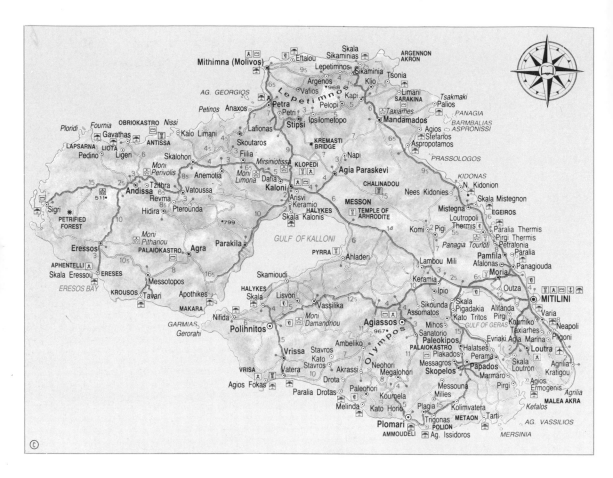

GEOGRAPHY. Lesbos or Mytilene is the third largest of the Greek islands, after Crete and Euboia. It lies at the very edge of the northeast Aegean, only 6.5 nautical miles from the coast of Turkey. 1,630 sq. km. in area, with 370 km. of coastline, it is 187 nautical miles from Piraeus and has a population of 88,601. Lesbos comprises a separate Prefecture, also including Lemnos and Aghios Efstratios. There are daily car and passenger ferries from Piraeus and once a week a boat to Thessaloniki and Kavala. There is also a link with Chios and, via the Piraeus -Kavala route, with Samos, Ikaria, the Dodecanese, Cyclades and Crete. Local services operate between Lemnos, Aghios Efstratios and Kavala. In the summertime a local craft sails to A'ivali in Turkey (16 nautical miles). There are daily flights from Athens. Although the terrain is mountainous (highest peak Olympos, 940 m. a.s.l.) there are fertile valleys in between and water in abundance,

especially on the south coast round the gulf of Gera. The second largest bay, that of Kalloni, lies between the north and east parts of the island, which are mainly of igneous rocks and have sparse vegetation cover. Indeed, the formation of the island is attributed to volcanic activity, since it must originally have been joined to the coast opposite. The numerous thermal springs and petrified forest at Sigri are probably also due to this vulcanicity.

Lesbos casts its own magic spell on those who come here. It is quite unlike other islands with its verdant scenery, indented coastline with secret coves, and monuments of all eras, little wonder visitors flock here in thousands, each guaranteed an unforgettable stay. Facilities for tourists are of a high standard and the good road network enables those with their own transport to drive around easily. The capital is Mytilene from where all roads radiate to the island's towns and villages.

121. Lesbos. View of the capital Mytilene.

121

HISTORY. The island's privileged position, in conjunction with its exceptional geomorphology and natural environment, determined its fate throughout the centuries. It was first inhabited in prehistoric times (3000 BC and in circa 1000 BC Aeolian colonisers settled here, establishing several important cities - Mytilene, Methymna, Eressos, Antissa, Pyrra, Arisbe. Antissa was laid waste by the Romans in 168 BC, Pyrra's decline had already set in in Hellenistic times and Arisbe was destroyed quite early. Home of poets, philosophers, historians and musicians (Pittakos, Theophrastus, Sappho, Alkaios, Arion), Lesbos attained its zenith between the 7th and 6th century BC. It was captured by the Persians, joined the Athenian League for a short period and then passed in turn to the Macedonians, Ptolemies and Romans. In the Byzantine era it belonged to the Thema of the Aegean and was continually harassed by pirates. After the sacking of Constantinople by the Franks it belonged to the Latin Empire of Constantinople until 1247. In 1344 the emperor John Palaeologus ceded it to the Genoese. It was ruled by the Gatelousi family and experienced a second period of acme without losing its Byzantine character. From 1462 until the 1821 War of Independence it was occupied by the Turks. Liberated in 1912 it was immediately incorporated in the Greek state. Just 10 years later (1922) refugees from the disastrous Asia Minor campaign flocked here in their thousands and many settled. Even in modern times art and literature continued to flourish on Lesbos and it was the birthplace of several outstanding Greek painters and men of letters (Myrivilis, Venezis, Eftaliotis, Elytis, Theophilos).

SIGHTS-MONUMENTS. The island's capital, **Mytilene**, is built on the incredibly beautiful wooded slopes of a hill, the trees reaching

down to the seashore. The mass of its castle and the large statue of liberty on the quay are the dominant features. It is an amalgam of quaint old houses, multi-storeyed buildings and Neoclassical mansions (*Pyrgelia*), interspersed with squares and parks. In the old part of town the streets are narrow, the houses low and the castle looms large over them and the market. The impressive castle, which stands on the site of the ancient acropolis, was originally built by the Byzantines and subsequently rebuilt by Francesco Gatelouzos in 1373. Nowadays it is one of the largest extant castles in the Mediterranean and one of the best-preserved in Greece. Directly opposite the castle is the ancient theatre, dating from Hellenistic times. Very near the theatre are the ruins of a Roman villa in which 3th century AD mosaics were discovered, with scenes from the comedies of Menander. North of the theatre sections of the polygonal fortification wall of the Classical period are preserved. There are also remnants of the Classical, Hellenistic and Roman cemeteries. Other places worth visiting include the Turkish hamam (bathhouse in the market) maintained by the municipality, churches and museums. The most important churches include St. Athanasios (1894) in the town centre and St. Therapon (cathedral) with its eraborately carved wooden iconostastis. In the Archaeological Museum, near the statue of Liberty, finds from excavations in various parts of the island are displayed, as well as the mosaics from "Menander's House". The Byzantine Museum has an interesting collection of icons and ecclesiastical keimelia. In addition there are: a Folk Art Museum, Museum - Library of Modern Art, Public Library and Lesbian House, arranged on the groung floor of the Marika Vlachou residence. At **Vareia,** a suburb of Mytilene, is the Theophilos Museum, bequest of the Lesbian art conoisseur Eleftheriadis (Teriade) who promoted the work of this Greek folk artist on an international scale. Very few notable examples of the many mansions (late 18th – early 19th century) which formerly embellished the town have survived. There are a few on the outskirts, along with the towers (*pyrgoi*), that is the many-storeyed fortified houses of the wealthy bourgeoisie, mainly used for summer vacations.

About 6 km. north of Mytilene, at **Moria**, one can see the remains of a Roman aquaduct (2nd/3rd century AD). 1 km. further on, at **Pamphila** are the "pyrgoi" of the Saltas and Chatzisavvas families) and yet another 4 km. away is **Pyrgoi Thermes**, so named after the many "pyrgoi" in the area. The village of **Therme** (11 km. from Mytilene) takes its name from the thermal springs there. Inhabited since ancient times, excavations have furnished evidence that Artemis Thermisia was worshipped here. Archaeologists have uncovered an Early Bronze Age installation (circa 3000 – 2000 BC), finds from which are on display in the Mytilene museum. The Byzantine church of the Virgin Tourloti, built in the 9th or 11th century, also merits a visit. 37 km. northwest of Mytilene is **Mantamados** where there is a monastery of the Taxiarchs (18th/ 19th century) which possesses a rare relief icon of the Archangel Michael. Mantamados is well- known on account of the tradition in pottery making which is still very much alive today. At **Aspropotamos**, southeast of Manatamados, is the Byzantine church of St. Stephen, the second on Lesbos. Further north, in the **Sarakina** valley, are the remains of a medieval castle and beyond here, at **Palaiokastro**, near the village of **Kleio** (6 km.) is a ruined Byzantine watch-tower. On the northeast edge of Mytilene is **Aghia Paraskevi** where there is a little chapel of St. Charalambos. Every fourth Sunday after Easter the renowned "feast of the bull" is held here, lasting for three days and including horse races, the slaughter of a bull and the distribution of the meat "keskeri" to the revellers. Not far from Aghia Paraskevi is the region of **Mesa** where there were sanctuaries of Zeus, Hera and Dionysos. The foundations of the Great temple (4th century BC) still exist, along with isolated fragments of marble

122. Lesbos. Plomari, the largest town on the island.

123-124. Two views of Mithymna, Lesbos, one of the most beautiful villages on the island, dominated by its massive Genoese castle.

123

124

from the columns and pediments. At **Klopedi** there are traces of the Archaic temple of Apollo, while at **Chalinadou** an Early Christian church of St. Paraskevi has been excavated. There is a medieval building at **Gefyra Kremasti** and, to the south, at **Achladeri**, lie the ruins of ancient *Pyrra* which was gradually abandoned in Hellenistic times. Finds from here can be seen in the Archaeological Museum. Northwest of Aghia Paraskevi is **Petra** (55 km. from Mytilene), built in a beautiful setting on the creek of a large, sandy bay. Here one should visit the mansion of the Varelitzidaina family, one of the most significant residences on the island, richly decorated and embellished with murals, as well as the churches of St. Nicholas (16th century) and the Virgin of Tenderness, built on a rocky eminence 27 m. high, from where there is a wonderful view. 7 km. north of Petra is **Methymna**, one of the most important cities on the island in ancient times. It is also known as **Molyvos**, the name given it in the Middle Ages and in order to reach it one must cross the plain of Kalloni, perhaps the most beautiful region on Lesbos. There has been habitation here since Neolithic times and a significant civilisation developed during the Bronze Age (2800 – 1100 BC). Cultural advancement continued up until the Roman period, which heralded its decline. When Molyvos was taken by the Gatelouzi family in 1355 it experienced a new floruit. Remnants of the fortification wall of ancient Methymna, originally 2900 m. long, have survived, along with the ancient aquaduct and ruins of an Archaic temple. Finds from the area are housed in the Town Hall. Methymna forms a crescent around the central nucleus of its castle. The streets are narrow, the houses high, and though there are almost no squares, there are numerous fountains decorated in relief and, of course, churches. The most noteworthy ones are that of the Taxiarch (built 1795) and St. Panteleimon (1844). There are also several Neoclassical houses and mansions at Molyvos, including some in excellent condition, such as the Yannakos mansion with its elaborately carved wooden ceilings and that of the Kralli family. Molyvos is a scheduled village. The summer courses of the University School of Fine Arts are held here. Since 1981 there has been an Art Gallery in the village. Argyris Eftaliotis' home was in Molyvos, his tomb is in the nearby village of Eftalou (3 km. south). Not only is **Eftalou** one of the loveliest bays on Lesbos, there is also a radioactive spring there. South of Methymna is **Kalloni** (40 km. northwest of Mytilene), also an important city in ancient times where, apart from the ruins of ancient and Byzantine edifices, ruins of a temple and castle on the height of Xirokastro, south of the town are preserved. The sheltered bay of Kalloni and its environs is one of the prettiest parts of the island. 5 km. northwest of here is the **Leimona monastery**, founded in the 15th century and housing a veritable treasury of precious manuscripts, icons and uniquely valuable items of folk art. The Byzantine **convent of Myrsiniotissa**, established in the 12th century, is situated 3 km. to the north. **Antissa** (73 km. from Mytilene) bears the same name as the ancient city destroyed by the Romans in 168 BC. Excavations have brought to light the remnants of a sanctuary of Geometric times (9th century BC). 3 km. east of Antissa is the **Perivoli monastery** in the katholikon of which are 16th century wall paintings and valuable icons. West of Antissa, on mount Ordymnos (511 m.a.s.l.), is the important nunnery of Ypsilos, founded, according to tradition, in the 9th/11th century, in which there is a small museum of icons, manuscripts and embroideries. Other features of interest in the Antissa region include the vestiges of the ancient city wall near the shore and the ruins of a medieval castle. South of Antissa (88 km. from Mytilene) is **Eressos** and 4 km. further south is its port, **Skala Eressou** which has a wonderful beach of golden sand and crystal clear sea. Ruins of ancient Eressos (sections of the polygonal wall) are preserved in the vicinity of the harbour and there are ruins of Byzantine defenses (towers) on the summit of the hill. The small museum next to the church of St. Andrew is worth a visit since it houses finds from tombs in the ancient cemetery and Early Christian artefacts. The excavated Early Christian church of St. Andrew (5th century) is of especial interest on account of its mosaic floors. There is another Early Christian church, a basilica, north of Skala Eressos, at Afentelli, dating from the second half of the 5th century AD. From Eressos one can visit the Pytharios monastery and **Palaiokastro** with its medieval ruins, **Sigri** (15 km. north of Eressos, built around a lovely cove, rather reminiscent of Cycladic scenery. At the water's edge are the remnants of a tiny castle of Turkish times. Sigri is famous for its petrified forest, that is fossilised tree trunks covered by volcanic material over a million years ago. Similar petrified vegetation can be seen on the islet of **Nisiopi**.

From Mytilene one can visit regions to the west and south, around the gulf of Geras, where there are many towns and villages. One of the most picturesque of these is **Ayasos** (28 km. from Mytilene), built amphitheatrically on the lower slopes of mount Olymbos. Local traditions are fervently adhered to here and attractive ceramics are produced. One should visit the 19th century church of the Virgin, its feast day, celebrated on the 15th August is the largest on the island and lasts three days. There is a small museum of icons and ecclesiastical plate adjacent to the church. Yet another charming town is **Polychnitos** (45 km. west of Mytilene), a coalescence of several small hamlets built on an eminence with a splendid view of the Aegean and the bay of Kalloni. **Plomari** (50 km. southwest of Mytilene) was originally a quaint little fishing village which has developed into an attractive town with well-ordered street system and several parks, very popular with tourists. Of especial interest is the village of **Vrissa** (53 km. southwest of Mytilene) with its old houses and cobbled streets. From **Vatera** (3 km. south), the harbour of Vrissa, one can go to cape **Aghios Phokas** where, beside the church, there are the ruins of the ancient temple of Dionysos, worshipped here in a major sanctuary (1st century BC). Among the features of interest on Lesbos the marble fountains in the villages, frequently carved with relief decoration, deserve mention.

There is no problem about where to swim on Lesbos with its seemingly endless beaches, all of which can be reached by bus or caique. There are lovely stretches of sand to the north of **Mytilene**, as far as **Skala Mistegnon**, as also at **Aghios Ermogenis**, which can be reached from **Loutra**, **Methymna**, **Eftalou**, **Skala Kallonis**. Some of the best beaches are at **Skala Polychnitou**, **Skala Eressou**, **Aghios Phokas**, **Aspropotamos**, **Petra** and elsewhere. All are excellent for fishing and sea sports also. In the island's interior one can mountaineer or shoot game and birds. Mytilene has plenty of hotels, pensions, rooms and apartments for rent, both in the capital and in its towns and villages, where one gains a more authentic picture of island life.

125

126

125-126. Two scenes from the Feast of the Bull at Aghia Paraskevi.

Chios

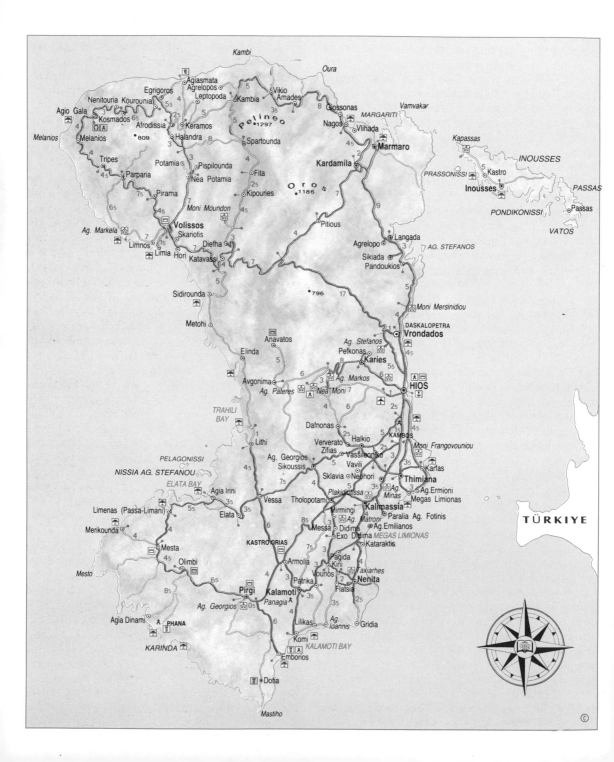

GEOGRAPHY. South of Lesbos (27 nautical miles) lies one of the most beautiful isles of the Aegean, Chios. It covers an area of 842 sq. km., has 213 km. of coastline and a population of 48,700. Chios is a separate Prefecture including the smaller islands of Oinouses, Psara, Antipsara and Pasas. It is 146 nautical miles from Piraeus with which there is a daily car and passenger ferry link. Once a week the boat on the Piraeus - Kavala route calls there, connecting Chios with Thessaloniki. There are also links with Lesbos, Syros and, again via the Kavala - Piraeus line, with the Dodecanese, Crete and the Cyclades. There is a local service to Psara, Oinouses and, in the summer, to Çesme in Turkey. Daily flights to and from Athens. The island's terrain is semi-mountainous (highest peak Pelinaios, 1297 m. a.s.l.) with several valleys intersecting the mountain ridges. The coast follows the configuration of the ground, steep rocky cliffs in the west and north and flat, sandy shores in the south and east. The mild climate, verdant vegetation, traditional villages and many monuments attract an ever-increasing number of visitors, even though tourist facilities are not particularly developed. The east and southeast parts of the island are the most densely populated and more villages are concentrated there, whereas the north is only sparsely settled.

HISTORY. In antiquity the island was known as *Makre* and *Pityousa* and has been inhabited since prehistoric times. In the 8th century BC Ionian colonisers settled here, developing a significant civilisation so that the island's floruit endured until the 6th century BC. During the Persian Wars Chios was captured by the enemy, afterwards it joined the Athenian League and then passed to the Macedonians. It was eventually taken by the Romans. In Byzantine times it belonged to the Thema of the Aegean and, like all the islands, was a victim of constant piratical attacks. It was a bone of contention between the Venetians and Latin emperors and in 1344 passed to the Genoese, under whom it experienced a new period of acme, commercial and economic, mainly due to its monopoly in the trade of mastic. It was ruled by several noble families, the most important being the Giustiniani. In 1566 Chios was captured by the Turks, who granted it special priveleges which prevailed— until the 1821 War of Independence. In 1822 the Chiotes were massacred by the Turks, which event, along with the later earthquake in 1881,

wrought the destruction of many of the island's monuments. Chios was liberated in 1911 and incorporated in the Greek state. Adamantios Korais and Yannis Psycharis were both from Chios.

SIGHTS-MONUMENTS. The island's capital, **Chios** is also its main port and is located more or less in the middle of the east coast of the island. The oldest quarter is that around the castle, built in Byzantine times (10th century), many Genoese and Turkish influences are also preserved. In addition to sections of the ramparts, towers and a gate are also preserved.. The wall was separated from the harbour by a moat, which no longer exists. Within the walls is the old Turkish quarter, ruins of the Giustiniani palace, the mausoleum of the Turkish admiral, Kara Ali, who ordered the 1822 massacre, a Byzantine chapel, Byzantine cistern and Turkish baths. Notable monuments in the town include the Early Christian basilica of St. Isidore, in which a significant 7th century mosaic floor was found, and the cathedral (metropolis). In the Korais library, one of the finest in Greece, there is a collection of rare books and manuscripts and, on the second floor, the Philippos Argentis collection of folk art is displayed. There is also an Art Gallery and Archaeological Museum in which finds and coins from excavations throughout the island are exhibited.

South of the town of Chios (6 km.) is **Kampos**, a particularly beautiful region with richly planted orchards and mansions set in their midst, the summer residences of the island's leading families. Most of them date from the 18th century and their architecture has distinct Genoese influences. Nowadays many have been abandoned but that on the Argentis estate has been restored and is in good condition, as is the Kazanova mansion near the torrent of Kokala, the Mavrokordatos residence at Frangovouni and those of the Zygomalas (Merminga) and Kaloutas families. Further south, near the village of **Vavyloi,** stands the Byzantine shurch of the Virgin of Krina, a 12th century building in which three layers of wall-paintings have been revealed. Also in the vicinity is the Genoese settlement of Sklavia where there are remains of medieval houses and churches. Close to the village of **Aghios Georgios Sykousis** stands the church of that name, in its present form a 19th century structure, but originally built in the 12th century. Continuing southwards, at the village of **Kal-**

limasia, on a knoll beside the Zevoi tower, stands the 13th century church of the Virgin of Sicily. There is another Byzantine church of St. John Argentis (14th century), in which notable wall-paintings can be seen, at **Katarraktis**, 15 km. south of Chios. At **Nenitas** (19 km. south of Chios) is the monastery of the Taxiarchs and at **Kalamoti** (20 km. south of Chios) the important monument known as the Virgin of Agrelopos (basilica in the orientalising order) in which there are 14th century wall paintings. To the north (approx. 2 km.), near the village of **Armolia**, in a moderately good state of preservation, is the Kastro Apolychnon, one of the major fortresses on the island, built in 1440.

In this part of southern Chios there is a considerable number of medieval villages, founded in the 14th and 15th century, of outstanding architectural interest since they are built like fortresses and the houses are mainly of medieval aspect. These villages were fortified against piratical raids and in order to facilitate the better exploitation of mastic, they were also known as the Mastichochoria. Most of the villages were destroyed or damaged in the 1881 earthquake and their character altered. Pyrgi and Mesta are the best-preserved. **Pyrgi** (22 km. south of Chios) is a scheduled village (state protected) with a distinctly medieval appearance, the house facades being embellished with geometric and linear designs, and fortress-like atmosphere. The central fortification with its large tower still stands, as well as two important churches: Holy Apostles and Dormition, and a Folk Art Museum. South of Pyrgi, at **Dotia** an interesting Genoese tower has survived. 9 km. southeast of Pyrgi at **Emboreion,** excavations conducted by the British School of Archaeology have brought to light remains of buildings, a temple of Athena, on top of which an Early Christian basilica with baptistry was built. 7 km. from Pyrgi is yet another medieval village, **Olympoi**, in which the central bastion has also survived. South of here, beside the sea at **Fana** are remnants of the sanctuary of Apollo (an early Classical edifice). The best-preserved medieval village, however, is **Mesta** (40 km. southwest of Chios and 11 km. from Pyrgi). Even though its cen-

128

129

127. *Chios. View of the capital.*

128. *Chios. Pyrgi, typical house facades.*

129. *Chios, Pyrgi.*

130

131

tral tower no longer stands, because a large basilica was erected in its place during the 19th century, the corner bastions of the defensive wall, gates, central square and narrow alleys are preserved and the houses all date from the 14th and 15th century.

North of the town of Chios (5 km.), in the locality known as Vrysi tou Papa, near **Vrontados**, stands the monument popularly known as *Daskalopetra* and associated in local lore with Homer. It is actually an outdoor sanctuary of the goddess Cybele and the view of the sea from here is magnificent. The tomb of Yannis Psycharis is not far away. At Vrontados there are two museums sponsored by local cultural associations: that of the «Philoproodos Omilos» (folk art and ecclesiastical objects) and that of the Intellectual and Cultural Movement (folk art). North of the Village (2 km.) is the Mersinidiou monastery and near **Langada** (9 km. from Chios) is the ancient *Delphinion* where excavations of the British School of Archaeology have brought to light the main Athenian naval base (5th century BC). The north side of the island differs considerably from the south both in its natural environment and density of settlement; the villages are fewer and smaller than in the south. The largest is **Kardamyla** (27 km. from Chios), built in a richly vegetated region. At **Volissos** (40 km. northwest of Chios) there is a well-preserved Venetian fortress on top of the hill and the monastery of St. Markella. At **Aghio Gala** (98 km. northwest of Chios), close to the village of **Ayasmata** with its undeveloped curative springs, the earliest remains on the island (Neolithic period) were discovered inside a cave. There has been no intervention in this cave to attract the public, even though it is full of stalagmite and stalactite formations. Just by the cave mouth is the Byzantine chapel of St. Thalelaios with significant wall-paintings.

The most important monument on Chios is **Nea Moni**, some 15 km. west of the main town. The monastery was founded in the middle of the 11th century by the emperor Constantine the Dueller (Monomachos) and is dedicated to the Dormition of the Virgin. Its katholikon (of octagonal type) is decorated with marble revetments and mosaics, among the finest ex-

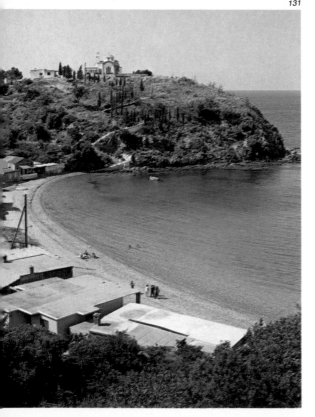

130. Kardamyla. Partial view.

131. The beach at Vrontados.

132. Anavatos. Partial view of this impressive, fortress-like village.

amples of Byzantine art and contemporary with those at Daphni and Hosios Loukas. The refectory, a side chapel, underground cistern and bastion on the west face have survived, as well as a few deserted cells and ruined buildings of 18th and 19th century date. Nea Moni is generally regarded as one of Greece's outstanding Byzantine monuments. To the north (14 km.) is **Anavatos**, a semi-abandoned fortress-like village with impressive houses and Postbyzantine churches, notably that of St. George. Medieval towers which served as reconnaissance posts still stand at intervals along the coast (Pasha Limani below Mesta etc.).

The shores of Chios are excellent for both swimming and fishing and can be reached by bus, private transport or caique. For those with a boat a sail all around the island is a memorable experience (refuelling stations in the harbour at Chios, Kardamyla, Pasha Limani). The mountains provide good hunting. Tourist facilities are of a high standard and accommodation is available in hotels, rooms and furnished apartments.

Oinouses

Lying opposite the northeast tip of Chios (9 nautical miles) and very close to the Asia Minor coast is Oinouses, which belongs administratively to the Prefecture of Chios. It is just 14 sq. km. in area, has 48 km. of coastline and 703 inhabitants. There is a daily boat service from Chios.

The island is renowned for its illustrious tradition in seafaring. There is no provision for tourists and it is visited exclusively by expatriate sailors and ship-owners who mainly return for the summer vacation. Its small natural harbours with their little beaches, mansions, churches and Maritime Museum are the sole features of interest.

133. *Nea Moni, one of the most important Byzantine monuments in Greece.*

134. *View of Oinouses.*

Psara

GEOGRAPHY. 48 nautical miles northwest of Chios is Psara, 40 sq. km. in area, 36 km. of coastline and population 460. Communication with the island is only possible via Chios. It is a small island with a great history, tiny beaches and clean sea.

HISTORY. Psara was inhabited in Mycenaean times and during antiquity Bacchus was worshipped here. The islanders then, as always, were mainly mariners. In the 15th century Palaiokastro was built on the promontory of Chersonisos. Psara made a valiant contribution to the Greek War of Independence and because of the islanders' heroic resistance the island was burnt in 1824. There were very few survivors of the holocaust and they sought refuge on Euboia and Syros. The hero of the Revolution, Konstantinos Kanaris was from Psara. Apart from sailors and other natives living elsewhere, who return to spend the summer, the other vistors are transcient.

SIGHTS-MONUMENTS. **Psara**, the island's capital, is a small village built on the creek of the bay of Limena. Features of interest on the island include the old mansions, churches —particularly that of St. Nicholas where the Insurrection was declared— the monastery of the Dormition of the Virgin. In its church are two marble reliefs with representations of double-headed eagles and some rare volumes, printed in Venice and Moscow are kept here. There is a small Archaeological Museum in the main village with finds from excavations on the island. Almost the entire population lives here. Small boats sail from the harbour to the tiny, sandy coves, or even to nearby Antipsara. For those wishing to stay a little longer, there are two hostels in the village of Psara and a few rooms for rent.

135. Psara. View of the small village.

135

Samos

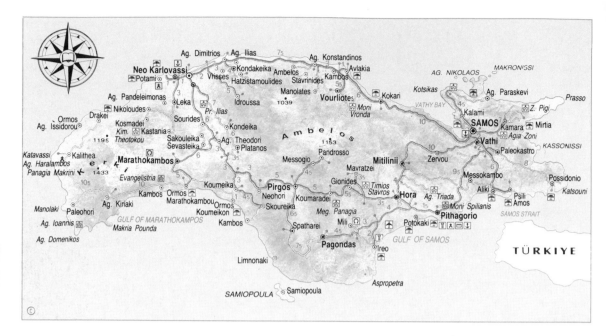

GEOGRAPHY. In the easternmost reaches of the Aegean, very close to the coast of Asia Minor (18 nautical miles), Samos is an island of exceptional natural beauty. 476 sq. km. in area, with 159 km. of coast, it is 175 nautical miles from Piraeus and has a population of 40,519. With well-developed tourist facilities, there are also daily car and passenger ferries from Piraeus and a link with Kavala once a week on the route Kavala - Piraeus. There are also connections with Ikaria, a regular service to Paros and, less frequently, with Syros and Phournoi. The boat travelling to the remoter islands on the Kavala - Piraeus route links Samos with the Dodecanese, Cyclades and Crete. Local craft go to Chios, the Dodecanese and Turkey. In the summer hydrofoils operate between Kos, Rhodes (twice a week) and (once a week) Leros and Patmos. There are daily flights to and from Athens. The island's capital is Samos and the main harbours are Vathy, Pythagoreion and Karlovasi. Despite the dominant mountainay massifs (highest peak Kerki, 1440 m. a.s.l.) the island's terrain displays considerable variety and small plains alternate with hilly regions, terminating in the gentle coastline, in complete harmony with its lush vegetation. Small towns and villages are scattered throughout and these, along with its many antiquities, monasteries and chapels make Samos a favourite island with tourists who can choose the kind of holiday which suits them, quiet or cosmopolitan.

HISTORY. Geologically, Samos was formed as a result of major tectonic upheavals, being separated from Asia Minor with which it was united (Quarternary period). In ancient times it was known by several names: *Dryousa, Elaiousa, Kyparissia* and even *Parthenia,* since it was the birthplace of Hera and here she was espoused to Zeus. The first inhabitants were Karians and Lelegians. Ionian colonisers arrived in around 1000 BC. During the 6th and 5th century BC Samos experienced a considerable acme, especially in 540 BC when the tyrant Polykrates came to power. Samos was conquered by the Medes during the Persian Wars and became a member of the Athenian League once they were over. In 440 BC, however, Samos renounced this alliance and the Athenians responded with intransigence, laying waste the island. Nevertheless, Samos fought alongside Athens against Sparta during the Peloponnesian War and afterwards passed in turn into the hands of the Macedo-

136. Samos. Vathy.

137. Karlovasi, view from above.

36

37

nians, Egyptian Ptolemies and Romans. During the Byzantine period it belonged to the Thema of the Aegean and was in a state of decline, harassed by pirates. When Constantinople fell to the Franks in 1204 the island was ceded first to the Franks, then to the Venetians and, from 1453 onwards, when Constantinople was taken by the Turks, the Samiotes fled their homes and sought refuge on Chios. Thus the island remained more or less desolated until the middle of the 16th century when the Turkish pasha, to whom it had been granted, introduced a series of measures (privileges, administrative independence, religious freedoms) which successfully attracted new settlers and its repopulation was effected. Even though it played an active role in the 1821 War of Independence it was not united with Greece until 1912. During the 80 year interim phase it had a special status of autonomy under Turkish suzereinty. It suffered extensive destruction during the Second World War.

SIGHTS-MONUMENTS. The island's capital, **Samos (Vathy)**, is built amphitheatrically around the harbour (Vathy), an inlet in the homonymous gulf. Exhibited in its museum are finds from excavations of the German Archaeological Institute at various sites on the island: Prehistoric, Geometric and Archaic pottery, wooden objects, sculpture, artefacts of ivory and bronze, votives and clay figurines. There is also a Museum of Ecclesiastical Art in town, a Byzantine Collection, Art Gallery, Folk Museum and Municipal Library. In the immediate environs are the monasteries of the Lifegiving Source (18th century) and Holy Girdle (17th century) with intricately carved iconostases and important icons. 10 km. south of Samos is **Pythagoreion**, colloquially known as *Tigani* (frying pan) on account of its shape, a name which prevailed from the 16th century until 1955. Prior to that it was called Samos. Excavations carried out by the German Archaeological Institute on the hill of the ancient acropolis have furnished evidence of occupation in prehistoric times, circa 3000 BC. The city was enclosed by a wall (6400 m. in perimeter) and Polykrates is accredited with its construction. Even today certain sections of it,

138. *Kokkari, partial view of the village.*

139. *Pythagoreio, partial view from the castle.*

140-141. *Karlovasi. Making pottery, a tradition still continued.*

140

141

teresting finds and fascinating details concerning its construction. Another of the town's sights is the Panaghia Spiliani cave, very near the chapel of the Virgin Spiliani.

6 km. south of Pythagoreion is the **Heraion**, the island's most important sanctuary in antiquity where the goddess Hera was worshipped. In the course of excavations directed by E. Buschor various buildings have been brought to light, remnants of altars (from the 10th century BC) and temples belonging to different chronological phases, the earliest being of 8th century date. This temple was replaced in the middle of the 7th century BC by a larger edifice, work of the Samian architect Roikos and regarded as one of the Seven Wonders of the ancient world, which was destroyed by fire in 538 BC. Rebuilding commenced during the reign of Polykrates but today all that remains is a single column "in situ". The road west of Vathy leads to Karlovasi and some 10 km. beyond Samos, in this same direction, is the lovely seaside village of **Kokkari** with churches to the Virgin and St. Nicholas. **Karlovasi** is situated 32 km. northwest of Samos and is the second largest town on the island, a sprawling yet picturesque conurbation. The church of the Virgin at **Potami,** 2 km. from Karlovasi, dates from the 11th century and replaced an Early Christian basilica of the 6th century. South of Karlovasi, beyond the village of Leka, is the monastery of Prophet Elijah (founded in the 17th century) and to the west, nestling in the foothills of mount Kerki, are the monasteries of the Annunciation (10th century) and the Dormition of the Virgin, close to the village of Kosmadaioi. At the entrance to the nearby Sarantaskaliotissa cave is a chapel to the Virgin. The cave of Pythagoras, higher up, where Pythagoras is traditionally reputed to have sought refuge, was also used by ascetics in Early Christian times. At **Kallithea,** on the far west of the island, are churches of St. Charalambos, in which there are 14th century wall-paintings, and the Virgin of Makrine (inside a cave in a virtually inaccessible location), in which there are also 14th century wall-paintings. South of Kallithea, at **Palaiochori**, there is the remote monastery of St. John, beside the sea. However, the island's most important monasteries are to the west of Vathy (25 km.) on the road to Pyrgos: those of the **Holy Cross (Stavros)** and the **Great Virgin (Megali Panaghia)**. The former was founded in 1582 and acquired its present aspect in 1838 when it was repaired, the iconostasis, pulpit and epi-

towers and gates, are still quite well-preserved. This wall girt the east mole of the harbour, the Kastelli hill, Ambelos hill and the monastery of the Virgin Spiliani, the hill on which the Kastro of Logothetis stands, and is reinforced by some 35 bastions. Adjacent to the Kastro of Logothetis, a fortification erected between 1822/24, stands the church of the Transfiguration, built in 1833 to commemorate the island's salvation in 1824.

The **Eupalineion aquaduct** is one of the major feats of ancient engineering, designed by Eupalinos from Megara and commissioned by the tyrant Polykrates who wished to convey water into the city from the source in the Ayades region. The aquaduct was discovered in 1881. In 1971 excavations revealed both in-

scopal throne in the katholikon date to that time. The monastery of the Great Virgin was established a little later than that of the Holy Cross and has a valuable iconostasis and wall-paintings. One may descend from here to the nearby village of Myloi and thence to the Heraion. In the fields around the *Heraion* (most easily reached from Chora) stands the Pyrgos of Sarakini, a three-storey, tower-like structure built in the 16th century which now belongs, along with the metochion, to the Patmos monastery of St. John the Theologian. The oldest monastery on the island, that of the **Virgin Brontiani,** founded in 1566, is situated to the west of Samos, near the village of Vourliotes. There is yet another monastery, less well-known, in the vicinity of cape **Kotsikas** on the island's east coast. The region is ideal for those who enjoy exploring and seeking out tiny bays in which to swim. One may hire a boat in the nearby village of **Aghia Paraskevi,** with its lovely beach at **Galazio,** and cross to the opposite islets of **Aghios Nikolaos** and **Makronisi** (uninhabited). There are other delightful beaches to the east of the town of Samos (6 km.) in the gulf of Myrtia. The rather remote beach at **Laka** is also beautiful and the offshore islet of Kasonisi is deserted. The shores at **Kokkari** (10 km. west of Samos), **Karlovasi, Potami, Poseidonio** (7 km. southeast of Samos), along the entire coast from **Psili Ammos** (6 km. south of Samos) as far as the **Heraion,** and the beaches in the gulf of **Marathokampos** are all fine for swimming, fishing and seasports. Not only can one enjoy a swim on the island of **Samiopoula,** off the south coast between **Pythagoreion** and **Marathokampos**, it is also possible to stay there. For those with sporty inclinations the island's mountainous hinterland is just the place for climbing, hiking and shooting, while those with a boat can visit its more secluded coves. Refuelling stations at Vathy and Pythagoreion. One is assured a comfortable stay on Samos since there are plenty of hotels, large and small but generally well-appointed, as well as rooms and furnished flats to let.

143

144

142. *The only extant column of the temple of Hera (Heraion).*

143. *Wonderful beaches and a verdant landscape are the main features of Samos.*

144. *Gulf of Marathokampos, yet another lovely beach on Samos.*

Ikaria

GEOGRAPHY. 10 nautical miles southwest of Samos is Ikaria, another of the large islands of the eastern Aegean. It covers an area of 255 sq. km., has 102 km. of coastline and 7,559 inhabitants. Ikaria and Phournoi belong administratively to the Prefecture of Samos. There are car and passenger ferries from Piraeus, 114 nautical miles away (daily in the summer), and connections with Samos, Paros and, (again in the summer) Syros and Phournoi. The boat to the far -flung islands on the Kavala - Piraeus route (once a week) links Ikaria with Kavala, the Dodecanese, Crete and the Cyclades. There is also a local service to Phournoi. The island's main town and chief harbour is Aghios Kirykos. Essentially a mountainous island (highest peak Aitheras, 1040 m. a.s.l.) with rocky coastline, Ikaria is famous for its numerous radioactive therapeutic springs. Apart from a few outcrops of marble, the island is mainly of schistose formations. In recent years its popularity with visitors has grown and it is an excellent spot for quiet, family holidays, even though tourist facilities are still under-developed. The climate is mild but blustery, since strong southeast winds blow in the winter and northerlies in the summer. The island's towns and villages are located mainly on tracts of flat land along the coast, with a few settlements in the mountains.

HISTORY. Ikaria assumed several names in antiquity: *Makris, Doliche, Ichthyoessa, Ikaros, Ikaria*. It was here, so myth relates, that Ikaros fell to his death, which is why the surrounding sea is called the Ikarian. It is also claimed as the birthplace of Dionysos. In the middle of the 8th century BC, or thereabouts, Ionian colonisers from the Asia Minor littoral settled here. It was captured by the Medes during the Persian Wars and afterwards became a member of the Athenian League. Ikaria took part in the Peloponnesian War as an ally of Athens. We have little information on the island's fate from the 4th century BC onwards. In Byzantine times it belonged to the Thema of the Aegean and those who provoked the emperor's displeasure were banished there. In 1191 it was ceded to the Venetians and ruled by a succession of noble families (Maonesi, Giustiniani) until it was taken by the Turks in 1567. Ikaria was finally liberated and incorporated in the Greek state in 1912.

SIGHTS-MONUMENTS. Aghios Kirykos, the island's capital, is built on its southeast side, facing Patmos. Churches include the cathedral (metropolis) and that dedicated to St. Nicholas. A small archaeological collection is housed in the Secondary school, as well as a folklore collection of exhibits associated with the island's historic past. About 1 km. to the east of the capital is the spa **Therma** with its radioactive springs. Remains of ancient baths have been found here and, according to inscriptions, the region was known as *Asklepeion*. A short distance to the north of the town are the ruins of the ancient city of **Drakano** (nowadays Fanari); a Hellenistic tower (3rd century BC) and section of the fortification wall are preserved. 38 km. northwest of Aghios Kirykos, is the second port of Ikaria, **Evdilos**, and near the village of **Kampos** (40 km.) are remains of the other important ancient city, *Oinoe*. Finds from here are exhibited in a small archaeological collection at Kampos. Some 2.5 km. west of here the Byzantines built a new city, called *Doliche,* a name which, like *Palatia,* held sway on account of the impressive Byzantine edifices in which the exiled nobles lived. Other interesting monuments hereabouts include the Byzantine church of St. Irene, while 3 km. further south stands the 10th century Byzantine castle of **Nikaria**.

At **Armenistis**, 51 km. northwest of Aghios Kirykos, graves of the 5th century BC have been unearthed, 4th century BC funerary stelae and, northwest of the church of St. Charalambos, the foundation courses of the defen-

145. Ikaria. Aghios Kirykos, partial view.

sive wall. Near the sea at **Na,** west of Armenistis, the remnants of the temple of Tauropolos Artemis are visible, from which significant finds dating from the 7th – 5th century BC have been recovered. The villages of the Mesaria region **Akamantra**, **Dafni**, **Kosoikia**, **Petroupoli** look out to sea. The southwest side of the island, particularly the villages of **Raches, Langada** and **Karkinagri**, has its own charm.

All the island's villages can be reached by bus and there is also a local caique service from Aghios Kirykos to the south coast. Beaches for swimming are those around **Aghios Kirykos**, **Evdilos**, **Yaliskari**, **Armenistis** (here the sea deepens suddenly). The best beaches are at **Mesakte** and **Livadi**. One can go by caique to **Therma**, **Fanari** and **Karkinagri** and even to the neighbouring islands of Phournoi and Thymaina where there are other delightful beaches and secluded coves.

Phournoi

Between Ikaria, Samos and Patmos is a cluster of tiny islands: Phournoi (or Korsoi), Aghios Minas and Thymaina, all of which belong to the Prefecture of Samos. Phournoi, the largest of these, is 30 sq. km. in area, has 126 km. of coastline and 1,203 inhabitants. It is 9 nautical miles from Samos with which there is a local caique service. Phournoi has been inhabited since antiquity and in the Byzantine era was a haven for pirates. Its population is mainly involved in fishing. Though there is no road network, the lovely beaches and picturesque bays make it a pleasant place for those seeking holidays "away from it all".

DODECANESE

The archipelago of the Dodecanese lies at the northeast edge of the Aegean. It consists of some 200 islands and islets, of which only 27 are inhabited, comprising a separate Prefecture in close proximity to the Turkish coast. The islands cover a total area of 2,705 sq. km. and have a population of 145,071. Though most of them are rather flat, tracts suitable for cultivation are limited to Rhodes, Kos, Kalymnos and Leros. Characteristic features of these islands are their mild climate and length of coastline. Little wonder that tourists flock here, both to the immensely popular large islands and to the smaller ones. With a common history within the context of the Hellenic world, there is a wealth of monuments, traditional architecture and outstandingly beautiful yet distinctly insular landscape. The capital, administrative and economic centre of the Prefecture is Rhodes.

Between East and West, in a vital geographical position, the Dodecanese have been inhabited since earliest times. Finds from the Palaeolithic and from the Neolithic era testify that most of the islands were settled in prehistoric times and in the Bronze Age Minoans, Achaeans and Mycenaeans came there. In around 1100 BC they were succeeded by Dorian colonisers, as well as Ionians who settled on Patmos and Leros. During the 8th century BC many of the islands enjoyed a period of economic and intellectual acme and founded colonies in the West. In the 6th century BC the three cities of Rhodes (Ialyssos, Lindos and Kameiros) comprised, along with Kos, Halicarnassus and Cnidus, the so-called Dorian Hexapolis. The islands were captured by the Medes during the Persian Wars and after the enemy was vanquished, at the battle of Salamis, they joined the Athenian League. In 408 BC the three cities of Rhodes were united in a single state. Kos experienced a period of zenith between the 4th and 3rd century BC, mainly due to the activities and fame of its Medical School, which was headed by Hippokrates. The Dodecanese continued to flourish in art and commerce until their capitulation to the Romans in 146 BC. In Byzantine times they belonged to the Thema of the Aegean. Though the Dodecanese maintained an independence after the Fall of Constantinople to the Franks, in 1309 they were captured by the Knights of the Order of St. John who remained there until 1522, when Rhodes finally fell to the Turks. Ottoman rule lasted untill 1912, in which year the islands came under Italian jurisdiction and so remained until 1945. In 1948 they were finally incorporated within the Greek state.

The visitor to the Dodecanese acquires yet another picture of island life and may revel in their natural beauty. The large islands, primarily Rhodes, are endowed with a plethora of monuments and rich variety of scenery, as well as a distinctly cosmopolitan atmosphere, all of which have gained it world-wide fame. The smaller and less frequented islands also have their own "couleur local" and tranquil rhythm of life. Churches, castles, mansions, vernacular architecture, narrow alleys, indented coastline, these are the principal characteristics of all the islands.

Rhodes, Kos, Kalymnos, Carpathos, Patmos, Leros, Astypalaia, Nisyros, Telos, Chalki, Symi, Kasos, Leipsoi and Kastellorizo; each with its own special charm, radiant in the sunlight.

Rhodes

GEOGRAPHY. Cross-roads of civilisations, with an age-old history and astonishing natural beauty, Rhodes is the largest island in the Dodecanese and the fourth largest island in Greece. It lies at the northeast limit of the Aegean, is 1398 sq. km. in area, has 220 km. of coastline and a population of 87,831. There is a regular car and passenger ferry from Piraeus, 260 nautical miles away, connecting the island with the rest of the Dodecanese, Crete and the Cyclades. Local boats also link it with all the islands of the Dodecanese and Samos. During the summer hydrofoils make trips to Kos, Symi, Patmos, Leros, Chalki, Nisyros and Telos. Excursion craft also operate in the summer sailing to Kos, Symi and Chalki. The boat plying the Piraeus-Kavala route to the outlying islands links Rhodes once a week with Melos, Pholegandros, Anaphi, Santorini, the islands of the north and east Aegean, Crete and Kavala. Throughout the year there is a weekly ship to Limmasol in Cyprus and Haifa in Israel. There are frequent flights from Athens and regular ones to Kasos, Leros, Carpathos, Kos, Crete and Mykonos. Last but not least, Rhodes is a port of call for numerous cruise liners. The island's main town and harbour is Rhodes, focus of the extensive network of roads leading to its many towns and villages. Three mountainous massifs dominate the island (highest peak Atavyros, 1215 m. a.s.l.), separated by fertile valleys and plains with lush vegetation, woodland and running water in plenty everywhere, excepting the south of Rhodes and the area around mount Atavyros.

A mild climate, unique and varied landscape, wonderful sea, monuments of all periods and antiquities; Rhodes is a mosaic of all these elements and its beauty defies description. An international tourist centre with sophisticated ambience, Rhodes is ideal for holidays all year round.

HISTORY. The island's geographical position, between Occident and Orient, was the major determinant factor throughout its history. Fruit of the union of Helios and the nymph Rhoda, according to myth, Rhodes was first inhabited in Neolithic times. During the Late Bronze Age (1550 – 1100 BC) Minoans settled there (Ialysos) and were succeeded in around 1400 BC by Achaeans who established installations all over it. The Dorians arrived here in about 1100 BC, founding three important cities, Lindos, Ialysos and Kameiros. In 700 BC these joined the Dorian hexapolis, along with Cnidus, Halicarnassus and Kos. Thenceforth Rhodes' power was in the ascendancy and it soon dominated the whole of the Dodecanese. This economic, cultural and artistic zenith was sustained throughout the 5th, 4th and 3rd century BC. During the Persian Wars Rhodes fought under duress alongside the Persians but subsequently joined the Athenian League (478 BC). In 411 BC the three cities united and in 408 BC founded the city of Rhodes by common concensus. Situated in the north of the island, on the coast, it was laid out in accordance with plans made by the architect Hippodamos from Miletus on exactly the same site as the modern city. Rhodes enjoyed exceptional splendour throughout the 3rd century BC and dominated the Aegean. Its coinage had a wide circulation and this commercial and economic apogee was accompanied by fervent cultural and artistic activity. Despite natural disasters and enemy incursions, which beset Rhodes following the Roman conquest, it never lost its pre-eminence and continued to be a major naval and mercantile centre. The Byzantine era was one of decline until 1309 when Rhodes was sold to the Knights of St. John, which heralded a new floruit. It was at this time that the imposing medieval town was built, with its magnificent buildings and enormous castle. Rhodes was captured by the Turks in 1522 and they remained until 1912 when it passed to the Italians. In 1948 it became part of the Greek state.

SIGHTS-MONUMENTS. **Rhodes**, the island's capital, built on its northeast tip is a combination of medieval atmosphere and worldly sophistication. One can visit the medieval town, ancient acropolis, Byzantine and Turkish monuments, walk around the fortification walls and then get to know the new town with its exciting hustle and bustle.

The harbour, **Mandraki**, with its picturesque windmills and countless craft moored beside the quay, was first arranged in antiquity. In all probability the gigantic statue of the Colossus of Rhodes stood here. The church of St. John

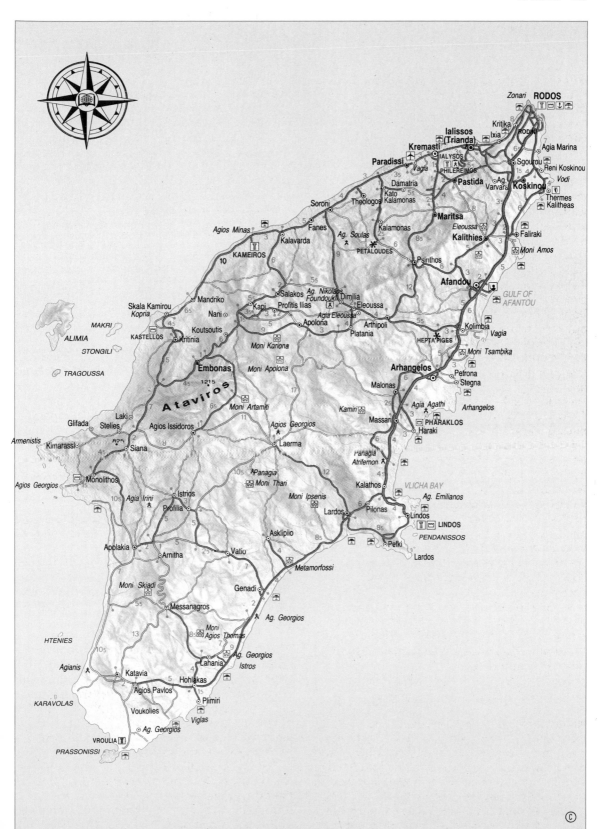

RODOS
Zonari

Kritika
Ixia
RODINI
Ialissos
(Trianda)
Kremasti
IALYSOS
Paradissi
PHILEREIMOS
Vagia
Sgourou
Agia Marina
Reni Koskinou
Pastida
Vodi
Damatria
Ag.
Varvara
Koskinou
Kato
Soroni
Theologos
Kalamonas
Thermes
Kalitheas
Agios Minas
Kalamonas
Maritsa
Fanes
Eleoussa
Kalavarda
Ag. Soulas
Kalithies
Faliraki
KAMEIROS
PETALOUDES
Moni Amos
10
Psinthos
Afandou
Mandriko
Salakos
Ag. Nikolaos
Foundoukli
Dimilia
GULF OF
AFANTOU
Skala Kamirou
Kopria
Nani
Kapi
Profitis Ilias
Eleoussa
MAKRI
Agia Eleoussa
Kolimbia
Vagia
ALIMIA
Koutsoutis
Apolona
Arthipoli
STONGILI
KASTELLOS
Kritinia
Platania
HEPTA PIGES
Moni Tsambika
TRAGOUSSA
Moni Kariona
Petrona
Arhangelos
Embonas
Moni Apolona
Stegna
1215
Malonas
Agia Agathi
Arhangelos
Atáviros
Kamiri
Moni Artamiti
Massari
PHARAKLOS
Laki
Agios Georgios
Haraki
Glifada
Stelies
Agios Issidoros
Armenistis
Kimarassi
Laerma
Panagia
Atrifernon
Siana
Agios Georgios
Monolithos
Panagia
Moni Ipsenis
Kalathos
VLICHA BAY
Agia Irini
Moni Thari
Lardos
Ag. Emilianos
Istrios
Pilonas
Profilia
Lindos
Asklipiio
LINDOS
Apolakia
Vatiu
Pefki
PENDANISSOS
Arnitha
Metamorfossi
Lardos
Moni Skiadi
Genadi
Messanagros
Ag. Georgios
HTENIES
Moni
Agios Thomas
Ag. Georgios
Agianis
Lahania
Istros
KARAVOLAS
Katavia
Hohlakas
Agios Pavlos
Plimiri
Voukolies
Viglas
Ag. Georgios
VROULIA
PRASSONISSI

at Mandraki merits a visit, as does the Governor's palace and the Murat Reis mosque, built on the site of the church of St. Anthony which was demolished by the Turks. The market and shopping centre known as the Nea Agora is just behind Mandraki. One enters the old town through the Freedom Gate. Here the history of the time of the Knights of St. John comes to life at every step. One proceeds to the Collacium where the Knights lived, and then to the palace of the Grand Master of the Order. One walks along the cobbled Street of the Knights, flanked by the "Inns" of each of the "Tongues" of the Order and should visit the Arsenal (formerly the Hospital of the knights) and Museum of Decorative Arts. In the Rhodes Archaeological Museum, housed in the later Infirmary or Hospital of the knights, finds from excavations all over Rhodes, as well as elsewhere in the Dodecanese, are displayed. The most impressive building of all is the Grand Master's Palace which was originally constructed in the 14th century and which survived intact until 1856. In 1939 it was restored by the Italians, new grandiose additions made, since it was intended to serve as a residence for king Victor Emmanuel II and Mussolini. It is indeed an impressive edifice consisting of numerous halls and chambers, the floors of which are set with Roman and Early Christian mosaics, mainly brought from Kos. In Socrates Street one may see the Clock Tower, several mosques (Suleiman's mosque, Aga mosque, Kavakli-Mestits on the site of an Early Christian basilica, Demirli mosque on the site of a Byzantine church, and others). There is also the Mercantile Court and Aristotle street with its rather oriental ambience. Important churches include that of the Virgin (15th century), St. Panteleimon and the ruined church of the Virgin of Victory, built after the successful repulsion of the besieging Turks in 1480. Close by is St. Catherine's Gate leading also to the Harbour Gate and St. Paul's Gate. The town is girt by a wall 4 km. in perimeter and at set times there are organised walks upon it, a truly memorable experience. These ramparts were built in the 14th century, replacing an earlier Byzantine enceinte. A large number of Early Chris-

147

148

146. Rhodes. Entrance to the harbour of Mandraki with the famous bronze deer.

147. Mandraki, the New Market-place and the Grand Master's Palace.

148. Entrance to the Grand Master's Palace.

149

150

tian churches have survived in Rhodes, including the outstanding 5th century basilica (at the intersection of P. Melas and Cheimaras Streets). Other significant churches are the Virgin of the Castle (11th – 12th century), St. Phanourios (for some time the mosque Plial el Din) which is of 13th century date and has important wall-paintings and St. George, which has 14th – 15th century wall-paintings. The ancient city of Rhodes, founded in 401 BC extended northwards and eastwards of the acropolis (Monte Smith) and the medieval town of the Knights stands on top of a greater part of it. The summit of Monte Smith, from where there is a magnificent view over verdant land and azure sea, was the ancient acropolis. Remnants of the temples of Athena Polias and Zeus Polieus are preserved and, to the west, the temple of Apollo. Restored and ruined edifices can still be seen, including the theatre and stadium (2nd century BC), both restored by the Italians, and the gymnasium. The new town is also an interesting place with its numerous Italian colonial style buildings and many churches. There is also a Municipal Art Gallery, Islamic Library and rich Folk Art collection.

A visit to the island's interior is an unforgettable experience on account of the wonderful scenery and abundance of monuments in every village and hamlet.

15 km. southwest of the town of Rhodes, near the village of Trianda, on top of mount Philerimos is the ancient site of Ialysos, one of the island's three Dorian cities. The foundations of the temple of Athena and Zeus Polieus are preserved (4th century BC), as well as remnants of Byzantine and medieval buildings. Here too is the important church of the Virgin of Philerimos which belonged to a 15th century monastery built by the Knights of St. John. Yet another significant church is that of Ai Yorgi tou Chostou in which there are 14th and 15th century wall-paintings. There is also a well-preserved 4th century BC Doric fountain and a 134-stepped Way to Golgotha with mosaic plaques of the Twelve Stations of the

149. Traces of the temple of Pythios Apollo on the ancient acropolis of Rhodes.

150. Hippokrates square with fountain.

151. The church of the Virgin at Fileremos.

152. Kameiros. Restored columns of a Hellenistic house.

151

152

Cross along its right side. the **Valley of the Butterflies** (20 km. south of Rhodes) is a densely wooded region which attracts myriads of brightly coloured butterflies between June and September and is a popular tourist haunt.

Another of the major archaeological sites on Rhodes is **Kameiros**, one of the three Dorian cities. Built in a valley it has neither a city wall nor an acropolis and its houses and temples were revealed in excavations conducted by the Italians. The restored columns of a Hellenistic house are particularly impressive, as is the Doric stoa in the agora and part of the temple of Athena. South of Kameiros is **Kastello**, a castle built by the knights on the pinnacle of an imposing crag. At **Embonas** (13 km. southeast), one of the quaintest villages on Rhodes with lovely traditional houses, local customs are still very much alive and many villagers still wear Rhodian costume. The most impressive fortress is that of **Monolithos** (92 km. southwest of Rhodes). This is an inland village on the south side of the island, far off the tourist track and rather difficult to get to. The knights built the castle in the 15th century at the very top of a precipitous cliff beside the sea, from where one has an unrivalled view. Other interesting villages on the south coast are **Mesanagros** (106 km. from Rhodes) and **Kattavia**, famed for its woven goods. The now-ruined Skiadi monastery merits a visit to see the important wall-paintings in its katholikon and the Ypseni monastery near Lardos is also of interest. **Archangelos** is a particularly pretty village (south of Rhodes) with dazzling white houses, then there is Malonas from where one can visit the castle of Faraklos, one of the largest and mightiest on Rhodes. Further south (58 km. from Rhodes) is **Lindos**, perhaps the most beautiful village on the island, with its narrow streets and fascinating houses in which the traditional interior decoration is still kept with copious wood-carving and the famous "Lindian" plates. An inscription bearing the date 1489/90 is preserved in the parish church and the coat-of-arms of Grand Master d'Aubusson. The village is dominated by the ancient acropolis built at the edge of a steep rock. Remnants of the sanctuary and temple of Athena Lindia (4th century BC) have been uncovered and partially restored, as also the Stoa and Propylaia. There are also traces of the temple of Dionysos and, on the west slope, the ancient theatre is preserved in quite good condition. Graves have also been brought to light in the area, including that popularly known as the tomb of Kleoboulos. Just inside the entrance to the acropolis is the ruined castle of the knights and Byzantine church of St. John. At the base of the large stairway leading up to the acropolis there is a large Hellenistic relief of a trireme carved in the rock and to the right of it steps of the ancient flight of stairs are preserved.

At **Thermes Kallithea** (10 km. southeast of Rhodes) there are therapeutic springs. Kallithea is a particularly attractive region on the coast, very richly vegetated. **Afantou** is yet another delightful village (20 km. south of Rhodes) which developed in the days of the corsairs and was so named because it was not visible from the sea. There is a golf course nearby. Villages in which the vernacular heritage of Rhodes is still much in evidence include **Koskinou** (8 km. southeast of Rhodes) where the house interiors are decorated with Rhodian ceramics and woven items. **Kremasti** (12 km. southeast of Rhodes) is a tourist village, surpassed by **Faliraki** (14 km. southeast of Rhodes) which is even more cosmopolitan. Other places worth visiting are **Asklipeio**, and the church of **Aghios Nikolaos** at **Fountoukli**.

Beaches and stretches of coast suitable for swimming and sea sports abound on Rhodes. Within the main town the beach between the yacht club and Hotel Mediterranean is fully equipped for all manner of sea sports. The beaches at **Kanaris quay**, **Faliraki** and **Lindos** are lovely and the bays at **Kremasti** and **Kameiros** large. The eastern shores are more sheltered. There are stretches of sand at **Afantou**, **Koskinou** and the entire strip of coast as far as **Lindos** and **Prasonisi**. There are an athletics stadium, riding club, volley court, tennis courts, golf course and two water skiing schools on Rhodes. Fishing is particularly good at Kallithea, Kameiros, Lindos and Vlychoi bay. In the mountains of the hinterland and the Lindos area one can shoot small game and birds. There are scores of hotels of all categories, as well as pensions, rooms and apartments to let. The visitor is assured an enjoyable and comfortable stay. Those with a private yacht or boat can refuel at the harbour and at Mandraki boats can also be hired for those wishing to make excursions to nearby islands.

153. Lindos. The acropolis, village and harbour.

154. Lindos. The large Doric stoa and the temple of Athena on the left.

153

154

Carpathos

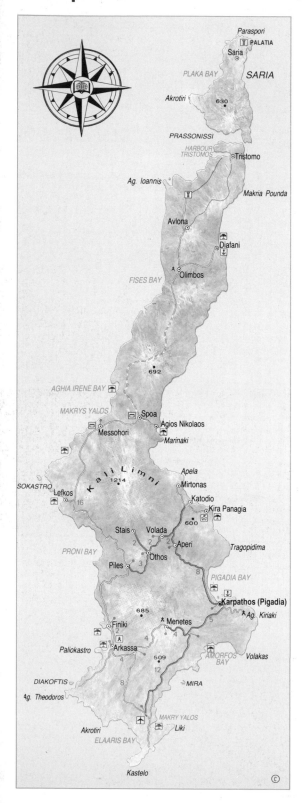

GEOGRAPHY. Carpathos, the second largest of the Dodecanese, lies between Rhodes and Crete. It is 301 sq. km. in area, has 160 km. of coastline, a population of 4,645 and is 227 nautical miles from Piraeus. There is a car and passenger ferry from Piraeus throughout the year, linking it also with other islands of the Dodecanese and Crete. The boat on the Piraeus - Kavala route links Carpathos with Melos, Pholegandros, Santorini, Anaphi, Crete, the rest of the Dodecanese, the northeast Aegean islands and Kavala. A local boat service operates between Kasos, Chalki and Rhodes. There is an air service, via Rhodes, to Athens and flights to Kasos and Crete. Carpathos is a mountainous island (highest peak Kalolimni, 1,215 m. a.s.l.) with only a few plains in the south. At its northernmost tip a narrow channel separates it from the islet of Saria. The island's main town and port is Carpathos (Pigadia) and there is a second harbour at Diaphani on its northeast side. The island is distinguished by its picturesque serenity. Beautiful bays, the traditional rhythm of life and architecture, hospitable people compose the picture of Carpathos today and one is assured of pleasant, peaceful holidays there.

HISTORY. Information on the island's history is somewhat scant but there were four important cities in ancient times, as evident from their participation in the Athenian League. From the 5th century onwards it was included within the sphere of influence of Rhodes until, like the other islands, it was captured by the Romans. During the Byzantine period it was destroyed several times. After the Fall of Constantinople to the Franks the island was governed by Leon Gavalas until the mid-16th century (1538) when it was captured by the Turks. Carpathos took part in the 1821 War of Independence and even experienced a brief phase of autonomy until 1832 when it was retaken by the Turks. From 1912 onwards it, like the rest of the Dodecanese was administered by the Italians and was not incorporated in the Greek state until 1948.

SIGHTS-MONUMENTS. The island's capital, **Carpathos (Pigadia),** is located on the southeast side of the island, probably on the site of ancient Poseidio, ruins of the acropolis of which have been recognised on the hill Kavos.

155

The houses in Carpathos are mainly modern, built by emigrants to the United States, and do not conform to the traditional style of architecture.

The village of **Menetes** (8 km. southwest of Carpathos) has been inhabited since the Middle Ages and has interesting churches (St. Mamas, the Dormition), as well as several houses with Neoclassical elements. 16 km. southwest of Carpathos is the village of **Arkasa,** identified with the ancient city of *Arkesia.* Remnants of the city wall are preserved near the top of the hill. From the ruined Byzantine church of Holy Wisdom (5th century) exceptional mosaic floors have been removed (nowadays in the Rhodes Museum). The villages to the north of Pigadia are of especial interest since many of the houses are authentic examples of vernacular architecture. Those below Volada are known as the Kato Choria (lower villages), while those north of Mesochori are called Pano Choria (upper villages). The most notable of the Kato Choria is **Aperi**, the island's administrative centre from the early 18th century until 1892. The castle built here was to protect the populace from piratical raids. **Volada** (10 km. northwest of Carpathos) has many old Carpathian houses with their original interior decoration, **Othos** (13 km.) has a local museum of folk art and domestic utensils in one of its old houses and **Pyles** (13 km.) is worth a visit. At **Mesochori** (31 km. northwest of Carpathos) one can visit a genuine Carpathian house with its characteristic wood-carved decoration and pebble mosaic floor. At both Mesochori and **Spoa** (northeast) there are ruins of medieval towers. Without doubt the most fascinating village on Carpathos is **Olymbos** (Elymbos). It was founded some time between the 10th and 15th century by shepherds and inhabitants from Vrykounta at the northernmost tip of the island which had been destroyed by earthquakes. Olymbos is situated in a rather inaccessible region and was originally girt by a defensive wall of which some remnants survive. Nothing remains of the tower (Pyrgos) which once stood at the very top of the village. The villagers lived both inside and outside the castle. In the centre of the village is the large church of the Virgin,

156

155. *Carpathos. Partial view of the village of Olympos (Elymbos).*

156. *The nowadays half-ruined windmills dominate the village of Elymbos.*

157

158

while other notable churches are that of St. Onouphrios and of the Holy Trinity. With its old houses, typical vernacular architecture and richly adorned house interiors, Olymbos is a living museum. The villagers speak their own local dialect in which there are many vestiges of Doric Greek, and proudly maintain their heritage and customs, the women still wear traditional costume all the time. There are several ruined windmills in prominent positions and the entire area commands a spectacular view of the Aegean. Olymbos is best reached from the sea, from the harbour of **Diaphani**, which can be reached by local boat from the town of Carpathos or the regular ship from Piraeus calls there. One can take a caique from Diaphani to the islet of **Saria** just off the north tip of the island.

There are plenty of lovely beaches on Carpathos, in the vicinity of the harbour (Pigadia) and on its north coast **Phoiniki, Afiarti, Platyalos,** which can be easily reached by bus. **Diaphani, Mesochori, Tristomo** and **Saria** can be easily reached by caique. Apart from swimming the sea is also fine for fishing. Visitors may stay in hotels, pensions, rented rooms and flats both in Pigadia and Diaphani. There are also rooms to let at Mesochori, Olymbos, Othos and Arkasa. Refuelling station for yachts at Carpathos (Pigadia).

157-158. Scenes from everyday life in Elymbos where the villagers keep their customs alive and the women wear traditional costume all the time.

Kasos

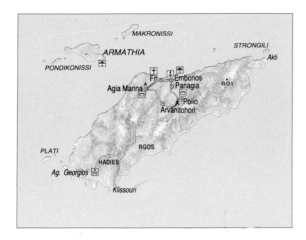

GEOGRAPHY. Very close to the southwest coast of Carpathos and 27 nautical miles from Crete, Kasos is the southernmost island of the Dodecanese. 66 sq. km. in area, it has 50 km. of coastline, a population of 1,184 and is 220 nautical miles from Piraeus. There are car and passenger ferries from Piraeus twice a week, as well as the rest of the Dodecanese and Crete. The boat on the Piraeus - Kavala route to the outlying islands connects it with Melos, Pholegandros, Anaphi, Santorini, Leros, Leipsoi, the northeast Aegean islands and Kavala. A local service operates among the Dodecanese and there are flights, via Rhodes, to Athens. A predominantly mountainous island (highest peak Prionas, 600 m. a.s.l.), the coast has steep cliffs with very few stretches of sand and there is minimal touristic development. The island is ideal for those seeking peace and quiet, close to nature.

HISTORY. Phoenicians are mentioned as the island's first inhabitants and its history has always been linked with that of neighbouring Carpathos. In historical times its fate differed little from that of the rest of the Dodecanese and its capital was *Polion*. From the end of the 13th century it belonged to the Knights of St. John until about the middle of the 16th century when it was subjugated by the Turks. An island with a great tradition in seafaring, its boats played their part in the 1821 Struggle for Independence. In May 1824 Kasos suffered the worst catastrophe in its history when it was set on fire by the combined Turkish and Egyptian fleet. There was only a handful of survivors. Kasos became part of the Greek state in 1948.

SIGHTS - MONUMENTS. The island's capital, **Phry** (Orphys), is built at the far end of the gulf of Bouka. Several old captain's houses set on the hillside are still preserved. In the local museum there is a small archaeological and folk art collection. 1 km. southwest of Phry, at **Aghia Marina,** there are several churches, as well as the *Ellinokamara*. On the other shore of the gulf, east of Phry, is **Emboreios** with its three-aisled church of the Virgin. 3 km. southeast of here is the old capital of Kasos, **Polion,** where there are remains of a fortress and church of the Holy Trinity. There are notable churches at **Panaghia** (1 km. east of Phry), dedicated to the Virgin and housing the coffin of Hosia Kassiani and another of the Sts. Anargyroi. At **Chadies** (12 km. southwest) is the monastery of St. George and at **Apokrani** that of St. Mamas. Although the steep coast of Kasos is not really suitable for swimming it offers good fishing.

159. Kasos. View of the harbour.

159

Symi

GEOGRAPHY. Just a few metres from the Asia Minor coast and only 20 miles from Rhodes projects the lovely island of Symi. It is 58 sq, km. in area, has 85 km. of coastline and a population of 2,273. It is 230 nautical miles from Piraeus with which there is a car and passenger ferry link twice a week, via Amorgos, Astypalaia, Nisyros Telos and Rhodes. Once a week there is a boat to Kalymnos, Kos, Kastellorizo and another to Carpathos, Kos and Crete. A local craft travels to the rest of the Dodecanese and Samos all year round, while there is a daily service to Rhodes and a hydrofoil linking Symi with Rhodes and Kos. The island's capital is Symi. Its terrain is mountainous with small valleys in the interior and its climate mild and dry. The coastline follows the configuration of the land, there are sheer cliffs in places and small sandy beaches in others. Symi is still an unspoilt island with no cars and plenty of steep stepped streets. The small coastal villages, its elegant capital and quiet life style are appreciated by those who want a restful vacation in a tranquil environment.

HISTORY. The island was inhabited in prehistoric times and myth relates that this was the birthplace of the Three Graces. In antiquity it was also known as *Aigle, Metapontis* and, finally, Symi after the nymph of that name, wife of Poseidon and mother of Chthonios. Prometheus, son of Iapetos, sought refuge on Symi when banished by Zeus and, according to myth, lived there till the end of his days. Lelegians, Rhodians, Argives and Lacedaemonians all came to Symi and were later followed by the Romans, Byzantines and the Knights of St. John. In 1522 Symi fell to the Turks. Throughout its history Symi served as a trading and commercial station. From 1373 the Knights of St. John helped promote marine and mercantile activities by granting the island special privileges which the Symiotes managed to maintain during the period of Turkish rule. In fact the island achieved a considerable degree of self-government in the Ottoman period. Such was the acme in those days that Symiotes bought tracts of land on the opposite coast of Asia Minor. For many years Symi was renowned for its shipwrights, fishermen and sponge-divers and the island amassed both wealth and glory. A reminder of this former pre-eminence is the copy of the trireme – like the relief at the base of the acropolis of Lindos on Rhodes – nowadays by the harbour. Symi played an active role in the 1821 War of Independence but did not manage to secure its liberation. The island's decline was signalled by the appearance of steam ships and continued during the Italian occupation from 1912 onwards. It was in Symi that the Protocol delivering the Dodecanese from the German army of occupation to the Allies was signed (8th March 1945). It was incorporated in the Greek state in 1948.

SIGHTS - MONUMENTS. The island's capital, **Symi**, is divided into **Ano Symi** (called Chora by the locals) and **Kato Polis** (Yalos or Aiyalos) and is located on the north side of the island. Many of the beautiful Symiote houses which once embellished the water's edge still stand though all around are burnt-out shells of others, mostly destroyed by incendiary bombs in the last war. The majority of houses at Yalo date to the 19th century, those in Chora are significantly older. As one climbs up the steep, stepped street from the main square (*Plateia tis Skalas*), to left and right rise impressive Neoclassical houses. Not only are the external embellishments, doors and windows, preserved, but the wood-carved interiors also. Symi has a great tradition in wood carving, which formerly played its part in the island's econo-

160. Symi. Partial view of the town with its many lovely Symiote houses dating from the 19th century.

160

161

162

my and, indeed, ship's carpentry is still an important and well-paid skill. In the local museum there are sculptures and inscriptions of the Hellenistic and Roman era, Byzantine icons and coins, as well as folk art objects on display.

Apart from the mansions in Chora, there are many other sights of interest on Symi. The town is dominated by the castle of the Knights, built of ancient material and nowadays abandoned. Here too stands one of the most charming churches on the island, the Great Virgin. There are other interesting churches, many with mosaic decoration, and several monasteries. At **Pedi** (2 km. east) are those of St. George and of the Holy Trinity. At **Emboreion** (4 km. north) there are Byzantine remains and a church of the Virgin. Important monasteries are those of the **Great Saviour** and **St. Michael Roukouniotis**.

After the town of Symi (Yalos and Chora) the most interesting place on the island is the monastery of the **Taxiarch Michael Panormitis,** patron saint of Symi. The monastery was built at the beginning of the 18th century in the sheltered bay of Panormitis, hence the epithet, on the southwest coast. Boats call here daily, both from the town of Symi and from Rhodes, from where one-day excursions are organised. On the Taxiarch's feast day, November 8th, and at Whitsuntide, pilgrims flock here not only from the whole of the Dodecanese, but from Crete and other parts of Greece. There are facilities catering for visitors at Panormitis for they come not only for the monastery but also the gorgeous scenery and environment. One can reach here by caique from the harbour. Caiques also sail to the picturesque bay of **Aghios Emilianos** and the tiny islet opposite where the chapel to the saint stands, to the beach at **Nanou**, perhaps the best on the island, to **Marathounta**, **Disalona** and the islets of **Aghia Marina** amd **Nimos**. The beaches at **Yalos**, **Pedi** and **Emboreion** (Nimborio) are easily reached on foot or by caique and are ideal for swimming. Private boats can anchor in the many bays (Yalos, Pedi, Aghios Emilianos, Nimborio, Panormitis). There is a refuelling station at Yalos. Accommodation is available in hotels (two at Yalos), rented rooms, houses and hostels in Chora, Pedi, Yalos and Panormitis.

161-162. Scenes from everyday life on Symi.

Chalki

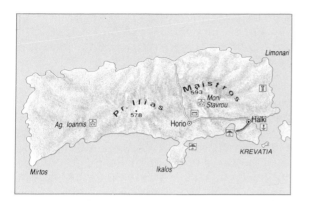

GEOGRAPHY. The small island of Chalki to the west of Rhodes has recently been declared an international meeting place for the world's Youth Movements. It is just 28 sq. km. in area, has 34 km. of coastline, a population of 334 and is 302 nautical miles from Piraeus. There is a boat from Piraeus, via the outlying islands, linking it also with Amorgos, Pholegandros, Melos, Santorini, Anaphi, the rest of the Dodecanese, Crete, the islands of the north and east Aegean and Kavala. A local service links it with Carpathos, Kasos and Rhodes and in the summer there is a hydrofoil service from Rhodes (harbour and Kameiros) once a week. The island's capital is Chalki (Nimborio). A mountainous island (highest peak Merovigli, 650 m.a.s.l.) with no provision for tourists, it is fine for those wanting a true taste of island life with only basic amenities.

HISTORY. Chalki was inhabited in ancient times and seems to have been named after the copper mines there. Excavations have shown that it experienced a period of acme in antiquity (10th – 5th century BC) but later sunk into oblivion. In the 13th century it was captured by the Venetians. Its recent history is much the same as that of the other islands of the Dodecanese and it became part of the Greek state in 1948.

SIGHTS-MONUMENTS. The island's capital and port is **Nimborio**, built amphitheatrically on its southeast side on the creek of the bay of Nimborio. The former capital, **Chora**, nowadays deserted, was in the island's hinterland in order to escape the menace of pirates. There are many abandoned houses at Chora which in its hey-dey was a thriving community of some 4000 souls. The ruined medieval castle still stands, built on the site of the ancient acropolis, as does the church of St. Nicholas with its significant wall-paintings. Other places of interest on the island include the **monasteries**, of the **Taxiarch Michael**, of **St. John**, the **Holy Trinity** and the **Holy Cross**.

One can reach the beaches on both the north and south coast of the island by caique or by walking from Nimborio. There are good fishing grounds between Chalki and the islets of Alimia and Erimonisa. Accommodation is available in three pensions and a few rooms to let. There is no refuelling station for yachts.

The nearby islet of **Alimia** can be reached by caique from Chalki or excursion craft from Rhodes. The fishing is excellent and visitors can stay in the small hospice in the monastery of St. George. The handful of houses belong to farmers from Chalki.

163. Chalki. Partial view of the capital Nimborio.

Telos

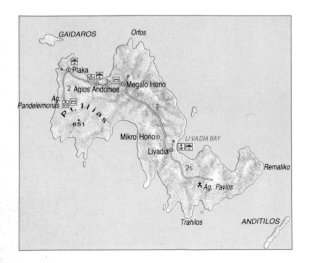

GEOGRAPHY. Telos, one of the smallest islands of the archipelago, lies between Nisyros and Chalki to the north of Rhodes. It is just 63 sq, km. in area with 63 km. of coastline, a population of 301 and is 290 nautical miles from Piraeus. There is a twice weekly car and passenger ferry link with Piraeus and a connection with Amorgos, the remaining Dodecanese and Crete. A local service operates with the rest of the Dodecanese and Samos and small boats make frequent trips to Chalki. A hydrofoil also operates between Rhodes and Telos. The island's capital is Megalo Chorio and its port is Skala, the main harbour is Livadia. With its many monuments, small settlements and lovely beaches, Telos is a pleasant place for a quiet vacation.

HISTORY. Long before the first human inhabitants reached Telos a species of prehistoric elephant evidently lived there, skeletons of which have been found in the Charkadion cave. Around 1000 BC the Dorians settled on Telos and in the 7th century BC, according to Herodotus, the Teliotes joined the Rhodians in founding the colony of Gela in Sicily. In the 5th century BC Telos became a member of the Athenian League but it later switched its loyalties to Sparta and after 394 BC became independent. It remained independent and flourishing until at least the end of the 4th century BC when it allied itself with Kos. Subsequently it remained a dependency of Rhodes until its subjugation by the Romans. Throughout the

Roman occupation, Byzantine times, up until the 14th century, its fortunes declined. In 1310 it was captured by the Knights of St. John and at that time was apparently known as (e)Piskopi. In 1522, after countless attacks, it finally fell to the Turks and its subsequent fate was the same as that of the other islands of the Dodecanese.

SIGHTS - MONUMENTS. Megalo Chorio, the island's capital is located in its interior, on the north side, most of its old houses being built amphitheatrically around the slopes of the hill of Aghios Stefanos. Most of the finds from the ancient cemetery are nowadays housed in the Rhodes Museum and a bronze hydria is in the British Museum, London. At the top of the hill are the walls of the castle of the Knights and within its ruined interior one can see the remains of a cistern and a large church with 16th century wall-paintings. Other places of interest in Chorio include the church of the Taxiarch. In the centre of the island is the nowadays abandoned village of **Mikro Chorio,** to the northwest of which are remnants of a medieval tower. Southeast of here is Livadia (6 km. from Megalo Chorio) the second port on the island where larger vessels drop anchor. It is a picturesque modern settlement with island architecture in a verdant environment. Other places of interest on Telos include the Monastery of St. Anthony, beside the sea, and of St. Panteleimon, patron saint of the island, dated to the 18th century and situated in a particularly beautiful region. It is enclosed within a high wall and there is a square tower at its entrance. At **Aghiosykia** there is a ruined medieval castle.

Telos has several sandy beaches with clear blue sea, accessible on foot or by farm vehicle. The most beautiful is **Erystos** (2.5 km. from Megalo Chorio), while the bay of **Livadia** is particularly picturesque and the swimming good at Aghios Antonios and Plaka. There is small game in the island's mountainous interior, particularly partridge. Visitors may stay in the hotel at Livadia or in the few rooms for rent there and at Erystos. Private yachts can replenish water supplies at Livadia.

164. Telos. Partial view of Megalo Chorio and the castle of the Knights.

Nisyros

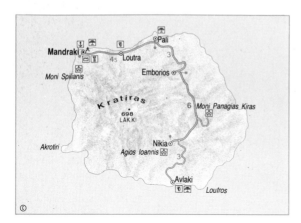

GEOGRAPHY. Nisyros, between Kos and Telos, is a quiet island off the tourist track, dominated by its white houses, blue sea and now extinct volcano. Area 41 sq. km., length of coastline 28 km., population 916 and distance from Piraeus 200 nautical miles. There is a boat from Piraeus three times a week all year round, with the other islands of the Dodecanese and Crete. A local connection operates with Telos, Symi, Rhodes, Kos, Kalymnos, Patmos, Leros and Samos. During the summer there is a hydrofoil once a week to Rhodes and Kos. With its tranquil atmosphere and picturesque appearance, Nisyros is just the place for a vacation away from it all, though there is little tourist development and only rudimentary facilities.

HISTORY. Inhabited since antiquity, the island was then known as *Porphyris* and myth relates that it was joined with Kos, being rent asunder by Poseidon while pursuing the giant Polybetes who is said to have created its volcano. Homer mentions that the island took part in the Trojan War. During historical times its fate was the same as that of the rest of the Dodecanese. In the 14th century it was captured by the Knights of St. John who built a castle there in 1315. Afterwards it was taken by the Turks and occupied by the Italians in 1912. It became part of the Greek state in 1948.

SIGHTS - MONUMENTS. The island's main town and port is **Mandraki** on its northwest side. Its medley of stark white and brightly col-

oured houses contrasts markedly with the dark, sombre volcanic rock on which they are built. Sections of the ancient harbour wall are preserved at Mandraki, as well as the area of the ancient cemetery. The town is dominated by its castle from where there is a superb view out to sea. Perched at the very edge of the rock is the church of the Virgin Spiliani, founded in 1600 and associated Venetian castle at **Emboreio** (8 km. southeast of Mandraki), a village surrounded by greenery and with mineral springs.

The quaint fishing village of **Paloi** is 4 km. northeast of Mandraki.

Without doubt the most impressive feature of Nisyros is the crater of its extinct volcano on the Lakki plateau. It is 260 m. in diameter and has a maximum depth of 30 m., steps lead down to its heart. The soil here is soft, there is a lingering odour of sulphur and hot vapours issue from the ground. Close to the volcano is the upland village of **Nikia** with a handful of inhabitants.

Loutra (1.5 km. east of Mandraki) was renowned in antiquity as a spa with therapeutic sulphurous springs. The island's shores are suitable for fishing and swimming. There is a lovely sandy beach at Mandraki. East of here is the large black pebble beach at Choklaki, the result of volcanic activity. Other delightful beaches are at Paloi and Aghia Irini. The sea at Avlaki is crystal clear. The beaches can be reached on foot or by bus. One can take a caique to the tiny islet of **Yali,** 4 nautical miles from Nisyros. There are small hotels and rooms to let at Mandraki and a hostel at Paloi. Yachts can moor in the harbour but there are no refuelling facilities.

165. Nisyros. View of the capital Mandraki with the castle.

166. Nisyros. The castle from the sea.

Astypalaia

GEOGRAPHY. Rather isolated from the rest of the Dodecanese and nearer the Cyclades, Astypalaia lies between Amorgos, Anaphi and Kalymnos. It is also known as *Astropalia* and *Stampalia,* reminders of its Venetian occupation. 97 sq. km. in area, with 110 km. of coastline and 1,030 inhabitants it is 180 nautical miles from Piraeus. There is a ferry boat service four times a week during the summer and three times a week in winter. There are also boat connections with the Cyclades, the Dodecanese and, via the route to the outlying islands, with Crete. The island's terrain is mountainous (highest peak Vardia, 482 m. a.s.l.) and in effect consists of two peninsulae (south and north) linked by a narrow isthmus 105 m. wide. The morphology of the land has affected that of the coastline which is indented with many small coves and larger bays. The island's capital Astypalaia is the focus of all routes to the rest of the island with its few villages and scattered farmsteads. Its harbour is called Pera Yalos. With its tardy way of life, lovely beaches and small bays, Astypalaia is a perfect place for quiet holidays away from tourists.

HISTORY. Excavations have shown that Astypalaia was inhabited in prehistoric times, first by Karians and Phoenicians and later by Cretans, Mycenaeans and Megarites. In antiquity the island was known by several names (*Pyrra, Pylaia, Theon Trapeza, Ichthyoessa*) and evidently experienced something of an acme, as the many inscriptions found there suggest.

This floruit continued into Roman times when the island was a trading station and anchorage from which anti-piratical raids were launched. In Byzantine times it belonged to the Thema of the Aegean and it was during this period (9th century) that the castle of Aghios Ioannis was built on the southwest side. From 1207 onwards it was ruled by the Venetians and in 1537 was sacked by Barbarossa. It took part in the Struggle for Independence in 1821 but remained under Turkish rule until 1912 when it was taken by the Italians who held it until 1948 when, along with the other isles of the Dodecanese, it was incorporated in the Greek state.

SIGHTS - MONUMENTS. The island's capital, **Astypalaia**, is built amphitheatrically on a hill on its south side presenting a delightful vista with its white houses clambering up from the harbour to the hill top, dominated by its magnificent castle. The picture is completed by the windmills strung out along the crest of the hill on the outskirts of the village. The wall of the castle comprises numerous houses, the so-called *Xokastra,* the oldest part of the settlement. The castle entrance is on its southwest face and within its confines are two important churches, St. George and the Annunciation. The church of the Virgin Portaitissa, just below the castle, is one of the most beautiful in the Dodecanese. Only another three villages on the island have a permanent population: **Analipsi (Maltezana)**, **Livadi** (2 km. south of Chora) and **Vathy** (19 km. northwest of Chora). Sights of interest include the monastery of the Virgin Poulariani (17 km. northeast of Chora) and that of St. John the Baptist (12 km. west of Chora).

Both facilities for tourists and the road network are underdeveloped. However, there are many lovely beaches which can be reached by bus from Chora, **Livadi**, **Pera Yalos**, **Maltezana**, or caique **Aghios Konstantinos, Vathy**. Accommodation is available in rented rooms. Yachts can replenish their water supply in the harbour.

167. Astypalaia. View of Chora, dominated by the Venetian castle on its summit.

Kos

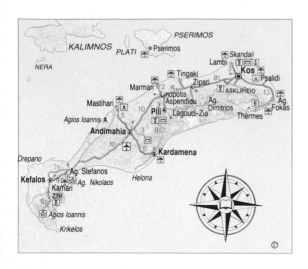

GEOGRAPHY. Kos, between Kalymnos and Nisyros, is the third largest of the Dodecanese. It is 290 sq. km. in area, has 112 km. of coastline and 20,350 inhabitants. All year round there are daily car and passenger ferries from Piraeus, 201 nautical miles away, as well as regular connections with the rest of the Dodecanese and Crete. The boat to the outlying islands on the Piraeus - Kavala route links Kos with Melos, Pholegandros, Santorini, Anaphi, the Dodecanese, islands of the north and east Aegean and Crete once a week. There is also a ship to Limmasol in Cyprus every week. Local services operate to other islands of the Dodecanese and during the summer months there are hydrofoils to Rhodes, Symi, Patmos, Nisyros and Samos. Small boats also ply the route from Kos to Kalymnos, Nisyros and Pserimos. In the summer excursion craft sail to Kalymnos, Pserimos and Nisyros and many cruise liners also drop anchor here. There are flights to Athens, Rhodes, Leros and Mykonos via Rhodes. The island's capital and main port is Kos and its second harbour is at Mastichari. With its rich natural vegetation, woodland and running water Kos is quite unlike the other islands of the Aegean. There is an abundance of antiquities and monuments of all eras, there are excellent tourist facilities, highly developed transport and road system and one is guaranteed a delightful vacation.

HISTORY. The island was first inhabited in Neolithic times, as indicated by traces preserved in many places, especially at Kefalos. In Mycenaean times (15th–12th century BC) the island was evidently densely populated and took part in the Trojan War. In around 700 BC it joined the Dorian hexapolis, along with Halicarnassus, Cnidus, Lindos, Ialysos, Kameiros, the religious centre of which was the sanctuary of Apollo at Cnidus. At the beginning of the 5th century BC Kos was conquered by the Persians. It joined the Athenian League as soon as these hostilities ceased. Around the middle of the 4th century BC (366 BC) the city of Kos was built and this remained the island's centre until the 6th century AD when it was destroyed by a terrible earthquake. Kos was the birthplace of Hippocrates (460–357 BC) the Father of Medicine and was renowned for its Asklepieion. In Roman times it faded into oblivion though it enjoyed something of a floruit in the Early Christian and Byzantine era. Towards the end of the 14th century it passed into the hands of the Knights of St. John who built their own city on the very site of the ancient agora. During the 15th and 16th century the Knights erected the castle which still stands today, sentinel of the harbour entrance. The Ottomans captured Kos in 1422 and it remained under Turkish occupation until 1912 when it was taken over by the Italians. In 1933 Kos was smitten by yet another catastrophic earthquake and between then and 1943 the Italians carried out extensive excavations on the island and the modern town was developed. Only in 1948 was Kos incorporated in the Greek state.

SIGHTS-MONUMENTS. **Kos**, the capital of the island, is located on its northeast side. Its oldest quarter is that around the harbour where the Knights of St. John built their city on the site of the ancient one. Excavations have brought to light foundations of diverse ancient buildings of both Hellenistic and Roman times. Sections of the Classical defensive wall and foundations of a stoa and small temple, possibly of Herakles, have also been revealed. A monumental basilica was erected adjacent to this temple in Early Christian times. Almost in the centre of the city stood a magnificent sanctuary of Aphrodite, while parts of the ancient agora and the great stoa,

of which two columns have been restored, have been uncovered to the west of it. Also at the western edge of town, buildings dating from Hellenistic and Roman times have been uncovered; Roman baths, the portico of the Hellenistic gymnasium, the odeum and a Roman villa which has been largely restored. Other features of interest in the town include the enormous plane tree which, according to tradition was planted by Hippocrates who used to teach in its shade. There are numerous notable churches both in town and on the outskirts, some with valuable wall-paintings and iconostases, and some dating to Early Christian times. Finds from excavations all over Kos are exhibited in the Archaeological Museum although many items (mosaic floors and statues) have been transferred to Rhodes. In antiquity Kos was famous as the island of the god Asklepios and the physician Hippocrates, founder of modern medical science. 15 km. southwest of Kos is the **Asklepieion**, situ-

168. Kos. Aerial photograph with the castle of the Knights on the left.

ated in a particularly beautiful area with cypress trees in abundance and a spectacular view of the Asia Minor coast opposite. A temple of Apollo originally stood on this site and the sanctuary of Asklepios was founded in the 14th century BC. During the 3rd century BC a large altar was built, embellished with sculptures reputedly fashioned by the son of Praxiteles. The sanctuary is built on four terraces and the various edifices were constructed at different times. The most important of these was the actual temple of Asklepios, a Doric peripteral building which stood a smaller temple in the Ionic order, close to the altar. Parts of the Roman temple still survive, as well as traces of the Roman baths. The Asklepieion was an important healing institution in ancient times, rivalling our modern hospitals. It was excavated by the Italian School of Archaeol-

170

ogy, which was also responsible for its restoration, giving us some idea of its appearance in Hellenistic and Roman times.

14 km. south of the harbour is the region of **Afendio**, comprising five settlements built on the hillside, overlooking the open sea. A little further south (16 km. from Kos) is **Pyli**, consisting of three villages in a lush, verdant setting. A sanctuary of Classical times has been discovered here, finds from which are exhibited in the Kos Museum. Above the village are the remains of a Byzantine castle, within which the church of the Presentation of Christ is preserved and from where there is a superb view towards Kalymnos and Pserimos. 9 km. further south (25 km. from Kos) is **Antimacheia**, a cluster of four settlements built on a plateau. The airport is nearby and its port is **Mastichari**, the second largest of the island's harbours. Southeast of Antimacheia (29 km. from Kos) is **Kardamaina** which has developed into an attractive, well-planned holiday resort. Between here and Antimacheia are the ruins of a large Venetian castle with well-preserved walls, a few houses, two churches and a cistern for water. The castle was probably built in 1494 on the site of the preceding Byzantine fortress. At **Kefalos** (43 km. southwest of Kos) there are ruins of ancient temples and a small theatre. There is an Early Christian basilica at **Aghios Stefanos** and at **Mastichari**. Among the lovely coastal villages are **Tingaki** (14 km. west of Kos) and **Aghios Fokas** (8 km. east of Kos).

Amenities and facilities on Kos are of a high standard, guaranteeing a pleasant vacation for all visitors. The beaches are excellent for swimming, fishing and sea sports and those on the east coast, in close proximity to the main town are particularly beautiful. On many others the trees grow down to the water's edge. Apart from the beach at Marmari, all the others can be reached by bus. There is an organised spa at **Thermes** (11 km. southwest of Kos) and other therapeutic springs near Kardamaina. In the harbours of Kos, Mastichari, Kefalos and Kardamaina there are yacht marinas but there are refuelling facilities only at Kos. Accommodation is available in hotels, pensions, furnished flats and rooms.

171

169. *Kos. Partial view.*

170. *Kos. Many of the buildings of the ancient town have been revealed in excavations.*

171. *Kos. The Asklepieion.*

Kalymnos

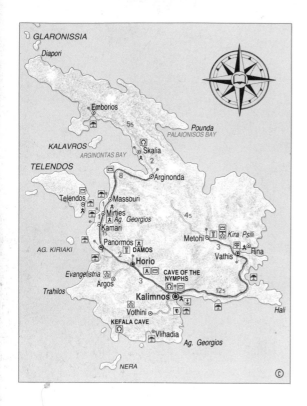

GEOGRAPHY: Between Kos and Leros lies the fourth largest of the Dodecanese, Kalymnos. It is 111 sq. km. in area, has 96 km. of coastline, a population of 14,295 and is 183 nautical miles from Piraeus. Passenger and car ferries link Kalymnos with Piraeus, the Cyclades and Crete. The boat on the Piraeus-Kavala route to the outlying islands connects it with Melos, Pholegandros, Santorini, Anaphi, Crete, the other islands of the Dodecanese, as well as those of the north Aegean. There is a local boat to Rhodes, Symi, Telos, Nisyros, Kos, Leros, Leipsoi, Patmos and Samos and a frequent service to Kos, Pserimos, Leros and Telendos. Via Kos there is an air link with Athens. Kalymnos is a mountainous island comprising three more or less parallel ranges extending from northwest to southeast, between which lie two fertile plains on which the two main villages are located, Vathy (north) and Kalymnos (or Pothia) (south). The island's other villages are built on the west coast and the northern part of the island is virtually uninhabited. The configuration of the coastline follows that of the terrain and is markedly

indented with many bays and coves. The main town is a good starting point for visiting the island's villages and other places of interest. Many Kalymnians are still involved in sponge diving, for which it was formerly renowned. There is little touristic development and visitors to Kalymnos must be prepared for a quiet holiday with only basic amenities.

HISTORY. The island has been inhabited since Neolithic times and during the Bronze Age (circa 1000 BC) there was a culture strongly influenced by that of Crete, as evident from finds at Vathy and Emboreion. The first inhabitants seem to have been Karians from the coast of Asia Minor, succeeded by Dorians in 1000 BC or thereabouts. Throughout antiquity Kalymnos was closely linked with Kos and the littoral of Karia opposite. In the mid-5th century BC it was annexed by Artemisia, queen of Karia, to whom it was subject. It then became a member of the Athenian League, belonged to the Egyptian ptolemies for a brief interval and from the middle of the 3rd century BC was united with Kos. After the Roman conquest it belonged to the province of Asia and in Byzantine times to the Thema of the Aegean. During this period the Kastelli, a mighty fortress, was built on the island. In 1204 it passed to the Venetians and, shortly afterwards, to the Knights of St. John who built the castle at Chorio, Pera Kastro or the Kastro tis Chrysocherias. Between 1522 and 1912 it was subject to the Turks and then occupied by the Italians. Kalymnos became part of the Greek state, like the other isles of the archipelago, in 1948.

SIGHTS - MONUMENTS. The island's capital, **Kalymnos (Pothia),** also its main harbour, was built in about 1850 when the inhabitants abandoned the former capital village of Chorio. Excavations have shown that Pothia was inhabited in antiquity. The present town, a mixture of old and new buildings, many of them brightly coloured, is charming to behold. **Chora** or **Chorio** (3 km. northwest of Pothia) is a much older settlement and there stands the

172. Kalymnos. View of the capital Pothia from the harbour.

173. Kalymnos. The harbour.

ruined castle built, according to tradition, by the Knights of St. John on the site of the previous Byzantine stronghold. Material dating from the 4th century BC and Hellenistic times is preserved in its now destroyed interior. There is another medieval castle to the north of Pothia, Pera Kastro, also known as the *Kastro tis Chrysocherias* after the church within its enceinte, where there is an icon of the Virgin with gilded hands. At the foot of the hill on which the castle stands is a small chapel of Christ and three disused windmills. Finds from excavations indicate that there was a settlement in the area in Mycenaean times. Northeast of Pothia is the cave of **Epta Parthenon** (Seven Virgins) or of the **Nymphs**, a place of cult in antiquity from which various votives

have been recovered and even Neolithic tools. On the road between Chorio and Panormos is the church of Christ of Jerusalem, the most important monument on Kalymnos, dated to the 6th century. A three-aisled basilica built mainly of ancient architectural material, this church stands on the site of the ancient sanctuary of Delian Apollo, which must have been particularly important judging from the finds and inscriptions found here. There is another basilica to the southeast, with a mosaic floor similar to that in the church of Christ. In its foundations a marble torso of a statue of Asklepios was discovered, now on display in the museum at Pothia, along with finds from other ancient sites on the island. The museum is housed in a Neoclassical building in which, apart from the archaeological artefacts, there is the original decoration and furniture.

At **Damos**, north of the village a Hellenistic

cemetery has been revealed, as well as foundations of houses and traces of walls, evidence of the presence of an important ancient city. Throughout the region, as far as the gulf of **Arginota**, there are ancient remains in abundance, indicative of a significance in those days. There are remnants of fortifications at **Xirokampos**, **Vryokastro**, **Anginaries**, while at **Kastri** parts of two Hellenistic towers have survived. Included among the island's places of interest is the **cave of Skalia** or **Daskaleio** with its rich decoration. The churches of St. Nicholas at **Skalia**, an Early Christian basilica at **Myrties** and the chapel of St. John at **Melitzacha** are all of interest. There are remains of a medieval fortress at cape Aspropounti, known as **Kastelli** or **Palaiokastro**. The church of the Holy Apostles, south of Chorio, is reputed to have been founded in the 11th century. Southwest of Pothia is the **Kefala** cave, also with elaborate formations. It was a cult cave in antiquity and later a refuge for pirates. Access to the cave is easiest by caique from the sea.

On the southeast side of the island is the most fertile valley, **Vathy**, with the village of the same name and two hamlets, **Metochi** and **Rina**. Neolithic finds have been recovered at Vathy. On the slopes of mount Kyra Psili stands the monastery of the Virgin Kyra Psili and a ruined fortification. In the area between Vathy and Metochi numerous traces of buildings of Classical, Hellenistic and Roman times can be discerned. There is a Postbyzantine church of the Taxiarch (17th century) near **Metochi** and at **Rina**, with its charming little harbour, the church of the Virgin Chosti, dated to the 11th/12th century and other Byzantine remains. In contrast to the southern part of the island, the north is virtually uninhabited and the sole village is **Emboreios** (20 km. northwest of Pothia). The church of St. Peter at **Palaionisos**, southeast of Emboreios, is of interest on account of its wall-paintings.

One of the loveliest beaches on Kalymnos, **Masouri** (9 km. northwest of Pothia) has developed into a tourist centre, that at **Myrties** (7 km. northwest of Pothia) is fringed by greenery and pretty summer cottages, while the seemingly endless beach at **Panormos** (5 km. northwest of Pothia) is surrounded by verdant countryside. There are other good beaches to the south of Pothia and at **Vlychadia** on the south coast there are therapeutic springs. Regular trips are organised from Kalymnos to the nearby islet of Pserimos and from Myrties frequent excursions to Telendos. On both islets there are delightful beaches. Apart from swimming one can go fishing or enjoy sea sports off the shores of Kalymnos and there is game in its interior. Accommodation is available in hotels, pensions, rooms or apartments. Refuelling station at Pothia.

Telendos

Just 700 m. off the west coast of Kalymnos, opposite Myrties, is the tiny islet of Telendos with about 90 inhabitants, mainly fishermen who live around its harbour. Up until the 6th century BC it was joined to Kalymnos and only became an island after the earthquake of 535 BC. On mount Aghios Konstantinos, on its north side, stands a chapel of St. Constantine and a ruined medieval castle. Telendos, which can be reached by caique from Kalymnos, has several lovely beaches on its west shore. A few rooms are available for those wishing to stay here.

Pserimos

A small island southeast of Kalymnos with a population of only 72, it is an idyllic spot for those seeking isolation. Caiques from both Kalymnos and Kos make excursions to the island which has many sandy beaches and lots of yachts drop anchor here. There is a hospice in the monastery of the Virgin and a handful of rooms to let.

Leros

GEOGRAPHY. Leros, situated between Kalymnos and Patmos, has a strange beauty. It is 53 sq. km. in area, has 71 km. of coastline, 8,127 inhabitants and is 178 nautical miles from Piraeus. There is a car and passenger ferry from Piraeus and a connection with the rest of the Dodecanese and Crete. The boat to the outlying islands on the Piraeus - Kavala route links it with Pholegandros, Anaphi, Santorini, the rest of the Dodecanese, the islands of the north and east Aegean, Crete and Kavala. There is a local service to Patmos, Arkoi, Leipsoi, Agathonisi, Samos, Kalymnos, Kos, Nisyros, Telos, Symi, Rhodes; and from Aghia Marina to Patmos, Leipsoi, Arkoi and Agathonisi. In the summer a hydrofoil operates between Leros and Rhodes, Kos, Patmos, Samos. There is an aeroplane from Athens, Kos and Rhodes. The island's capital is Aghia Marina and its main port is Lakki. There are small settlements all over Leros which is traversed by a series of hills with small fertile plains and valleys between, like the inlets in its bays. The coastline follows the lie of the land and is indented with bays and coves, little harbours and headlands. The varied landscape, healthy climate and quiet way of life make Leros a good venue for restful holidays.

HISTORY. The island was inhabited in Neolithic times, as evident from traces preserved in the region of Partheni. In antiquity it was known, together with Kalymnos, as the *Kalydnai* isles or *Kalydna*. Archaeological remains scattered throughout the island testify to its continuous habitation in ancient times. The island seems to have taken part in the Trojan War and later became a member of the Alliance of Ionian cities, centred on Miletus. Due to its safe harbours it enjoyed economic and commercial prosperity until the Roman conquest, after which its fate was the same as the other islands of the archipelago. In 1316 it was sold to the Knights of the Order of St. John and belonged administratively to Kos. In 1522 it was captured by the Turks who remained until 1912 when it passed to the Italians. They transformed it into a naval base and as a consequence it suffered heavy bombing during the Second World War. In 1948 it was incorporated in Greece and in recent times was a place of exile for political prisoners.

SIGHTS - MONUMENTS. The island's capital today, **Aghia Marina,** is built in about the middle of its east side and actually comprises three settlements adjacent to each other, Aghia Marina, Platanos and Panteli. This is the main traditional village on the island with its brilliant white houses and narrow alleyways in the old quarter, its Neoclassical mansions and massive Venetian castle. The most important monument is the castle built on the eastern edge of the town. It occupies the site of the ancient acropolis and acquired its present aspect during the time of the Knights. This castle was also important in the preceding Byzantine period and it was here that Hosios Christodoulos, founder of the Monastery of St. John on Patmos, first arrived. It is to him that the destruction of all the ancient edifices and temples, extant until then (11th century) is attributed. When the Knights of St. John acquired the island (14th century) they repaired and enlarged the castle. Nowadays the restored enceinte survives and within its precincts is the church of the Virgin of the Kastro, originally the katholikon of a monastery, as evident from the ruined cells all round it. There are also ruins of various buildings and houses, for the castle was inhabited up until the 18th century.

174

Behind the castle stand the windmills. Other places of interest include the Public Library, in which a small archaeological collection is housed, the church of St. Paraskevi and a few buildings in which the local vernacular architecture is combined with Neoclassical elements.

Southwest of Aghia Marina (4 km.) is **Lakki** the island's main harbour built at the far end of a sheltered bay. During the Italian occupation it served as a naval base and the Italians supervised the painting of the town with its wide streets and gardens. Many Bauhaus style buildings were built at this time. The churches of St. John the Theologian, St. Spyridon, St. George and St. Zacharias are of interest. Further south, at **Xerokampos** (8 km. south of the capital) the ancient acropolis of the 4th century BC is located on top of hill. A medieval fortress was also erected here, though this has now been completely destroyed.

Northwest of Aghia Marina (5 km.) is **Alinda** a seaside village in the midst of greenery. Just north of here (9 km. northwest of Aghia Marina) is **Partheni**, a tiny village on the creek of the homonymous gulf, surrounded by trees. Its name is evidently derived from the ancient

174. Leros. Aghia Marina, the harbour and the castle.

word Parthenos (chaste), an epithet of the goddess Artemis who, we gather from literary sources and inscriptions, was worshipped here. The church of the Virgin Kioura merits a visit.

The loveliest beaches on Leros are on its east side —at **Aghia Marina, Panteli, Vromolithos, Alinda**— and can be reached on foot or by car. The northern coast is rockier with small sandy coves— **Aghios Stefanos** at Partheni, **Blefountis bay**. The south shores of the island —**Lakki, Merikia, Xerokampos**— can be reached by car or caique from Aghia Marina and have stretches of sand both large and small. There is a large beach at **Gourna** on the west side of Leros.

The harbours and anchorages on Leros are ideal for private craft and the island is surrounded by uninhabited islets where the fishing is excellent. Refuelling facilities at Lakki. Although accommodation is available in hotels, pensions, rooms and apartments there is often a problem of where to stay during the summer season.

Patmos

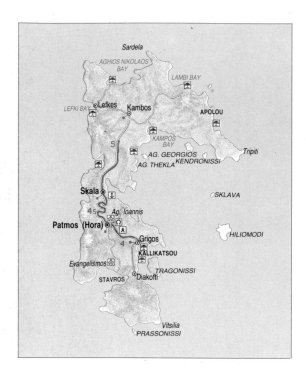

GEOGRAPHY. The holy isle of Patmos lies between Ikaria and Leros. It is 34 sq. km. in area, has 63 km. of coastline, 2,534 inhabitants and is 163 nautical miles from Piraeus. There are car and passenger ferries from Piraeus to Skala, the island's main port, as well as connections with the rest of the Dodecanese and Samos and there is a regular link also with Leros, Kos, Leipsoi, Arkoi and Agathonisi. During the summer there are hydrofoils to Rhodes, Kos, Leros and, once a week, Samos. Many cruise liners call at Patmos in the summer. It is one of the smaller inhabited islands of the Aegean, merely a narrow strip of land with numerous rocky hills, scant vegetation and two main villages: Chora and Skala. In two other regions there is a scattered population: Groikos and Kampos. Its mild, healthy climate, sunshine virtually all year round, indented coastline with delightful bays and coves and numerous chapels testifying to the island's sanctity combine to form a picture of unique beauty.

HISTORY. Very little is known of the island's past though there seems to have been an important city there in antiquity, as testified by finds of the 6th and 4th century BC recovered from excavations in the region between Skala and the bays of Merika and Chachlakia. The island is referred to as Patmos in a 5th century BC inscription and here, according to mythological tradition, Orestes sought refuge from the pursuit of the Furies. During Roman times Patmos was a place of exile and between 95 and 97 AD the Apostle John was banished here and composed the wonderful text of the Apocalypse. In the ensuing centuries the island was constantly plagued by pirates and was more or less abandoned. In 1088 the monk Christodoulos Latrenos arrived here with the intention of building a monastery in honour of St. John. Even today the three chrysoboulls with which the Emperor Alexis I Comnenus granted the island to the monk Christodoulos, supporting it and exempting it from taxation, are preserved in the katholikon. It took five years to build the monastery and both monks and lay folk assisted him in this task. The laity were forbidden to live within the monastery and settled in Choridakia and Evdilos until 1132, when the monks permitted them to live outside its walls. In the subsequent centuries Patmos enjoyed peace and prosperity and acquired a mighty mercantile fleet. In 1659 it was sacked by Morosini. In the 18th century the famous Patmian School was founded from which many enlightened priests graduated. Between 1821 and 1832 the island enjoyed a brief interval of independence from the Turks but they returned and remained until 1912, when it was occupied by the Italians. It became part of the Greek state in 1948.

SIGHTS-MONUMENTS. From about 1600 onwards the island's main harbour has been **Skala**. This is where the boats drop anchor and from where one can visit Chora and the other villages on the island. Its dazzling white houses with their flower-filled courtyards and balconies compose a pleasant picture as they cling to the slopes of a low hill. On the *Kastelli* hill above the harbour there are ruins ot the 4th century BC fortification and ancient tombs and pottery have been found here.

The island's capital, **Patmos** or **Chora**, is built 3 km. southeast of the harbour. It extends beneath the impregnable walls of the monastery of St. John, indeed an impressive sight with its white houses, narrow streets, man-

175

sions, captain's residences at the very edge of the rock and Neoclassical edifices. Without doubt the most important monument is the **fortress-monastery of St. John the Theologian**, built in the centre of Chora at its highest point. The imposing mass of its walls looms large over the entire environment. It is a purely Byzantine structure girt by defensive walls and battlements and within its precinct are the katholikon and five chapels. In one of these the relic of Hosios Christodoulos, its founder, is housed. The monastery library is one of the best and most modern in Greece, of invaluable importance for scholars. It includes some 900 codices, 2000 printed volumes and 13,000 manuscripts and papers. One of the oldest works in its possesion is the so-called Gospel of St. Mark, dated to the 6th century, penned in gold and silver letters on purple vellum. Thirty-three folios are in Patmos, the rest are in Vienna, the Vatican, the Byzantine Museum Athens and the British Museum London. In the sacristy of the monastery many precious objects are housed: icons (particularly valuable are those of St. Nicholas —mosaic— and of St. Theodore), crosses, ecclesiastical plate, jewelery and vestments. From the monastery terrace there is an unrivalled view of the Ae-

175. Patmos. Skala, the present harbour of the island, as seen from Chora.

gean and on a clear day one can see the islands of Kalymnos, Leros and even Amorgos, Naxos, Mykonos and Paros, and to the east, as far as Samos and Ikaria. The Easter celebrations in Chora are especially moving and impressive, with the re-enactment of the Last Supper and the ceremony of the Washing of the Feet on Maundy Thursday by monks and the abbot of the monastery in the main square.

About half way along the road from Chora to Skala is the **Cave of the Apocalypse** where St. John dictated the text of the Revelation to his pupil Prochoros. Just inside the mouth of the cave is the chapel of St. Ann, founded by Hosios Christodoulos. Next to the cave is the building of the Patmian School, an institution established at the beginning of the 18th century which made a significant contribution to the Greek Struggle for Independence in 1821. Today it is a training college for the priesthood. 5 km. southeast of Chora, just before the village of **Groikos,** is the chapel of St. John the Theologian, built on top of a Roman building. **Kampos**, 11 km. north of Chora, is one of the most fertile villages on Patmos in the midst

of verdant countryside.

One can sail all round the island in a caique and discover the beautiful beaches at **Kathisma tou Apollou,** the bay of **Lambi, Livadi ton Kalogiron,** the **gulf of Lefki** and **Merika**. The beach at **Groikos** is also suitable for swimming and has golden sands, just as at **Kallikatsou** with its weird rocky landscape. A caique sails from Groikos to the lovely beach at **Diakofti** on the south coast. There are also secluded sandy beaches on the neighbouring islets of **Arkoi** (8 nautical miles northeast of Patmos with only 68 inhabitants but very nice beaches) and **Agathonisi** (a little island east of Patmos ideal for those seeking solitude) which can be reached by caique. Visitors may stay in hotels, pensions, rooms or apartments.

Leipsoi

Yet another group of tiny islands, the main one being Leipsoi or Leipso, lying between Leros and Patmos. 16 sq. km. in area, with 35 km. of coastline and a population of 574. There is no provision for tourists and only basic amenities for those seeking peace and quiet close to nature. One can reach Leipsoi from Piraeus with the boat on the Piraeus - Kavala route to the outlying islands (once a week) which also links it with the Cyclades, the islands of the northeast Aegean, Kavala, Crete and the rest of the Dodecanese. There is a local service once a week to other isles of the archipelago and Samos. Small craft operate between Leipsoi and Patmos (every day during the summer), Arkoi and Agathonisi. The lovely sandy beaches and sparkling sea are marvellous for both swimming and fishing and accessible on foot. There is a hotel and few rented rooms. The natural harbour is a safe anchorage for yachts but the only refuelling facilities are on Patmos.

176. The roof terraces of the Monastery of St. John.

177. Inside the Monastery of St. John.

178. Part of Chora with the fortified monastery of St. John above.

Kastellorizo

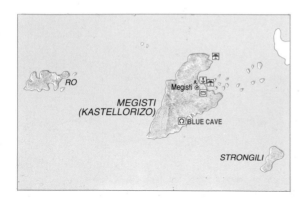

GEOGRAPHY. Kastellorizo, guardian of Greece's easternmost borders, lies 72 nautical miles southeast of Rhodes, only 1.5 miles from the Turkish coast. It is barely 9 sq. km. in area, has 19 km. of coastline, a population of 222 and is 328 nautical miles from Piraeus. Boats from Piraeus are infrequent, once a week all year round. The island is linked once a week with Amorgos, Astypalaia, Nisyros, Telos, Symi and Rhodes. There is a local, twice weekly, connection with Rhodes. The island has a wonderful warm climate, the sea is delightful, life is quiet, just the place for a relaxing holiday.

HISTORY. In antiquity the island was known as *Megiste* and was first inhabited in prehistoric times. There are marked traces of the Mycenaean presence and it is to this era that the gold wreath of vine leaves in the National Archaeological Museum, Athens dates. Also of prehistoric date are the remnants of Cyclopean walls, tombs and stone axes. The Dorian settlers built fortified acropoles on the site of the present capital and at *Palaikastro*. Apart from a brief period of independence, its fortunes were tied to those of Rhodes, from the 4th century BC until Roman times. Its geographical position has played a decisive role in its history. It was the target of piratical raids in the Byzantine era and was taken by the Knights of the Order of St. John in 1306. It was subsequently captured by the Sultan of Egypt, the king of Naples and, in 1512, by the Turks. The succession of pillaging and disasters suffered by the island forced its inhabitants to seek their fortunes at sea and, indeed, by the time of the 1821 Struggle for Independence its merchant fleet played an important role. From 1830 onwards the island secured special privileges and until 1910 enjoyed particular prosperity. In 1920 it came under Italian rule and was only incorporated in the Greek state in 1948. During the Second World War it was more or less razed to the ground by bombs, to which the many destroyed houses bear witness.

SIGHTS-MONUMENTS. The main harbour and village is **Kastellorizo** where all its inhabitants live. Nothing now remains of its glorious past except a few remnants; the outer bailey of its castle with a few towers, built in the 14th century by the Knights of St. John, ruined mansions of the ship owners and captains, and a few churches: St. Constantine (The Metropolis), built in 1833, St. Nicholas (11th century), the Virgin of the Fields (17th century) and St. George with its catacombs. In the small Archaeological Museum both ancient artefacts and items of folk art are exhibited. At Palaiokastro tombs, tools and ruins of the ancient acropolis are preserved. There are also the **monasteries of Prophet Elijah** and the **Holy Trinity**. Another of the island's sights is the **Blue Grotto**, (Parastas' cave), the largest and loveliest sea cave in Greece, renowned internationally for its stunning stalactitic formations, lit by the sun's reflected rays, a unique and unforgettable spectacle. In days of old it was a haven for pirates and nowadays seals bask within it. The grotto can be visited by boat, as also the nearby islets of **Ro** (6 nautical miles west) and **Strongyli** (5 nautical miles southeast). Accommodation is available in the municipal hostel and some rented rooms. The shores in the vicinity of the harbour are ideal for swimming and so is the beach at Mandraki. There is a refuelling station for yachts in the harbour.

179-180. Kastellorizo. The Harbour. Handsome two-and three-storey houses overlook the quayside, while behind the church bell-towers can be seen. The mansions maintain their nobility, a reminder of the days when Kastellorizo was densely populated and flourishing.

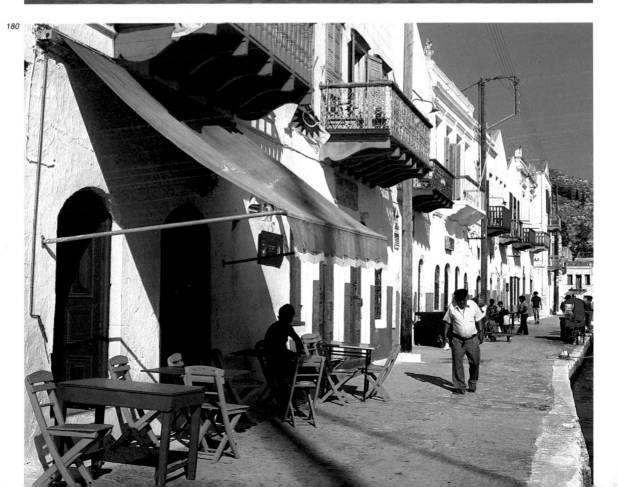

Crete

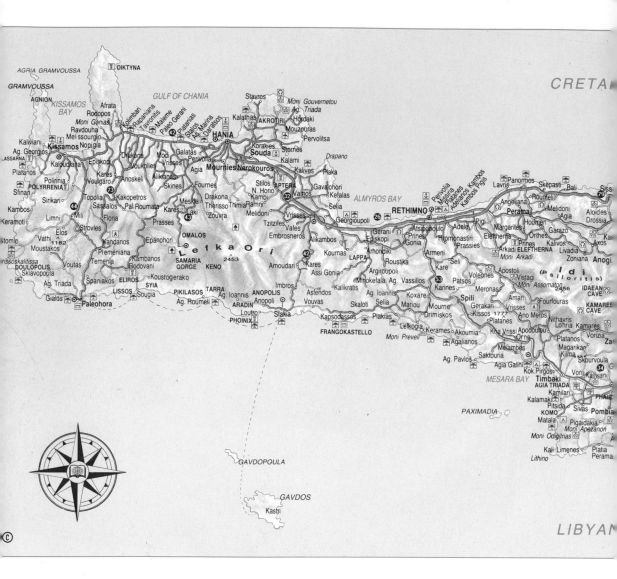

GEOGRAPHY. Crete is the largest of the Greek islands and the fifth largest in the Mediterranean. It is outstanding not only on account of its geographical situation but, primarily because of its long history and exceptional cultural contribution. The island is 8261 sq. km. in area, has 1046 km. of coastline and a population of 243,622. It is separated administratively into four Prefectures, coinciding with its geographical division. The Prefecture of Herakleion (capital Herakleion) and the Prefecture of Rethymnon (capital Rethymnon) in Central Crete, the Prefecture of Lasithi (capital Aghios Nikolaos) in East Crete and the Prefecture of Chania (capital Chania) in West Crete. The numerous islets fringing the shores of Crete also belong to it (Dia, Mikronisi, Chrysi, Gavdos).

HISTORY. The island's unique geographical position, in the centre of the Mediterranean, played a decisive role in its historical development for it has always been a crossroads of civilisations, as well as a focal point for all manner of invaders. During its turbulent history it suffered numerous plunderous incursions and conquests. It is impossible to give a detailed account of its history, sights and histor-

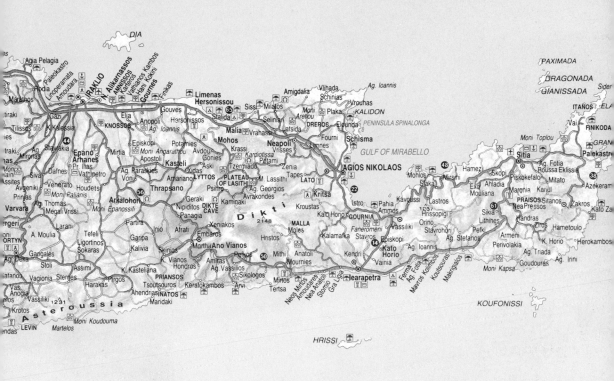

ical monuments in a brief text such as this, which only furnishes basic, essential information.

Crete is characterised by its diversity of landscape and marked contrasts. The island is dominated by a major mountain range extending from west to east, the highest peak being Mt. Ida -Psiloreitis (2948 m. a.s.l.). There are fertile valleys between the mountains, extensive plains (Mesara, Hierapetra, Herakleion, Chania) and gorges, the best-known being that of Samaria. The most outstanding feature of the Cretan mountains are the plateaux large and small, the most famous of all being

those of Omalos and Lasithi. Variety is the key-note of the Cretan landscape. In some parts there are woods and forests, green plains and in others the terrain is barren. The climate in the south is mild but the winters are harsh in the mountains. The south coast of Crete, facing the Libyan Sea, is the most precipitous, while the north is much gentler and most of the conurbations have developed there.

The island was first inhabited in Neolithic times (6000 BC). Between 2800 and 1400 BC a unique civilisation developed there, one of the most important in the ancient world and called

181-182. Crete. Pictures of everyday life.

183. The folk dances of Crete are especially interesting. They are spirited and usually accompanied by traditional instruments.

181

182

Minoan after the mythical king Minos. Magnificent palaces were built (Knossos, Phaistos, Mallia, Zakros), as well as country houses, and art and commerce flourished. Crete's influence spread throughout the Mediterranean basin. The Minoan palaces were destroyed in around 1400 BC as a consequence of the eruption of the Thera volcano, Achaeans settled there and its acme in all aspects of life came to an end. There were gradual changes in the ensuing centuries up until 69 BC when Crete was captured by the Romans, becoming part of the African province of Cyrenia. In 330 AD it became a province of the Byzantine empire and its centre, as in Roman times, was Gortyn. This phase of prosperity continued until 824 AD when it was conquered by the Saracens who set sail from Crete on their hostile sorties

183

against other provinces of the Byzantine empire. In 961 AD the emperor Nicephorus Phocas liberated the island and installed Christian colonisers in order to swell the depleted population. In the years following, Crete once again was a hive of cultural activity, now centred on Herakleion. With the Fall of Constantinople to the Franks (1204) it came into the hands of Venice which purchased the isle for a token sum from Boniface Monferrat, to whom it had been presented by the Latin emperor of Constantinople. The Venetians assumed full command in 1210 and imposed the feudal system. The island was constantly plagued by insurrections until the mid-14th century when it was declared an independent republic. It then entered a phase of pre-eminence in sea-faring, commerce, becoming a major transit port.

In 1538 the coasts of Crete were laid waste by the pirate Khayr ad Din Barbarossa and thence forth the Turkish threat loomed ever larger. Its economic floruit under the Venetians was accompanied by notable cultural achievements during the 15th and 16th century, particularly in art and literature. From 1669 til 1898 the island was occupied by the Turks, intransigent and rapacious masters.

Crete took part in the Struggle for Independence in 1821 and in the Protocol of 1830 was ceded to Mehmet Ali of Egypt who held it until 1841. There followed another period of internal strife until the 1879 rebellion, after which Prince George was appointed Governor General. In 1912 Crete was incorporated in the Greek state. In 1923 refugees from Asia Minor flocked to the island and during the Second

184

World War it fought obdurately against the enemy occupiers. Among Crete's distingushed sons in the world of art and letters are Domenicus Theotokopoulos (El Greco) and Nikos Kazantzakis, and in the history of Modern Greece the politicians Eleftherios and Sophocles Venizelos. The island's capital today is Herakleion, population 102,398, a convenient place from which to get to know not only its environs but central Crete in general.

Central Crete

HERAKLEION

GEOGRAPHY. The capital of Crete, Herakleion, is a modern town with places of interest both in its centre and surrounding area. It can be reached by aeroplane from Athens or car and passenger ferry from Piraeus, 174 nautical miles away. There are also connections with the Dodecanese, the Cyclades and every ten days there is a liner to Limmasol in Cyprus and Haifa in Israel. The good tourist facilities and the highly developed transport and road system make Herakleion one of the most densely populated places of Crete.

185

HISTORY. Built by the Arabs in 824, on the site of the ancient city, it was formerly known as *Candia* (Chandax) after the protective moat surrounding it. Until its liberation in 961 AD by Nicephorus Phocas the Saracen pirates set sail from here. Herakleion experienced its greatest acme during the period of the Venetian occupation when its fortress was the most important on the island. It was besieged by the Turks in 1648 but did not capitulate until 1669. Its fortunes declined under the Turks and its population was massacred in 1828 and 1898. During World War II it suffered much damage.

SIGHTS-MONUMENTS. Places of interest in the city include:
— The cathedral of St. Minas (19th century), one of the largest churches not only of Crete

184. *Partial view of the harbour of Herakleion and the castle.*

185. *Herakleion. The Morosini fountain.*

186. *Partial view of Herakleion.*

187. *Herakleion. The Venetian fortress at the harbour.*

188

but in the whole of Greece, with important icons.

— The Morosini fountain (1628), opposite which is the basilica of St. Mark, in which cultural events are staged.

— The church of St. Titus which was converted into a mosque for some time, destroyed in 1856 and rebuilt in 1922.

— The Town Hall on the site of the 17th century Armory and the Loggia, a Venetian edifice frequented by merchants. Nowadays the original palace, destroyed during the last war, has been restored exactly.

— The Historical and Ethnographic museum with significant exhibits from Venetian and Turkish times.

— The Archaeological Museum, unique of its kind with a wealth of exhibits from the island's major excavated sites. In its 20 galleries, large and small, one gains an overview of Minoan civilisation and Cretan history and cannot but marvel at its exceptional works of art.

— The old town with its well-preserved Venetian walls, which in their present aspect date from the 16th to 19th century, with their numerous bastions and gates, as well as Venetian fortress, also in an excellent state of preservation, guarding the harbour entrance. On one of the bastions is the tomb of Kazantzakis.

6 km. southeast of Herakleion is **Knossos**, the most important centre of the Minoan civilisation. Excavations begun by Sir Arthur Evans in 1900 brought to light the splendid, labyrinthine palace with its chambers decorated with wall-paintings, bathrooms and porticoes. The palace occupied a vast area and is nowadays partially restored so that the visitor gains a picture of the wealth and might of Knossos and may conjure up visions of Theseus Ariadne and the mythical Minotaur. Finds from here are on display in the Herakleion Museum, including some of the magnificent wall-paintings which adorned its halls. The first palace was built in 2000 BC and destroyed in 1750 BC. The new palace was rebuilt on the same site and destroyed in 1400 BC along with the other

189

188. Knossos. Wall-painting of the Prince of the Lilies.

189. Knossos. The Throne Room.

190. Knossos. Part of the North Entrance to the palace.

191. Knossos. The Palace. The Hall of the Royal Guard decorated with the wall-painting of the figure of eight shields.

192

193

major Minoan centres. There is another interesting site to the south of Herakleion, **Archanes**, where another large Minoan palace has been excavated. On the summit of Mt. Yuktas (7 km. northeast) an equally significant Minoan shrine has been discovered. At **Vathypetro**, 5 km. from Archanes, one of the largest Minoan villas has been revealed from which excellent examples of Minoan pottery, nowadays kept in the Herakleion Museum, were recovered. There are 14th century wall-paintings in the nearby churches of the Taxiarch Michael, the Holy Trinity and the Virgin. 19 km. southeast of Herakleion, at **Myrtia,** is the Kazantzakis Museum. There are other important ancient sites at **Arkalochori** (32 km. southeast of Herakleion) where a Minoan cult cave has been discovered with rich finds, **Viannos** with its churches of the Archangel Michael and St. Pelagia, both with notable wall-paintings, and ancient **Lyttos** near the village of **Xidas** (50 km. southeast). To the east of Herakleion (8 km.) lies **Amnissos** with its cult cave of Eilithyia, while at **Nirou Chani** are the ruins of a Minoan villa. At **Gournes** (18 km. from Herakleion) Minoan buildings and rock-cut tombs have been uncovered. The port of ancient Lyttos was **Chersonisos** (26 km. from Herakleion) with ruins of Greek and Roman times at **Kastri**, as well as the ruins of two Early Christian basilicae. 34 km. east of Herakleion is **Mallia**, a lovely seaside village right next to the area of the ancient palace, one of the largest in Minoan Crete and contemporary with those of Knossos and Phaistos. A Minoan town has been excavated all around and to the north the cemetery of **Chrysolakkos**. On of the most important monasteries, not only of the Herakleion region but of Crete, is that of the Virgin at **Kera Pediada** (12th century) in which there are valuable Byzantine icons.

25 km. west of Herakleion is **Fodele** with its 11th and 12th century Byzantine churches and the house in which the painter Dominicus Theotokopoulos (El Greco) was born. At Tylissos (14 km. southeast of Herakleion) there are remnants of a Minoan villa (1800 – 1450 BC). From here one may visit **Anogeia** (700 m.

192. Tylissos. View of the archaeological site and ruined villa.

193. Aghia Triada. The royal villa.

194. Mallia. Aerial photograph of the palace.

195. Phaistos. The palace.

194

195

a.s.l.) built on the slopes of Psiloreitis (Mt. Ida), a village in which traditional Cretan mores are kept very much alive. A pathway leads from Anogeia to the cult cave known as the **Idaion Antron**. At **Asites** (24 km. southwest of Herakleion) stands one of the oldest monasteries in Crete, that of St. George Gorgolainis. Another important monastery is that of the Virgin Paliani at **Venerato** (20 km. south of Herakleion) and close to **Zaros** (14 km. southwest of Herakleion are the monasteries of Vrontisi, with its 14th century wall-paintings and a Venetian fountain, and of St. Phanourios Varsamonerou (14th century), also with outstanding wall-paintings. 4 km. from this monastery is the **Kamares cave** in which the distinctive polychrome Minoan pottery was first found. In the plain of the **Mesara,** one of the largest on Crete, is **Aghioi Deka** (45 km. southwest of Herakleion) with its Byzantine church and the graves of ten Christians martyred in the persecution of Decius and after whom the village is named. A short distance away are the ruins of the ancient city of **Gortyn** from which one has an idea of this city's importance in Hellenistic and Roman times. Incorporated in the wall of the Roman odeum is the renowned inscription of the Laws of Gortyn (500 BC). The archaeological collection on site comprises finds from excavations there. Close at hand is the **Basilica of St. Titus** (7th, 8th century AD) of which only the apse now remains. Northeast of the city is **Lavyrinthos**, a labyrinthine quarry of poros stone which has been traditionally associated with the Minotaur. At **Moires** (53 km. southwest of Herakleion) is the monastery of the Virgin Hodegetria and 10 km. west of here is the archaeological site of **Phaistos**. The important Minoan palace revealed here was contemporary with those of Knossos and Mallia. West of Phaistos was a smaller yet significant palace or villa, **Aghia Triada** (61 km. southwest of Herakleion), set on the brow of a hill. 4 km. from Aghia Triada the road continues on to **Tympaki**, a large town in southern Crete, to the south of which is **Matala** with its world-famous and truly enchanting beach.

There are plenty of hotels, pensions, rooms

196. Matala. One of the most beautiful beaches of southern Crete.

197. Fodele. Byzantine church.

198. Aghia Galini. The little harbour and village.

and apartments throughout the Prefecture of Herakleion. Visitors may also engage in various sports such as tennis and there are basket and volley ball courts both in tennis and athletics clubs, as well as in many large hotels. There is a school providing instruction in water-skiing and wind-surfing at Chersonisos. The beaches at **Aghia Pelagia, Mallia, Chersonisos, Kaloi Limenes, Matala** and **Lenta** are ideal for swimming and fishing and all are accessible by bus or car. During the summer there is a caique service between Kalo Limenas and Lenta.

RETHYMNON

GEOGRAPHY. Rethymnon has its own particular scenic, beauty, especially its south coast beside the Libyan sea. Its important antiquities and places of interest, in conjunction with the good network of roads, attract an appreciable number of visitors, most of whom prefer quiet holidays. There is a car and passenger ferry from Piraeus via Herakleion and it is also linked to Athens by air, via Chania or Herakleion.

HISTORY. Rethymnon has been inhabited since prehistoric times and its fate has been more or less the same as that of the other cities of Crete. The modern town is built adjacent to the site of the ancient city of *Rithymne*. It was at its zenith in Venetian times when the ramparts were erected around the city and the small fortress of Fortetsa, which stands to this day, built at the tip of the peninsula. In 1645 the town was captured by the Turks. It suffered extensive damage during World War II.

SIGHTS-MONUMENTS. Nowadays one may visit the new town of **Rethymnon** with its modern buildings, as well as the old town with its quaint alleyways and, even today, distinctly Venetian atmosphere. Indeed, some Venetian edifices, gates, the walls, castle and Venetian loggia where the merchants met and which nowadays houses the Archaeological Museum, are preserved. The Lyceum of Greek Women in Rethymnon has a significant folk art collection and there is a Historical and Folklore Museum too.

The cave at **Gerani** 6 km. west of Rethymnon, with its rich stalagmite formations, has also yielded important archaeological and palaeontological material. 15 km. south of Rethymnon is the village of **Armenoi** and further south is the ruggedly beautiful Kourakliotiko gorge in which there is a church of St. Nicholas. Near the gorge entrance is the church of St. George with its rare wall-painting of the Holy Trinity. In a beautiful landscape beside the Libyan sea, 40 km.south of Rethymnon, stands the **Moni Preveli** a monastery dedicated to St. John the Theologian. The historic monastery of **Arkadi** is located 24 km. southeast of Rethymnon on the road to Herakleion. The monastery, which owes its present appearance to the 18th century, was one of the most important centres of resistance against the Turks and in 1866 its defenders, headed by the Abbot Gabriel chose a horrendous death when its powder-store exploded, rather than surrender to their attackers. Of the buildings within its confines the most important are the katholikon (1587) and its wonderful renaissance style gateway. There is also a small museum and charnel house. 24 km. east of Rethymnon are the ruins of ancient **Eleftherna**, a Classical and Roman city. The cave at **Melidoni** (28 km. east of Rethymnon) is one of the most famous in Crete, a place of cult in ancient times. In 1823 some 370 women and children who sought refuge from the Turks here, perished horribly from suffocation.

199. Rethymnon. Partial view of the town and port.

200. The Prevelis Monastery, built in a truly beautiful setting overlooking the Libyan Sea.

201. The lovely entrance to the historic Monastery of Arkadi.

200

201
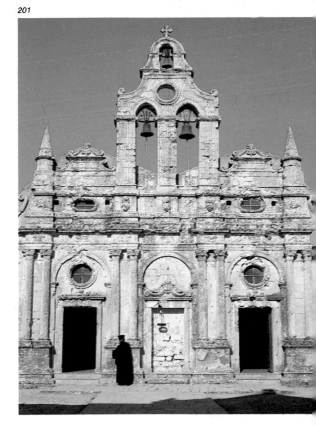

Southeast of Rethymnon is another important cave, that of **Zoniana** (43 km.), its extensive interior richly decorated. In the cult cave on the Nida plateau, known as the **Idaion Andron** (reached from Anogeia), Zeus was said to have been born and reared. One of the loveliest region in the Prefecture is **Aghia Galini** (61 km. from Rethymnon) with its gorgeous sands and interesting grottoes which can be reached by boat. The sea is warm throughout the year and the area has developed into a popular tourist centre. Other thriving restorts include **Adele** (8 km. east of Rethymnon) and **Bali** (31 km. east of Rethymnon). **Panormos** (19 km. east of Rethymnon) and **Plakias** (39 km. southwest of Rethymnon) are particularly picturesque villages.

Even though Rethymnon is one of the less developed parts of Crete, all facilities are available for an enjoyable stay. There is accommodation in hotels, pensions, rented rooms and apartments both in town and throughout the Prefecture, especially on the coast. Its sandy beaches are suitable for swimming and water-sports, as well as fishing. Swimming is very good at **Bali**, **Panormos**, **Aghia Galini**, **Moni Preveli**, **Plakias** and **Ammoudi**. All the beaches can be reached by bus or car and there are small caiques plying the sea between Aghia Galini and Matala and Aghios Pavlos and Plakias.

West Crete
CHANIA

GEOGRAPHY. The Prefecture of Chania with its historic capital, sights of interest, rich vegetation and uniquely beautiful gorge of Samaria has an especial charm. Chania can be reached be aeroplane from Athens or ferryboat from Piraeus. Once a week there is a boat from the Peloponnese, Kythera and Antikythera. There is a local craft sailing out of Palaiochora for the small island of Gavdos and from Chora Sfakion to Gavdos. Caiques make excursions along the south coast and to Gavdos during the summer months.

HISTORY-SIGHTS-MONUMENTS. The capital of the Prefecture, **Chania**, like Rethymnon has a distinctly Venetian atmosphere. It stands on the site of ancient *Kydonia* and its history and fate differs little from that of the rest of Crete. Chania has been its capital since 1850. In 1941 the famous Battle of Crete began at Maleme. Nowadays Chania consists of both the old town and the new, the latter built around the Venetian harbour. Sections of the Venetian ramparts are preserved in Chania and at Kastelli where there is the Venetian palace of the governor and the fortress of Firka. Other places of interest include the Municipal market, the house in which Eleftherios Venizelos lived, a few Turkish mosques and the Churches of St. Nicholas, St. Francis, the Russian church of St. Magdalene at Chalepa, and the monastery of the Virgin Chrysopigi and the Catholic monastery of Capuchin monks. The Archaeological Museum in the Byzantine church of St. Francis houses important finds from sites in western Crete. The Historical Museum, Municipal Art Gallery and Maritime Museum are also worth a visit.

To the west of Chania is **Aghia Marina** (10 km. from Chania) with its ruined Venetian and Turkish buildings, as well as a cult cave, Gerontospilios. The lovely seaside village of **Platanias** is 11 km. west of Chania and just beyond is **Maleme** (17 km. from Chania), renowned centre of the Battle of Crete in 1941. At **Kolymbari** (23 km. west of Chania) is the **Gonia monastery** (17th century), one of the major monuments of Crete. About 1 km. from the village the Orthodox Academy of Crete stands beside a beautiful bay. **Kastelli Kissamou**, at the far end of the homonymous bay, is a quite thriving small town. There are remains of the ancient city and acropolis at **Selli** and at **Krya Vrysi** a Roman aquaduct. There are Venetian fortifications around the old harbour. In one of the rooms of the Town Hall there is an archaeological collection. The ancient city of *Phalasarna* stood close to the village of **Platanos** (53 km. west of Chania). A short distance to the north is the **Gramvousa** peninsula with its offshore islet of that name on which there are ruins of yet another ancient city, **Polyrrhenia**.

At **Akrotiri** (8 km. northeast of Chania) are the tombs of Eleftherios and Sophocles Venizelos and on the headland are two important monasteries: the **Zangaroloi** monastery (17th century) and that of **Our Lady of the Angels** (Gouverneto) of 16th century date. Close to the monastery is the Gouverneto cave with its wonderful stalagmite and stalactite formations.

6 km. east of Chania is **Souda**, the harbour of Chania wich has developed rapidly in recent years. **Mournies**, 3.5 km. south of Chania,

202. Chania. Partial view.

203

204

is the home village of Venizelos and not far to the south (16 km. from Chania) is the historic village of **Theriso** where the Cretan Revolution was declared. One of the loveliest regions in Crete, and indeed in Greece as a whole, is the **Samaria Gorge,** 18 km. long and 3.5 km. wide, at the westernmost edge of the plateau of Omalos. The gorge is a national nature reserve and it takes about seven hours to walk down to the village of Aghia Roumeli at its exit. About half way along its course is the tiny village of Samaria with the church of Hosia Maria.

Beside a beautiful beach on the Libyan coast, 74 km. south of Chania, is the picturesque village of **Palaiochora**. There are many delightful beaches on the south coast of the Prefecture, linked by caique services from Palaiochora of Chora Sfakion. **Souya** (67 km. southwest of Chania) is a quaint fishing village popular with tourists. At the exit to the Samaria Gorge is **Aghia Roumeli** which is linked by boat only with the other villages on the south coast. 73 km. southeast of Chania is **Chora Sfakion** with its traditional architecture, always a centre of resistance to the diverse occupiers. To the east is **Frangokastello**, one of the loveliest 14th century Venetian fortresses with which many local traditions are associated (Drosoulites). The little island of **Gavdos**, 27 nautical miles from Chora Sfakion, is the southernmost inhabited point in Europe with a history lost in the mists of time, for according to mythology this was the isle of Calypso. Between Gavdos and Aghia Roumeli lies the islet of **Gavdopoula**. South of the **Monastery of the Virgin Chrysoskaliotissa** (85 km. south of Chania) is **Elafonisos**, easily reached from dry land since the channel is exceptionally shallow.

The shores of western Crete have wonderful sand and crystal clear seas. The beaches of north, west and east Chania can be easily reached by bus -**Kolymbari, Kalamaki, Akrotiri, Kissamos**. The beaches on the south coast are wonderfully secluded and can be reached in summer by daily caique trips, -**Palaiochora, Souya, Aghia Roumeli, Loutro, Chora Sfakion, Frangokastello**. All the villages, except Loutro

203. Chora Sfakia. Partial view.

204. Frangokastello, one of the loveliest Venetian fortresses in Crete.

205. The Samaria Gorge, a region of exceptional natural beauty.

205

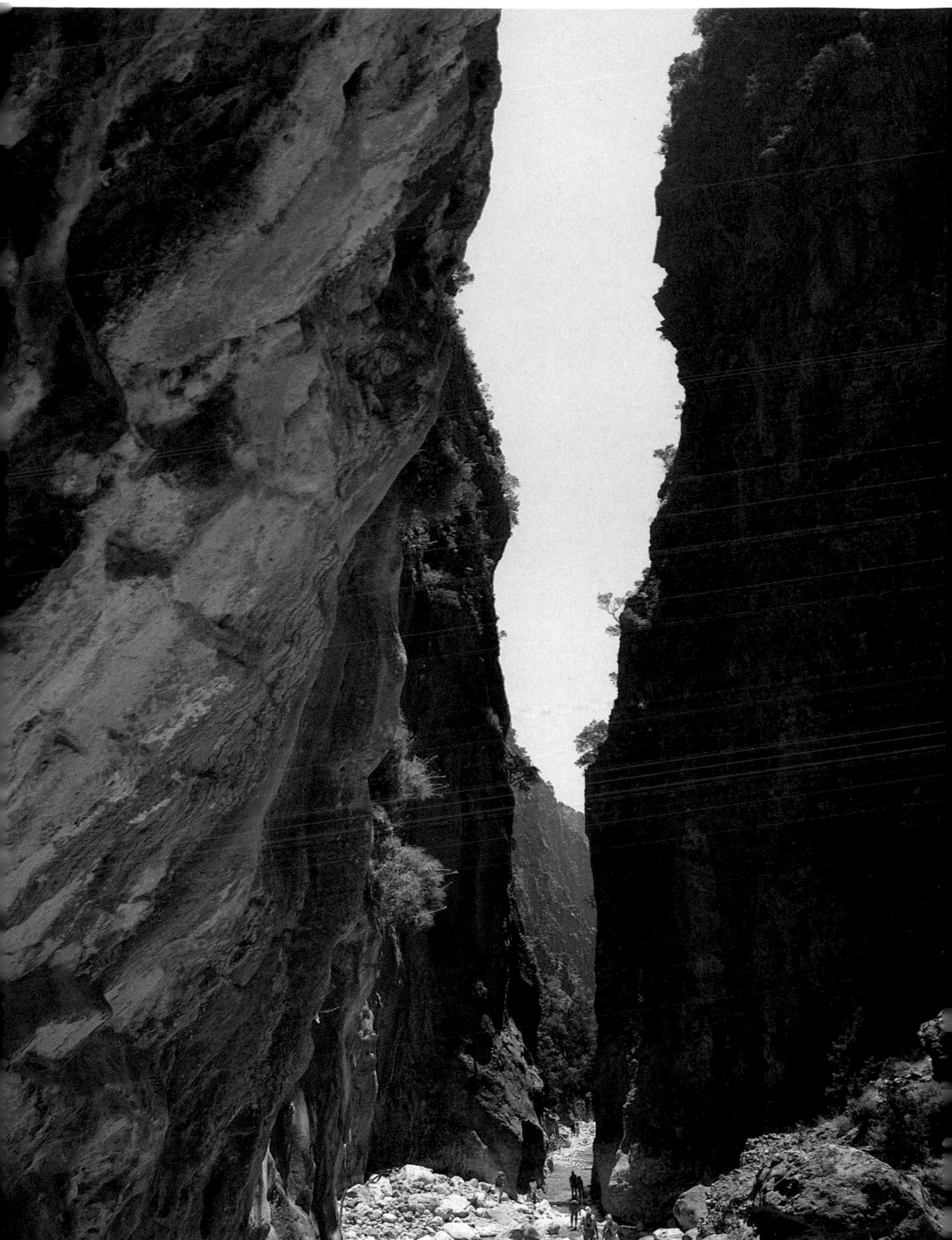

206

206. The Lasithi Plateau with its distinctive and ubiquitous windmills.

and Aghia Roumeli, are accessible by bus or car. The shores are fine for swimming, fishing and sea sports. The sandy beach at **Chrysoskaliotissa** is particularly beautiful. The Chania Yacht Club offers instruction in water skiing, sailing and swimming and there are tennis courts at Chania also. One can hunt small game in the hinterland of the Prefecture. The road from Omalos (not very good condition) leads to the White Mountains (Lefka Oroi) where there are small ski slopes. Accommodation is available in hotels, pensions, rooms and flats. The harbours have good moorings for yachts and there are refuelling facilities at Souda, Chania, Kastelli and Palaiochora.

East Crete

LASITHI

GEOGRAPHY. The Prefecture of Lasithi is one of the most attractive regions of Crete of particular natural beauty and archaeological interest. Its tranquil shores, well-organised tourist facilities and mild climate make it an ideal venue for vacations. This idyllic picture is completed by the lush vegetation, azure sea, numerous coves and some 5000 windmills. The capital of the Prefecture and its main port is Aghios Nikolaos. Siteia is its second most important harbour and Neapolis and Ierapetra are the other two main towns. The Prefecture is reached by boat or aeroplane, via Herakleion, though the ferry boat on the Piraeus - Kavala route calls at both Siteia and Aghios Nikolaos once a week, connecting Lasithi with Piraeus, the Cyclades, the Dodecanese, the islands of the north Aegean and Kavala. Excursion caiques sail from Aghios Nikolaos to Elounda and the islet of Spinalonga, and from Ierapetra to the islet of Chrysi. There is a bus service from Siteia and Aghios Nikolaos to Herakleion, Rethymnon and Chania.

HISTORY-SIGHTS-MONUMENTS. Aghios Nikolaos, capital of the Prefecture, is built at the far end of the gulf of Mirabello and is today a cosmopolitan holiday resort. It was named after the tiny chapel of St. Nicholas, one of the oldest in Crete (9th century). The Venetians built the mighty fortress of Mirabello here. The dominant feature of the town, an ideal centre from which to visit the rest of eastern Crete, is its lake, Almyri, Vromolimni or Voulismeni, which is linked to the new harbour by a canal. It is actually the sunken crater of a long extinct volcano. In addition to the Byzantine chapel one may visit the Archaeological Museum with its exhibit of finds from excavations carried out in eastern Crete. The road to the north of the town leads to one of the loveliest spots in Crete, **Elounda** (12 km.). Northeast of Elounda is the peninsula of Spinalonga, a rocky area which was a leper colony for many years, and dominated by the ruined Venetian fortress on its crest. At the very point the peninsula joins the land are the ruins of ancient *Olous* and an Early Christian basilica with mosaic floor has been excavated on the isthmus. Elounda has a cosmopolitan ambience. A little further north on a small island, opposite the village of **Plaka** (9 km.) are remnants of Venetian and Turkish

207. Aghios Nikolaos. Partial view.

structures, a fortress and chapel. 15 km. north of Aghios Nikolaos is **Neapolis** one of the most important towns in the Prefecture and capital of Lasithi from 1868 – 1903. There is a small Archaeological Collection of local finds and a Folklore Museum.

10 km. southwest of Aghios Nikolaos lies the ruined city of **Lato,** one of the most important in Crete. Nearby is one of the island's most renowned churches, **Panaghia Kera,** with 14th century wall-paintings. In the adjacent village of **Kritsa** there is another noteworthy church, of St. George, with early 14th century wall-paintings. Southeast of Aghios Nikolaos (10 km.) is the Minoan town of **Gournia** where the foundations of the houses and street system, dating from 1500 – 1450 BC are exposed. Finds from this area, as well as from

the small shrine and palace unearthed here, are displayed in the Herakleion Museum. To the north of Gournia is **Pacheia Ammos** (21 km. from Aghios Nikolaos), a charming coastal village, focus of many routes and tourist centre. On the south side of the island (36 km. from Aghios Nikolaos) is **Ierapetra,** one of the island's most thriving tourist centres. It is built on the site of the ancient city which flourished particularly in Roman times. The small archaeological collection includes finds from excavations here. There is also a small fortress and little house where Napoleon Bonaparte is reputed to have stayed a night en route to Egypt. West of Ierapetra (14 km.) is yet another significant archaeological site, **Myrtos** (52

km. southwest of Aghios Nikolaos), a beautiful seaside village with an archaeological collection of finds from the ancient settlement located at the southeast edge of the present village. East of Ierapetra there is yet another lovely settlement by the sea, **Makryyalos** (60 km. southeast of Aghios Nikolaos) where there are remnants of a Minoan villa and a monastery of St. John. There was another prehistoric settlement at **Lastro** (35 km. east of Aghios Nikolaos) and also a Byzantine church of St. George. At **Mochlos** too (48.5 km. east of Aghios Nikolaos) there are traces of a Minoan settlement. One of the main tourist centres on Crete is **Siteia** (68 km. east of Aghios Nikolaos), built amphitheatrically on the creek of a bay surrounded by greenery. Siteia was the birthplace of Vintsentos Kornaros. There is a

Folk Museum in which notable examples of folk art, as well as objects for everyday use are displayed. The Archaeological Museum is also worth visiting. From Siteia one may easily visit the archaeological sites of Praisos, Itanos and Zakros.

21 km. east of Siteia is the historic **monastery of Toplou** and, even further north is Vaï (98 km. east of Aghios Nikolaos) an exotic spot where the indigenous palm forest grows down to the sea. 2 km. from Vaï arise the ancient ruins of *Itanos*, yet another important Minoan city finds from which can be seen in the Herakleion Museum. **Palaikastro** (85 km. from Aghios Nikolaos) on the east coast was important in Minoan times and is today a major tourist spot. One of the loveliest parts of East Crete is **Zakros** with its narrow streets

and whitewashed houses set in the midst of a verdant landscape. 4 km. east of Kato Zakros a very important Minoan palace has been revealed, contemporary with those at Knossos, Phaistos and Mallia. The impressive finds from Zakros are exhibited in the Herakleion Museum.

Tzerniado (44 km. west of Aghios Nikolaos) is the main town of the Lasithi plateau (Oropedio). There are two Postbyzantine monasteries on the plateau, at Vidiani and Kroustallenia. Archaeological finds have been discovered at **Trapeza** and the **Dikte cave** near Psychro (48 km. west of Aghios Nikolaos), said to be the birthplace of Zeus. At the edge of the plateau is the Chavga gorge with a magnificent view, a centre for partisans during the German occupation.

The Prefecture of Lasithi boasts some of the finest beaches on Crete, all of which can be reached by bus or car: **Ammoudi**, **Elounda**, **Pacheia Ammos**, **Mochlos**, **Siteia**, **Vaï**, **Palaikastro**, **Kato Zakro**, **Makryyalos**, **Ierapetra**, **Myrtos**. One may take a caique from Ierapetra and visit the islet of **Chrysi** (9 nautical miles) with its gorgeous beaches and tropical vegetation. Similarly one can sail to the small island of **Aghios Nikolaos** in the bay of Siteia, and to **Pseira** opposite Mochlos in the gulf of Mirabello.

Accommodation is available in hotels, large and small, pensions, furnished rooms and apartments. The large hotels are equipped with tennis courts and facilities for water sports. There are volley ball and tennis courts at Aghios Nikolaos. The shores are ideal for fishing and there is small game in the interior.

209

210

208. Siteia. Another of Crete's delightful coastal towns.

209. Elounda. One of the charming regions of Crete.

210. Vaï. The beach with its exotic beauty.

IONIAN ISLES

The islands off the west coast of Greece are known as the Ionian isles or Heptanese. They comprise an archipelago of twelve islands, the six largest of which are more densely populated (Corfu, Paxoi, Lefkada, Ithaka, Cephallonia, Zakynthos), sharing a common history and more or less the same political identity. Kythera is often included with the Ionian islands although it lies off the southern tip of the Peloponnese, isolated from the other isles and has its own history and political physiognomy.

The islands cover a total area of 2,307 sq. km. and have a population of 182,651. In general their terrain is mountainous with numerous small fertile plains. Their coastline is indented with bays and coves and many promontories. According to the geologists they were formed as a result of geological disturbances resulting in their detachment from the Greek mainland with which they were originally joined. Myth relates that the islands were inhabited at the dawn of time and this is borne out by the archaeological evidence from Palaeolithic times (Cephallonia, Lefkada). During the Mycenaean age they enjoyed a remarkable floruit. This was the period of the crafty king of Ithaka, Odysseus, whose exploits in the Trojan War and adventures afterwards on his twenty-year voyage home are narrated by Homer.

During the 8th and 7th century BC Corinthians settled here, mainly in the northern islands of the group, founding an important city on Corfu. The secession of Corfu from Corinth at the end of the 5th century BC was the pretext for the Peloponnesian War. For a time the islands were subject to the tyrants of Syracuse, the kings of Epirus and Macedonia and, finally, the Romans (146 BC). They were harassed by pirates throughout Byzantine times until the Fall of Constantinople to the Franks (1204) when they passed under the jurisdiction of Venice, though the Serenissimo did not capture them until much later (1386). Under the Venetians the population was stratified into three classes: the Nobles (Nobili), Bourgeoisie (Civili) and Peasantry (Popolari). The Ionian islands remained a Venetian possession until 1797 and were only occupied by the Turks for a brief interval. In 1797 they came into French hands and remained so until 1815, with the exception of a short phase of Russian rule and another of autonomy under I. Kapodistrias. In 1815 the islands were captured by the British who ruled them until 1864, when they were incorporated in the Greek state. During the Second World War they were first occupied by the Italians and in 1943 by the Germans, only being liberated when hostilites ceased.

The long period of Venetian rule and easy communication with Italy and the West had a decisive influence of their character and yet, despite these centuries of various foreign masters, they always maintained and preserved their Greekness. At the same time there was a plethora of artistic and cultural activity, art and letters were cultivated and the Ionian isles set their seal on modern Greek literature.

The visitor will enjoy not only the natural beauties of these islands with their great diversity of landscape, but also their wealth of monuments. Many of the later edifices, both ecclesiastical and civil, are decidedly Italianate.

The mild climate, high standard of tourist development and ease of access make the isles an ideal place for holidays all year round.

211. *Corfu. Scene from everyday life.*

212-213. *The dances of the Ionian islands have their own style, continuing a centuries-old tradition. Dance from Zakynthos and from Corfu.*

212

213

Corfu

DIAPLO

Drastis

Perouladès
Avliotes

Agios Stefanos Magoulades
Kefali
Arilas

KRAVIA
Afionas

Akra Arilas

Makrades
Krini
ANGELOKASTRO
Moni Ag. Paraskevis
Paleokastritsa

LIAPADES
BAY

KOLIVRI

Sidari
Roda
Roda

Karoussades
Sfakera
Kavalouri
Platonos
Livadi Agrafi
Xanthates
Agii Douli
Velonades
Rahtades
Kavadades Armenades
Dafni
Valanio
Horepiskopi
Agros Kastelani Sokraki
Alkadades
Pagi Troumbetas
Ahmatades
Doukades
Lakones
Gardelades

Liapades

Kanakades
Marmaro
Gianades

Ag. Ekaterini

Pelekito
Agios Ilias
Riliatika Loutses Kassiopi
Aharavi
Ag. Pandeleimonas
Lafkio
Perithia
Agios Stefanos

Nimfes Episkepsi
Petalia
Klimatia
Zigos
Sgourades
Spartilas
Barbati
Ano Korakiana
Pirgi
Ipsos
Kato Korakiana
Gazatika
Dassia
Dafnila
Komeno

Gouvia
Kondokali

Tembloni
Evropouli
Afra Potamos
Ag. Alepou
Ioannis
Kanali
Kombitsi

Pelekas
Varipatades
Kalafationes
Kinopiastes
Sinarades
AEROSTATO
Kamara
Agii Deka
Ano
Agios Gordis Garoura
Kato Garouna
Pendati

Ano Kato
Pavliana
Vouniatades

Agios Mattheos
Moni Pandokratora

Pandokrator
906

Strinilas
Apolissi
Nissaki

Agios Markos

Agnissini
Gimari Kouloura
Kalami
Katavolos
Kendroma

Alikes

KERKIRA

Kanoni

PONDIKONISSI
Perama

Viros
Pondi

Gastouri
Benitses
Loukata
Tsaki

Kornata
Strongili
Ag. Ioannis Peristeron

Episkopiana
Moraitika

Messongi
Vranganiotika
Hlomatiana
Hlomos
Kouspades

GARDIKI

LAKE
OF
KORISIA

LAGOUDIA

Megalohoro

Agios Georgios
Marathias

PTIHIA
Ptihia

LAZARETO

SHQIPËRIJA
[ALBANIA]

Glifada

ROPA
VALLEY
Ermones
Vatos
Moni Mirtidion

Boukaris
Korakades
Petriti
Notos
Ag. Nikolaos
Argirades

Molos

Akra Lefkimi

LEFKIMMI BAY

Ano
Lefkimi
Perivoli
Vitalades

Kritika
Paleohori
Dragotina

Lefkimi

Neohori
Kavos
Sparteia

Asprokavos

GEOGRAPHY. Corfu, the northernmost of the Ionian isles and the second largest, is one of the loveliest islands in Greece. It is 592 sq. km. in area, has 217 km. of coastline and 96,533 inhabitants. It constitutes an independent Prefecture in which the islands of Paxoi, Antipaxoi, Ereikousa, Mathraki, Othonoi, Panaghia and the uninhabited islets of Pontikonisi and Ptychia are included. Corfu can be reached by aeroplane from Athens or by ferry boat from Igoumenitsa (18 nautical miles) and Patras (132 nautical miles). The liners from Patras continue on to the Italian ports of Ancona, Brindisi and Bari. There is a coach service from Athens and from Thessaloniki, via Igoumenitsa. Corfu is also linked to Cephallonia, Paxoi, Mourto Thesprotias and the islets of Ereikousa, Othonoi and Mathraki by a local boat twice a week from Sidari. During the summer months there is a daily connection with Brindisi and a regular service to Ancona and Bari by ferry boat from Igoumenitsa.

The island is dominated by two mountainous massifs (highest peak Pantocrator, 906 m. a.s.l.) which divide it into three parts. In the north there are olive groves, small verdant valleys and indented coastline with bays and coves. The central part, the most important, is literally drowned in vegetation, thickly wooded hillsides and small fertile plains. The southern section, also the narrowest, is flatter and has few trees. As a consequence of its clement clime and fertile soil the island is densely populated. Its capital is Corfu, from where roads lead out to the other towns and villages of the island.

Nowadays Corfu is an international tourist centre with excellent facilities catering for all tastes. Its lush green landscape, monuments and unusual architecture, as well as its marvellous beaches, attract a host of tourists throughout the year.

HISTORY. Because of its geographical location and favourable natural environment Corfu was inhabited even in Palaeolithic times (Aghios Matthaios 70,000 – 40,000 B.C.). According to myth it was named after the nymph Kerkyra (Greek name for Corfu is Kerkyra), daughter of Asopos, with whom Zeus fell in love and brought to this isle. Fruit of their union was Phaiakas and so Corfu was also known as the island of the Phaiakes. It was here that Odysseus met the daughter of Alkinoos, Nausika, as described by Homer in the Odyssey. Bronze Age installations (2000 BC) have been discovered on the west coast. In historical times Corfu was colonised by Eretrians (775 – 750 BC) and in 734 BC Corinthian colonisers founded the city of Kerkyra which quickly developed into a wealthy and powerful centre. In 432 BC Kerkyra sought the aid of Athens in its dispute with Corinth and so the Peloponnesian War broke out. At the end of the 4th century BC it passed into Spartan hands, was subsequently captured by Agathokles, tyrant of Syracuse, and then taken by Pyrrhus king of Epirus (281 BC). It was besieged by the Illyrians in 229 BC and not long afterwards fell to the Romans. In Byzantine times, though plagued by hostile incursions, it experienced a floruit and its first fortress was built then. It was ruled by a series of overlords and beset by many difficulties until the Fall of Constantinople to the Franks (1204) when it was taken by the Venetians who held it from 1207 until 1214, when it was annexed to the Despotate of Epirus. From 1267 it was ruled by the *Andegaves* until 1386 when it once again came under the suzereinty of Venice, which held Corfu until 1797. The Venetians ruled the island as a Venetian colony and made provision for its defense. Throughout the 15th century the Turks tried time and again to capture it, but to no avail. From the 17th century onwards there was a notable acme in art and letters which lasted well into the 19th century. Between 1797 and 1799 Corfu was a possession of the French Republic, then came the Russo-Turkish occupation, followed by a period of independence and in 1814 it was captured by the British who also took the other isles of the archipelago. In 1864 Corfu was incorporated in the Greek state. It was occupied by the Italians in World War II and by the Germans in 1943, who wrought considerable destruction in the battle fought for its capture.

SIGHTS-MONUMENTS. **Corfu**, the island's capital, is one of the loveliest towns in Greece, built more or less in the middle of the west side on the site of the ancient city of Kerkyra. In antiquity the city extended slightly further south and its centre was at Palaiopolis. A section of the ancient fortification wall still stands close to the present-day cemetery. The ancient acropolis stood on the hill of Mon Répos and Analipsis. Within the Mon Répos estate (originally the residence of the English Governors and later summer residence of the Greek royal family), significant temples have been revealed. The largest and most important

214

is that of Hera, dated to the 7th century BC, of which there are many dispersed parts. The best preserved temple on Corfu is that at Kardaki, dedicated to Apollo and dated to the 6th century BC. Another ancient monument brought to light is that of Menekrates (circa 600 BC) near which an Archaic lion, nowadays in the Corfu Archaeological Museum, was found. In the vicinity of the monastery of Sts. Theodore one can see the ruins of the famous temple of Artemis, established at the beginning of the 6th century BC. A pseudoperipteral temple in the Doric order and richly embellished. The west pediment, the oldest surviving stone pediment in Greece, with its representation of the Gorgon is exhibited in the Archaeological Museum.

One of the most magnificent Byzantine monuments on the island is the basilica at **Palaiopolis** (Aghia Kerkyra), near the entrance to Mon Répos. It dates to the 5th century and was built on the site of a 5th century BC temple. Sections of the mosaic floor form part of the Collection of Christian Art housed in the palace. Also noteworthy is the church of Saints Jason and Sosipatros, dated to the 12th century. There are a number of well-preserved Byzantine churches in Corfu, including that of St. Spyridon, perhaps the best-known. It was built towards the end of the 16th century to replace an earlier church at Saroko which had been destroyed. Saint Spyridon is the island's patron saint and his relic is kept in this church. Other important churches are that of the Virgin Spiliotissa (cathedral), built in 1577 and containing valuable icons, the Virgin Antivouniotissa (15th century), St. Nicholas ton Geronton (16th century), the Pantocrator (second half of the 16th century). Also of interest are the church of the Holy Trinity (17th century), St. John the Baptist (16th century), the Virgin ton Xenon (18th century), as well as the katholikon of the Platytera monastery (18th century). All these churches have significant wall-paintings and icons. There are also a few Ca-

215

214. Corfu. Tall old buildings on the waterfront.

215. Shopping street in Corfu and the church of St. Spyridon in the background.

216. Kanoni. One of the loveliest spots in Greece. The islet of Pontikonissi with the Vlacherna church.

217. View of the old fortress of Corfu from the north.

tholic churches in the town of Corfu: St. James (cathedral), St. Francis and the Virgin of Tenedos.

The Venetian fortifications of the town of Corfu are truly impressive, begun in the 15th century and maintained and added to until the demise of Venetian rule. As a consequence the town developed within a confined space and has multi-storeyed buildings and narrow streets. There was already a fortress on the headland on the east coast when the Venetians captured the island and a settlement had grown up outside its walls, Xopoli. The Venetians extanded and reinforced the defences with towers and bastions, enclosing the town and creating a new fortress in addition to the old. Access was through gates, the most impressive being that of St. Nicholas. Impressive too is the church of St. George on the south side of the old fortress (mid-19th century). The old town of Corfu with its narrow alleys, promenades, squares, shopping streets, mansions, public and private buildings is unique. The most handsome edifices are the Town Hall (originally the portico of the Nobles), the residence of the Catholic bishop, the Grimani barracks and Spilia barracks. Many private 17th and 18th century buildings still stand, unaltered, in their original state. The 19th century buildings are of interest, dating from the period of French and British rule, in particular the Reading Society (Anagnostiki Etaireia) founded in 1836, the Headquarters of the Prefecture (1840), built on the site of an earlier building in which Ioannis Kapodistrias was born, the Ionian Parliament and the palace of Sts. Michael and George (1819) which served as the residence of the British Governor and later the summer villa of the royal family. Nowadays the island's Archive, the Archaeological Service, Public Library and Museum of Asiatic Art are housed therein. One of the loveliest parts of town is the waterfront promenade —Mouraya— from where one has a panoramic view of both the old town and the new. In the Corfu Archaeological Museum the sculptures from the temple of Artemis are displayed, prehistoric pottery, bronze statuettes, coins and finds dating from the 4th century BC until Roman times. The Museum of Asiatic Art, unique in Greece, is of especial interest since it provides a complete picture of Oriental art. There is also a Municipal Art Gallery, the Dionysios Solomos Museum, Museum of the War of Independence and Historical Museum.

From the town of Corfu roads radiate to all parts of the island with its delightful scenery and picturesque villages. One of the most beautiful regions lies in close proximity, **Analipsis,** (3 km. south of Corfu) from where there is a magnificent view of the town and Mon Répos.

One of the best-known localities on Corfu, and indeed in Greece, is **Kanoni,** renowned for its unrivalled beauty. From here one can visit the monastery and church of the Virgin of Vlacherna, built on a tiny islet linked to the land by a narrow spit. Boats make trips from Kanoni to Pontikonisi, the little green island with the church of the Pantocrator, according to mythology the petrified barque of the Phaiakes. A narrow bridge links Kanoni with **Perama** on the other side. North of Corfu town, beyond the village of **Kontokali,** is **Gouvia** (5 km. from Corfu) on the headland of which are remains of the Venetian naval station. **Dasia** (13 km. from Corfu) has a cosmopolitan ambience and here is the Club Mediterranée.

Ypsos (15 km. from Corfu) is another tourist centre. If one takes the left fork at the crossroads here one may visit the quaint inland villages and the monastery of the Pantocrator, built on the site of a Frankish abbey.

One of the most popular haunts is **Nisaki** (22 km. north of Corfu) from where boats sail down to the town during the summer months. Another much-frequented spot is **Kassiopi** (36 km. north of Corfu), a charming little country town. The church of the Virgin Kassiopitissa stands on the site of the temple of Zeus. Remnants of the Frankish castle, one of the mightiest on the island, still survive. Another region favoured by tourists is **Roda** (54 km. north of Corfu) from where one can visit **Karousades** with the Theotokis family mansion.

At **Sidari** (35 km. north of Corfu) are ruins of the Venetian castle and the straits known as the "Channel of Eros". The village has a distinctive atmosphere and boats depart from here for the nearby islands of Othonoi, Ereikousa and Mathraki.

24 km. northwest of Corfu town is **Palaiokastritsa,** since the last century the best-loved resort of the native Corfiotes which nowadays attracts also a host of tourists, yet still retains its natural beauty unspoilt. The view out to sea is unique, particularly at sunset. Palaiokastrit-

218. Kassiopi. One of the most popular places on Corfu.

219. Kouloura. Another picturesque locality.

sa was the site of the palace of king Antinoos and the islet in the bay is said to be the petrified ship of Odysseus. The monastery here acquired its present aspect in the 18th/19th century but was actually founded in 1228. In the small museum there are precious Byzantine and Postbyzantine icons. North of Palaiokastritsa is **Bella Vista** from where one has one of the most superb views in the Mediterranean, and at nearby **Angelokastro** there are ruins of the Venetian castle.

At **Hermones** (16 km. west of Corfu), where Odysseus met Nausika as myth relates, the combination of azure sea and verdant land is quite spectacular. At **Glyfada** (16 km. southwest of Corfu) there is an extensive sandy beach, sparkling sea. From here one can visit the Myrtiotissa monastery and the nearby village of **Pelekas** with its outstanding view of the sea.

Ai Gordis (16 km. from Corfu) is a much-visited region and **Gastouri** (10 km. south of Corfu) is one of its most picturesque villages. Close at hand is the **Achilleion**, former palace of queen Elisabeth of Austria, on the first floor of which is a museum and on the second the casino. Another very popular cosmopolitan village is **Benitses** (16 km. south of Corfu). **Aghios Matthaios** (22 km. southwest of Corfu) is one of the island's largest villages and at **Gardiki,** slightly further south, a Byzantine castle built in the 13th century still stands. 45 km. southeast of Corfu is **Lefkimi**, an extremely attractive town, just south of which is **Kavos** from where small craft sail to Corfu town in the summertime. It is also the harbour for the boats to Paxoi.

There is no problem of where to stay in Corfu with its excellent hotels, pensions, hostels, furnished rooms and apartments. All the beaches can be reached by car and are perfect for swimming and sea-sports: **Mon Répos, Kontokali, Gouvia, Ypsos, Nisaki, Kassiopi, Sidari, Palaiokastritsa, Hermones, Glyfada, Pelekas, Myrtiotissa, Ai Gordis, Kavos, Benitses**. There are boats from Corfu town to **Nisaki**. Schools offering instruction in water-skiing, windsurfing and skin diving operate in Corfu. Many hotels have tennis courts, as does the tennis club, in the Répos valley there is a golf course and one can hunt in the mountains of the hinterland.

From Corfu one can visit the island of **Vido**, at the entrance to the harbour, on which there is a ruined Venetian fortress, and go by boat from Sidari to **Ereikousa** (3 nautical miles northwest) with 164 persons. Those with their own craft may visit both the nearby islets and the shores of the mainland. There are refuelling facilities in the harbour of Corfu.

221

222

220. Palaiokastritsa. Perhaps the nost enchanting corner on Corfu.

221. Sidari, the impressive beach.

222. Part of the extensive sandy beach at Glyfada.

Paxoi

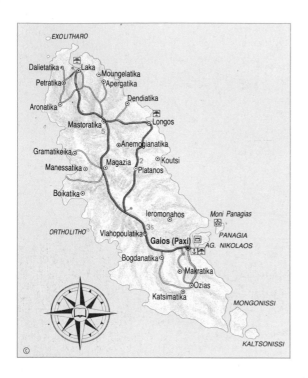

GEOGRAPHY. Paxoi and Antipaxoi lie to the south of Corfu. Paxoi covers an area of 25 sq. km., has 46 km. of coastline and a population of 2,247. Paxoi can be reached by ferry boat from Patras, Mourto Thesprotia (12 nautical miles), Igoumenitsa and by coach from Athens via Mourto. A local service operates between Antipaxoi, Corfu and Parga. The island's capital and main harbour is Gaios from where one can visit the island's other tiny villages. The tranquility and calm of Paxoi are particularly valued by visitors and holidaymakers there.

HISTORY-SIGHTS-MONUMENTS. Paxoi has been inhabited since ancient times and has always been closely associated with Corfu. Its main village stands on the creek of a picturesque bay in which lie the islets of Ai Nikolaos, with its ruined Venetian castle, and Panaghia, with a monastery dedicated to the Virgin. **Gaios** is noted for its distinctive Ionian architecture and the interesting church of the Holy Apostles. **Lakka**, 8 km. northeast of Gaios, is an extremely beautiful little village with a Byzantine church of the Presentation of Christ. Other pretty villages are **Longos** (6 km. north of Gaios) and **Otzias** (3 km. southeast of Gai-

os). Among the sights of Paxoi are its numerous littoral caves, large and small, which can be visited by small boat, and its many beaches, suitable for both swimming and fishing: Gaios, Otzia, Longos. Visitors may stay in hotels or rented rooms and flats. Those with their own boat or yacht can sail to Corfu, Parga, Mourto and Antipaxoi. There is a refuelling station at Gaios.

3 nautical miles from Gaios is **Antipaxoi,** just 5 sq. km. in area and home to 126 souls. There is a local boat service to Paxoi and, during the summer, a link with Corfu. One can also take a trip to the two offshore islands of **Exolitharo** and **Daskalio**.

223-224. Two views of Paxoi. The shores of Paxoi are particularly lovely. The verdant land meets the azure sea and the mild climate creates a magical atmosphere.

Lefkada

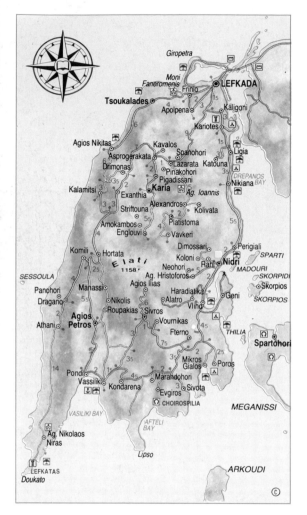

GEOGRAPHY. Lying just off the coast of Central Greece, Lefkada is more like a peninsula than an island. It is 303 sq. km. in area, has 117 km. of coastline and a population of 19,947. Lefkada, along with its neighbouring islets, inhabited and uninhabited (Kastos, Skorpios, Madouri, Meganisi, Sparti) comprises a separate Prefecture. The island can be reached by air, via Preveza, or car and bus. There is a local connection with Fiskardo in Cephallonia and Frikes in Ithaka. A caique sails between Nidri, Ithaka, Sami, Cephallonia, Meganisi and in the summer there are tourist excursion craft to the nearby islets of Sparti and Madouri. Buses also link it to Aktion in Preveza and Agrinion. The island has a mountainous interior (highest peak Elati, 1158 m. a.s.l.) and several fertile

valleys and plains. It has a rich vegetation cover, gentle coastline and lovely beaches. The high standard of tourist facilities and good road network make it an attractive place for holidaymakers who revel in its lovely landscape, numerous monuments and quaint villages.

HISTORY. Lefkada has been inhabited since Neolithic times. Excavations have brought to light Mycenaean installations and, according to the German archaeologist Dörpfeld, Homer's Ithaka was here, a theory with few supporters today. In around the middle of the 7th century BC colonisers arrived here from Corinth. Lefkada participated in the Persian Wars and sided with Sparta during the Peloponnesian War. In the 4th century BC it passed to the Macedonians, was sacked by Pyrrhus king of Epirus and then conquered by the Romans. In Byzantine times it was savagely attacked by pirates many times and from the 13th century onwards belonged to the Italian Orsini family. At the beginning of the 14th century it came into the hands of the d'Anjou family who held it until 1479 when it capitulated to the Turks. In 1684 it was captured by the Venetians, in 1797 by the French, in 1815 by the British and finally incorporated in the Greek state in 1864. Two highly important Greek poets are sons of Lefkada, Aristotelis Valaoritis and Angelos Sikelianos.

SIGHTS-MONUMENTS. The island's capital, **Lefkada**, is situated at its northeast edge facing the shores of Akarnania. It is a very attractive town virtually built in the sea and strong Venetian elements may be observed in both its architecture and lay-out. Its many churches, a lot of them privately owned, are well worth visiting. Their architecture and interior decoration is strongly influenced by Italian baroque. Some of the most interesting are those of St. Minas (1707), St. Spyridon (renovated in the 18th century) and that of the Pantocrator. In the small cemetery behind this church is the tomb of the poet Aristotelis Valaoritis. The Museum of Postbyzantine Art and the Folk

225. Lefkada. The island's capital with the mountains of Akarnania in the background.

Museum, with its large collection of folk art from Lefkada, as well as the archaeological collection of finds from excavations conducted by the German archaeologist Dörpfeld, all merit a visit. In the Municipal Library there is a notable collection of books and manuscripts. At the northern edge of town stands the castle of Aghia Mavra, built by the Orsini and renovated by the Venetians and Turks. On the south side of town is the church to St. John Anjousi, founded by the d'Anjou family. Below this church there are therapeutic springs. Not far from the town are two important monasteries, the Phaneromeni monastery with its superb vista of the open sea and that of the Virgin Megalovrysiotissa.

On top of the hill at **Kalligoni** (about 1.5 km. south of Lefkada) there are ruins of the prehistoric, Classical and Medieval acropolis of the island for this was the site of its ancient capital, traces of which can be discerned amongst the trees. On the acropolis sections of the Cyclopean fortification wall and cisterns can be seen and excavations have brought to light a small theatre of Hellenistic times. Just beyond here are the villages of Karyotes and Lygia and then the road continues on to Nydri, the most frequented place on the island after the capital.

Nydri is a modern village in the gulf of Vlychos and there are many lovely beaches in the vicinity. One can take a boat from here to the islets of **Chelonaki**, densely wooded, **Madouri**, where there is the Valaoritis family mansion, **Skorpios**, owned by the shipowner Onasis and **Meganisi**. Just opposite Madouri is cape **Aghia Kyriaki** on which stands a chapel of St. Kyriaki, on the site of an ancient temple, and alongside is the grave of Dörpfeld. Nydri is the port of call for the ferry boats from Sami in Cephallonia. Southeast of the capital (27 km.) is Poros with its port **Aspros Yalos**, which has a particularly delightful beach. One of the most beautiful regions is **Syvota**, at the far end of a narrow inlet where the sea is enchanting. Of the mountain villages one should visit **Karya** (15 km. south of Lefkada) in which the famous Lefkas embroideries are produced. Not only is the traditional architecture impressive but local customs are kept alive and many women still wear costume. 5 km. south of Karya is the highland village of **Englouvi**. One of the loveliest routes on the island is that along the west coast leading to the village of **Athani** and cape **Lefkata**. Between the monastery of St. Nicholas and this promontory there are remains of the temple of Apollo, one of the most significant in antiquity to which votives were sent from all over Greece. It was from this cape that Sappho flung herself into the sea and many others have followed here since, seeking consolation for unrequited love. Indeed these dives were famous in antiquity, being a kind of judgement imposed on those awaiting trial or those seeking a cure for their incurable love. To minimise risk of drowning those who jumped were equipped with feathers, checking their fall and boats awaited below to haul them out of the sea.

Vasiliki is the southernmost village on the island (40 km. south of **Lefkada**) and in recent years has grown into a bustling holiday resort. It is also the port for ferry boats from Fiskardo in Cephallonia.

Lefkada has many beaches for swimming: **Megali Ammoudia** near the main town, close to the castle, **Lygia, Nydri, Aspros Yalos, Vasiliki, Aghios Nikitas, Syvota**. The south coast is also good for fishing and there is hunting in the interior. The beaches on the nearby islets are also fine for both swimming and fishing and these can be reached by boat from Nydri. Accommodation is available in several hotels, rooms to let and furnished apartments. Those with yachts of boats can sail around the island, as well as explore its many offshore islets. There are refuelling stations at Lefkada and Nydri.

Meganisi

12 nautical miles southeast of the harbour of Lefkada is the largest of its offshore islands, Meganisi. It is 20 sq. km. in area, has 46 km. of coastline and 1339 inhabitants. Settled since prehistoric times, there are now three villages. One should visit the large coastal cave of Papanikolis, the second largest sea cave in Greece, to which boats make trips from Nydri.

226. Lefkada. Another corner of the town, a combination of the old and the new.

227. Nydri. The beach.

228. Vasiliki, one of the loveliest villages on the south coast of the island.

226

227

228

Cephallonia-Ithaka

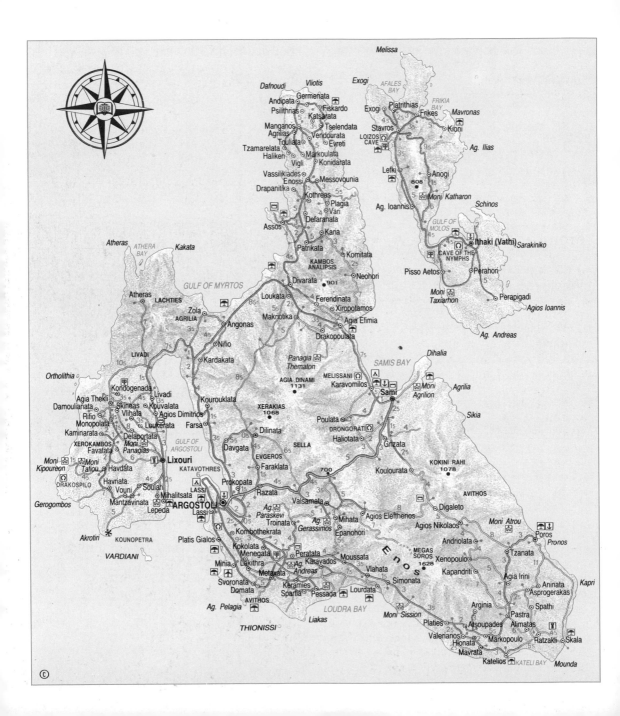

GEOGRAPHY. Cephallonia is the largest of the Ionian islands. It is 782 sq. km. in area, has 254 km. of coastline and a population of 27,649. Together with Ithaka and a few nowadays deserted islands it comprises an independent Prefecture. Cephallonia can be reached by ferry boat from Patras (56 nautical miles), Kylini (21 nautical miles) and Astakos (about 25 nautical miles). There is a bus connection with Athens, via Patras, Kylini and Astakos. There are also daily flights from Athens and a ´plane from Zakynthos. The ferry boats from Patras also connect the island with Ithaka, Paxoi, Corfu, Igoumenitsa and Italy. There is a local boat service to Ithaka, Lefkada and Zakynthos. Cephallonia is a mountainous island with rich vegetation, marked contrasts in landscape, numerous monuments and sights of interest, lovely villages and hamlets. The island's capital and main port is Argostoli. The varied scenery, wealth of monuments and good tourist facilities attract many visitors who are assured of spending an enjoyable vacation.

HISTORY. The earliest traces of human presence on the island go back to Palaeolithic times. The island was inhabited in the Neolithic period and, as evident from excavations in the region of Kokolata, experienced a flourit between 1600 and 1500 BC at which time it had, like Ithaka, close trading links with Nydri on Lefkada. During the Mycenaean age four cities flourished on the island: Krani, Pali, Pronnoi and Sami. Mycenaean cemeteries have been excavated at Kokolata, Diakata, Mazarakata, Parisata, Kontogennada, Lakithra and Metaxata. Pali took part in the battle of Plataeae (479 BC), while Krani, in opposition to the other cities, sided with Athens in the Peloponnesian War. In 187 BC the Romans captured Sami and became masters of the island. In Byzantine times pirates were a constant menace. The island was conquered by the Normans and ruled by the Orsini family from 1185 until 1478 and in 1485 was decimated by the Turks. From 1500 – 1797 it belonged to the Venetians, then passed into French hands when its fate was the same as that of the other Ionian isles. There followed a brief interlude of Russo-Turkish occupation, then rule by the French and the British. Cephallonia was finally incorporated in the Greek state in 1864. In 1953 it was devastated by an earthquake which considerably damaged the capital and its villages.

SIGHTS-MONUMENTS. Cephallonia's unusual shape is a result of geological disturbances and upheavals. The island's capital, **Argostoli,** is built on its west side. It was virtually destoyed in the 1953 earthquake and largely rebuilt so that it is a strikingly modern town in appearance. The Archaeological Museum deserves attention since it houses important finds from excavations conducted all over the island, but especially in the region of Kokolata and the cemetery of Mazarakata. Also of interest is the Korgialeneian Library on the ground floor of which is the historical archive and folk art collection. In one of the rooms of the library there is also a collection of valuable Byzantine icons. North of Argostoli are the famous sink holes or swallow holes, a rare geological phenomenon. 3 km. south of Argostoli is the cave in which the ascetic Gera-

229. Cephallonia. Assos. The village is famous for its panoramic view.

229

simos, patron saint of the island, lived in solitary contemplation. East of Argostoli stood one of the island's most important ancient cities, **Krani**. Remnants of its mighty acropolis are still preserved on top of the hill beside the Leivathous plain —the richest and most fertile region of Cephallonia— as well as the ruins of a Classical temple and Roman Stoa. At the nearby village of **Aghios Andreas** are ruins of the castle of St. George, built in the 13th century by the Italian lords of the island, since this was its medieval capital. At **Lakithra** (10 km. south of Argostoli) one may enjoy the wonderful view, just as Lord Byron did during his sojourn here. Mycenaean tombs have been discovered hereabouts. 14 km. south of Argostoli is the convent of St. Gerasimos in the Omaloi valley. In its church the saint's relic is preserved. At **Vlachata** (15 km. southeast of Argostoli) is the monastery of the Virgin of Sission. To the south and southeast side of the island are the picturesque villages of **Kateli, Skala** and **Poros** (43 km. from Argostoli). The ruined 3rd century villa on the shore at Skala has a lovely mosaic floor. At **Markopoulos** the "Virgin's little snakes" appear on her feast day, August 15th.

23 km. northeast of Argostoli is **Sami**, built close to the site of the ancient city, one of the major ones on the island. There are traces of the polygonal fortifications of the acropolis, ruins of a Roman building and the region is also renowned for its remarkable geological phenomeno. The abyssal cave at **Melissani** (2 km. from Sami) is well worth visiting and exceptionally beautiful as the sun's rays penetrate its collapsed roof and are reflected in the waters of its lake. There is another notable cave 5 km. from Sami, **Drongorati,** with elaborate stalagmite and stalactite formations. One of the loveliest routes is along the road from Argostoli to Sami where one can veer off into the densely wooded Ainos mountains from which there is a spectacular view. There are regular boat connections from Sami to Corfu, Paxoi, Lefkada, and Ithaka. North of Sami is the charming village of **Aghia Evfimia** (33 km. from Argostoli) where there is a ruined Roman villa. From here one can visit the Monastery of the Virgin of Thematon. **Assos** (40 km. north of Argostoli) is one of the most beautiful parts of Cephallonia with its impressive Venetian castle. On the slopes of the hill beneath is the modern village from which there is a splendid vew. **Fiskardo** (54 km. northeast of Argostoli) is the only Cephallonian

village which survived the earthquake in 1953. It is built in the far north of the island and has all the charm of a quaint seaside fishing port. It was named after the Norman Robert Giscard and the buildings clustered around the harbour are Venetian in style. Here too there are remnants of an Early Christian basilica and the Monastery of the Virgin Platytera. On the eminence known as *Spiliovouno* there are var-

ious hollows known as caves, which are of particular interest. Boats leave from Fiskardo for the island of Lefkada.

The lagoon at Koutavos separates Argostoli from **Lixouri**, the second most important town on the island (40 km. west of Argostoli and 3 nautical miles away by ferry boat). The town was founded in 1534 but destroyed in the 1953 earthquake and rebuilt on the same site. Now-

230. Cephallonia. Argostoli, the island's capital, is a modern town which was almost entirely rebuilt after the destructive earthquakes of 1953.

231. Fiskardo. One of the prettiest coastal villages, quaint and serene.

adays it is a modern conurbation with two important libraries —the Petritseios and the Iakovatios— including notable collections of ecclesiastical vestments and rare books. There is a small archaeological collection in the Municipal Library. South of Lixouri was the ancient city of *Pali,* known today as **Palaiokastro**. Only a few traces of its acropolis have survived, though there are remnants of the medieval fortress which stood here. In the nearby village of **Soulari** an important column capital was found, on display in the Argostoli Museum. Further south, at **Mantzavinata** is the famous Kounopetra, a curious geological phenomenon. 2 km. north of Lixouri is the monastery of the Virgin which has an ornate woodcarved iconostasis and precious icons in its katholikon. In the monastery of **Kipouria** (10 km. west of Lixouri) there are significant holy keimelia and Postbyzantine icons. At **Kontogennada** (12 km; northwest) Mycenaean tombs have been brought to light. Traces of the ancient city of *Pronnoi* are preserved in the locality now known as **Dakori**. A 6th century BC cemetery has been excavated here and there are remnants of an ancient temple on the summit of the acropolis.

Cephallonia boasts many lovely sandy beaches: at **Argostoli, Lixouri, Kipouria, Karavomylos, Sami, Aghia Evfimia, Assos**, the shores of **Leivathos, Skala** and **Poros**. All are suitable for swimming, fishing and water sports. At Argostoli and in the large hotels there are tennis and basket ball courts, as well as a school of sea sports offering instruction in water-skiing, windsurfing and canoing. There is no shortage of hotels, rooms and apartments on the island, as well as villas for rent. An enjoyable vacation is assured. Those with their own boat may investigate the coves and bays around the coast and visit nearby Ithaka. There is a refuelling station at Sami.

Ithaka

GEOGRAPHY. Ithaka, isle of the crafty hero of the Odyssey, king Odysseus, lies just 2 nautical miles west of Cephallonia. Area 96 sq. km., coastline 101 km. population 3,646. It belongs administratively to the Prefecture of Cephallonia. Its capital and main port is Ithaka (Vathy) with which there is a daily ferry boat connection from Patras (52 nautical miles away) and Astakos (about 26 nautical miles away). One may travel to Ithaka by bus via Patras and via Sami (Cephallonia). There is a link with Sami and Aghia Euphemia on Cephallonia, by ferry boat from Patras and Astakos. A local service operates from Nydri and Vasiliki in Lefkada. A narrow mountain range (highest peak Aetos, 808 m. a.s.l.) divides the island into two sections, north and south. The coastline follows the configuration of the land, being indented with numerous bays and coves. Ithaka is a verdant isle with picturesque little villages, a quiet way of life and interesting monuments in some parts. There is little tourist development but one is assured of a pleasant, relaxing stay, close to nature, and can make excursions to nearby Lefkada and Cephallonia.

HISTORY. Ithaka (or Thiaki as it is called by the locals) was first inhabited in prehistoric times and, according to Homer, was the home of king Odysseus whose palace was located by Schliemann on one of the summits of the prehistoric acropolis called "Castle of Odysseus" by the islanders. Excavations carried out by the British School of Archaeology have brought to light significant finds from the acropolis of both Classical and Hellenistic date, many of which are nowadays in the British Museum, London. Excavations have also shown that the island was first inhabited in around 3000 BC and throughout the Bronze Age it maintained contacts with the region of Nydri on Lefkada. Mycenaean sites have yielded an abundance of pottery. However, the island's acme evidently commenced after 1000 BC when it served as a trading station for the cities of the Greek mainland, particularly Corinth. Finds from a sanctuary on Mount Aetos bear witness to the island's many contacts with the cities of the ancient world. There was also a fortified acropolis on this peak and a second one at Aghios Athanasios near Stavros, while at Aghios Georgios a small sanctuary to an unknown goddess has been discovered.

In Roman times the island's fate was the same as that of the others in the archipelago. No monuments of Byzantine date have survived. During the Frankish occupation the island was attacked by pirates on numerous occasions and they used Vathy as a base for their forays. Ithaka belonged to the French in 1797 and then to the British, being incorporated in the Greek state in 1864.

In 1953 the island suffered considerable damage caused by earthquakes.

SIGHTS-MONUMENTS. The island's capital, **Ithaka (Vathy)**, is built at the far end of a closed bay and is the focus of roads leading to its villages and places of interest. There is a noteworthy library in the Cultural Society including rare editions, as well as a not inconsiderable library of theatrical works. About 1 km. west of Vathy is the cave of the Nymphs **(Andron ton Nymphon)** or **Marmarospilia** which is of outstanding archaeological interest. Here, according to tradition, the Naiads were worshipped and here Odysseus hid the treasures bestowed on him by the Phaiakes. South of Vathy (2 km.) at **Perachori** there is a church of the Dormition of the Virgin. From here one may visit the monastery of the Taxiarchs and clamber down to the east coast to the many delightful coves and inlets. Near Perachori is the Marathia plateau on which Eumaios, Odysseus´ faithful shepherd, tended his swine. Further south, at **Pera Pigali** is Arethousa's Fountain, identified with the Homeric Korakos Petra (Crow's Stone).

In the region of **Aetos** (5 km. southwest of Vathy) there are remains of the ancient acropolis which Schliemann claimed was the site of Odysseus´ palace. North of Vathy (about 10 km.) is the monastery of the Virgin Katharon. Not far to the north (15 km. northwest of Vathy) is **Anogi**, a mountain village overlooking the Ionian sea.

There is another village to the west, **Lefki** (13 km. northwest of Vathy).

232. Ithaka. View of the town.

One of the most beautiful villages is **Stavros** (16 km. northwest of Vathy) and from here one can visit **Polis**, which still keeps its Mycenaean name, a fact which adds credence to the view that the ancient city of Ithaka was located hereabouts.

At **Pelikata** (1 km. north) a prehistoric installation of the mid-2nd millennium BC has been unearthed and pottery and other finds from these excavations are kept in the small archaeological collection.

In the **Loizos cave**, on the north side of the bay, Mycenaean pottery has come to light and traces of a shrine. The northernmost of the island's villages is **Exogi** (22 km. northwest of Vathy).

The seaside villages of the north and northwest coast include **Frikes,** on the homonymous bay and **Kioni** (21 km. north of Vathy), a national heritage village which is developing into a tourist centre.

There is no shortage of beaches and bays on Ithaka; all can be reached by car **Tsiribi, Paliokaravo, Loutsa, Gidaki, Kioni, Polis, Ammoudaki** and are fine for swimming and fishing. There are just a few hotels, rooms and flats for rent. Those with their own boat can investigate secluded anchorages and coves, as well as sail to Cephallonia. Refuelling station at Vathy.

Zakynthos

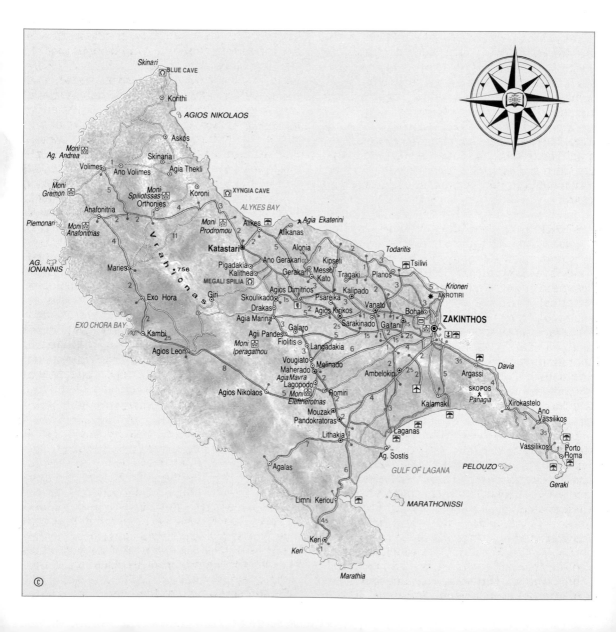

Skinari
BLUE CAVE
Korithi
AGIOS NIKOLAOS
Askos
Moni
Ag. Andrea
Skinaria
Volimes
Ano Volimes
Agia Thekli
Moni
Gremon
Moni
Spiliotissas
Orthonjes
Koroni
XYNGIA CAVE
ALYKES BAY
Anafonitria
Moni
Prodromou
Alikes
Agia Ekaterini
Plemonari
Moni
Anafonitrias
Katastari
Alonia
Todaritis
AG.
IONANNIS
Maries
Pigadakia
Ano Gerakari
Kipseli
Tsilivi
Kalithea
Gerakari
Messo
Tragaki
Planos
Kato
MEGALI SPILIA
Krioneri
Giri
Agios Dimitrios
Kalipado
AKROTIRI
Exo Hora
Skoulikado
Psareika
Drakas
Vanato
EXO CHORA BAY
Agios Kirikos
Bohali
Agia Marina
Sarakinado
ZAKINTHOS
Kambi
Galaro
Gaitani
Agii Pandes
Fiolitis
Davia
Agios Leon
Langadakia
Moni
Iperagathou
Vougiato
Melinado
Argassi
Maherado
Ambelokip
SKOPOS
Agia Mavra
Lagopodo
Panagia
Xirokastelo
Agios Nikolaos
Moni
Romiri
Ano
Eleftherotrias
Kalamaki
Vassilikos
Mouzaki
Pandokratoras
Lithakia
Laganas
Vassilikos
Porto
Roma
Ag. Sostis
PELOUZO
Agalas
GULF OF LAGANA
Geraki
Limni Keriou
MARATHONISSI
Keri
Keri

Marathia

GEOGRAPHY. South of Cephallonia (8.5 nautical miles) and west of Kyllini (about 10 nautical miles) lies the third largest of the Ionian isles, Zakynthos. It is 402 sq. km. in area, has 123 km. of coastline and a population of 30,011. Zakynthos can be reached by ferry boat from Kylini (17 nautical miles), bus from Athens, via Kylini, and train from Kavasila, via Kylini. There is a daily aeroplane from Athens and a flight from Cephallonia with which there is also a local ferry link. The island's terrain is mountainous (highest peak Vrachionas, 758 m. a.s.l.) with small fertile plains. The northern coast is rocky and precipitous, while the east and south shores are sandy, forming numerous bays and coves, the largest of which is Laganas.

Zakynthos is girt by many tiny islets resulting from the geological transformations to which it owes its shape. The island combines quiet rural life with cosmopolitan gaiety, it has beautiful green countryside, clean sandy beaches and a host of monuments, little wonder that visitors flock here in great numbers. The capital and main harbour is Zakynthos. The island has tourist facilities of a high standard and extensive road network enabling one to visit all the villages, both coastal and inland.

HISTORY. Zakynthos has been inhabited since prehistoric times, first by Achaeans from the Peloponnese. According to tradition, mentioned by Homer, the island takes its name from Zakynthos, son of Dardanos king of Troy. In historical times it was initially under the domination of Athens but during the Peloponnesian War came under the sovereignty of Sparta. It was subsequently subject to the Macedonians and eventually the Romans, under whom it experienced a degree of autonomy. In Byzantine times it was the object of hostile attacks and looting and in 1185 was seceded from the Byzantine empire, comprising, along with Cephallonia, the Palatine County of Cephallonia and Zakynthos. When the Franks captured Constantinople (1204) Zakynthos was ruled by the Orsini. From 1484 it belonged to the Venetians who held it until 1797. The population was stratified in three estates or classes, as in the other Ionian isles, and during this period Zakynthos was raided many times by the Turks. In 1797 the French assumed control, then came the Russo-Turkish domination, the autonomous Heptanesian state, British rule and, finally, incorporation in

Greece in 1864. In 1953 there was a severe earthquake, perhaps the major disaster suffered by the island. Since antiquity Zakynthos has been a hive of cultural activity and even in modern times art and letters flourished here. This was the birthplace of the national poet, Dionysos Solomos, of Hugo Foskolos, Andreas Kalvos and many other important authors and poets of recent times, in particular Grigorios Xenopoulos and Pavlos Matesi. A distinctive school of painting developed on Zakynthos (Zakynthos School) the main representatives of which are Panayotis Doxaras and Nikolaos Kantounis. Sculpture and other artistic activities similarly advanced.

SIGHTS-MONUMENTS. **Zakynthos**, the island's capital, is built on the southeast side of the island and acquired its present aspect after 1953 since the old town was largely destroyed in the catastrophic earthquakes. The town, with its impressive buildings, fortress, renowned churches, museums, charming squares and streets has an atmosphere of elegance and nobility. One can visit the Byzantine Museum with its large collection of Postbyzantine icons, iconostases, the interior of the little church of St. Andrew from Volimes and a number of works by local hagiographers. The Dionysios Solomos Museum in St. Mark's square includes a statue of the poet, his mausoleum, heirlooms and personal possessions. There are also various exhibits and momentoes of the 1821 Struggle for Independence, as well as the Historical Archive of Zakynthos. The churches of St. Nicholas of Molos, St. Dionysios, the island's patron saint whose relic is housed within, the Virgin Phaneromeni and Our Lady of the Angels are all worth a visit. 3km west of the town, just beyond the garden suburb of **Bochali,** stand the remnants of a medieval castle, built on the site of the ancient acropolis, with a magnificent view of the town and its harbour. Here too is the important church of the Virgin Chrysopigi in which there is a rare double-sided Byzantine icon. On the road leading to the hill known as **Strani** is the church of St. George ton Philikon and the grave of the poet Andreas Kalvos. It was on this hill, Strani, that Dionysios Solomos was inspired to write the Hymn to Liberty and his bust stands in remembrance. One of the loveliest regions of Zakynthos is **Akrotiri** with its many lovely villas set in the midst of greenery.

On the south side of town, near the bridge

over the torrent, is the restored church of St. Charalambos with significant icons and paintings of the saints. Not far away is the church of St. Catherine, metochion of the Sinai monastery. 3 km. southeast of Zakynthos is **Argasi,** one of the most picturesque seaside villages on the island. The monastery of the Virgin Skopiotissa on the summit of mount Skoros, on the site of the ancient temple of Artemis, is also worth seeing. **Vasilikos** is another lush green village (16 km. southeast of Zakynthos) with beautiful secluded beaches and just south of here is **Porto Roma** with its shady beach.

The largest bay on the island is that of **Lagana** (9 km. south of the capital) surrounded by rich vegetation and with a seemingly endless stretch of sand is a popular tourist spot, as is the beach at **Kalamaki.**

The inland village of **Lithakia** (13 km. south of Zakynthos) can be reached from **Agalas** which has a very special atmosphere. The road from Lithakia leads to **Keri** (20 km. southwest of Zakynthos) with its church of the Virgin Koriotissa. This is an area of touristic development and many visitors come specially to see the sunset. 6 km. west of Zakynthos is the lovely country town of **Machairado** with the church of St. Mavra which has an exceptional iconostasis and paintings of the saints. The road leads northwards through verdant villages.

At **Katastari** (15 km. north of Zakynthos) is the ruined monastery of St. John the Baptist and at **Aghios Nikolaos** (17 km. northwest of Zakynthos) is the monastery of the Virgin Eleftherotria. Close to the village is another monastery of the Virgin Hyperagathos. One of the prettiest villages is **Maries** where the famous Anaphonitria monastery, in which St. Dionysios was an ascetic, stands. At **Othonies** (26 km. northwest of Zakynthos) is the monastery of the Virgin Spiliotissa (mid-16th century) which has a valuable icnostasis. 33 km. northwest of Zakynthos is **Volimes,** a picturesque mountain village with important churches. From here one can take a boat to the famous Blue Grotto.

Among Zakynthos' many lovely beaches that at **Alykes** deserves a place (18 km. northwest of Zakynthos). Excursions are organised from Zakynthos to both Alykes and the Blue Grotto and one can also take a trip around the island by caique. The beaches at **Lagana, Argasi, Keri, Vasiliko, Alykes** are ideal for swimming, fishing and sea sports and can

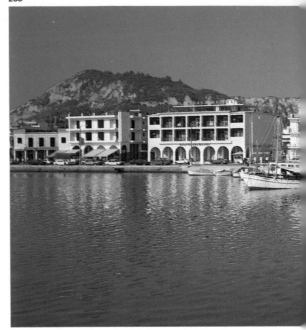

233

234

be reached by car. There are tennis courts in Zakynthos as well as in the large hotels which also have mini golf, sailing, water skiing and wind surfing facilities. Accommodation is available in hotels, pensions, rooms and flats. From Zakynthos one can visit the islets of: Aghios Ioannis and Plemonari (from the beach at Anaphonitria), Aghios Nikolaos (Katastari), Aghios Sostis, Marathonisi and Pelouzo.

To the south of Zakynthos lies a tiny archipelago, the **Strofades** (42 nautical miles) which can be visited by caique from the main harbour. On the largest of these is the 13th century monastery of the Transfiguration, dedicated to St. Dionysios. Those with private craft can both sail around Zakynthos and visit the offshore islets. Refuelling station in the main harbour.

233. Zakynthos. View of the harbour. In the background the hill of the castle, where traces of a medieval fortress can still be seen, giving a splendid vista of the town and harbour.

234. St. Mark's Square with the church of St. Mark and the Museum of Dionysios Solomos and Eminent Zakynthians.

Kythera

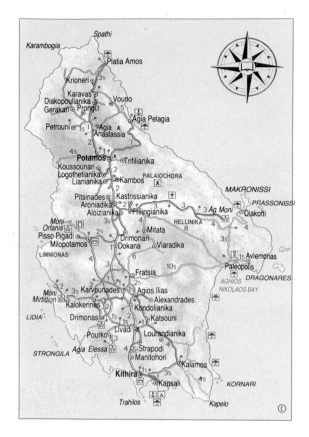

GEOGRAPHY. Kythera and Antikythera lie just off the southeast tip of the Peloponnese in the Myrtoon sea, seemingly cut off from the other insular groups. With a surface area of 278 sq. km. and 52 km. of coast, Kythera is 103 (Aghia Pelagia) or 125 nautical miles (Kapsali) from Piraeus. A mountainous island with several ranges, its highest peak is Myrmingari (506 m. a.s.l.) The main town is Kythera (Chora) with a population of 3,354. Passenger and car ferries link the island with Piraeus and twice a week with Monemvasia, Neapolis, Gytheion, Antikythera, Kastelli (Chania) in Crete, and once a week with Elafonisos, Gerakas and Kyparissia. Hydrofoils also ply the route to Piraeus, as well as to Neapolis, Monemvasia and Porto Cheli. There is also a daily flight from Athens.

Kythera has a clement, healthy climate with prevailing northerly winds in the summer. The sea is crystal clear and there are delightful coves and sandy beaches on its east side. At the "cross-roads" of the sea routes to the Ioni-an, Aegean and Cretan seas, Kythera is an ideal choice for a quiet vacation for, though there are several villages, tourists are few and far between and there has been little development in this sphere.

HISTORY. The island was known as *Porphyris* or *Porphyroussa* in antiquity and was associated with the goddess Aphrodite who was worshipped here (Kytheria or Ourania Aphrodite) in a splendid sanctuary on the southeast side of the island in the locality nowadays known as Palaiokastro. Pausanias, 2nd century AD, refers to the temple as the oldest and most sacrosanct within Greece and that the goddess herself was an armed xoanon. The island has been inhabited since earliest times and by 1700 BC there were already two major urban settlements, Kythera and Skandeia. Finds from excavations at Kastri confirm that the Minoans had already settled here at the beginning of the 2nd millennium BC and, indeed, in several places. They were followed by Phoenicians, as attested by its ancient name, and then by Mycenaens. At Palaiopolis, near Avlemonas, Mycenaean graves have been revealed. In historical times the island belonged to Sparta, being captured only very briefly by the Athenians (424 BC). In the 4th century BC it passed into Macedonian hands and in 395 AD to the Byzantines. During the 12th century frequent and violent piractical attacks forced the islanders to move their capital to Palaiochora. Throughout the Latin occupation the island was under Venetian suzereinty, its capital was renamed Tsirigo, the name by which the island itself was known. In 1536 it was sacked by Haradin Barbarossa, then conquered by the Turks for a short interval and united with Greece in 1864.

SIGHTS-MONUMENTS. The island's capital, **Kythera** (Chora) is built on a hill on its south side with a commanding view of the open sea, interrupted only by the tiny islet of Avgo. It is dominated by the massive and nowadays desolate Venetian castle, first built in 1316 and

235. Kythera. View of the harbour (Kapsali).

236. Chora. The impressive castle looms large over the dazzling white traditional houses.

235

236

237. Kythera. View of the harbour.

repaired several times. All the houses and churches within the castle are in ruins. People still live in the quarter known as Mesa Bourgo and some 16th and 17th century churches have also survived. The settlement of Chora, with its tiny cuboid houses, developed outside the castle walls. In the local Archaeological Museum there are finds from excavations conducted on the island, as well as on Antikythera and Avgo, the most important exhibit being the sculpted group of Aphrodite and Eros.

At a distance of 3 km. from Chora is the harbour of **Kapsali**, comprising two bays; Brostinos Yalos and Piso Yalos. Between the harbour and Chora is the Shrine of St. John ⁀he Forerunner at Gremnos where there is not ⁀ly a chapel but also a grotto with burbling ⁀ing of holy water. Another place of pilgrim- ⁀ is on the southwest side of the island, ⁀d the village of **Pourko,** where stands ⁀urch of the patron saint of Kythera, St. ⁀uilt in 1871 in commemoration of her ⁀m there at the end of the 4th century. ⁀way is **Livadi** with its late Byzantine ⁀t. Andrew in which traces of wall

paintings are preserved. From Livadi it is quite easy to visit the monastery of the **Virgin Myrtidiotissa** (11 km. from Chora) which has a unique vista out to sea. The monastery was founded in the mid-19th century and its katholikon, a replica of that of the Virgin on Tenos, was built specifically to house the icon of the Virgin discovered on the island in 1160 and formerly kept in a church in the castle. South of the monastery is the chapel of St. Nicholas Krasa, while south of the nearby village of **Drymonas** is the shrine of the Sts. Anargyroi, a private monastery built in 1825.

On the west side of the island (17 km. from Chora) is the very beautiful region of **Mylopotamos,** thus named after the 24 windmills which once stood here. Not far away are the remnants of a Venetian castle, dated to the mid-16th century, and a short distance beyond is the cave of St. Sophia, with its stalagmitic and stalactitic formations, regarded as one of the most spectacular in Greece. The church of the Shrine of the Virgin of the Orphan, about 3 km. to the northwest, is built in a cave and the silver-invested icon is incorporated within its iconostasis.

Proceeding northwards from Mylopotamos, one comes to **Arodianika** (the road to the airport commences here) and then to **Potamos,** the island's commercial centre, where there are several churches with important icons. The inhabitants of **Karavas** (34 km. from Chora), north of Potamos, evidently came to Kythera from Koroni in the Peloponnese in around 1600.

Five km. east of this village, renowned for its springs, is the harbour of **Aghia Pelagia** with its lovely sandy beach. 5 km. south of Potamos, just beyond the village of **Trifyllianika**, is **Palaiochora**, built in the 12th century when the Kytherans were forced to vacate their capital in order to escape the piratical raids. According to tradition, in its heyday, Palaiochora, dedicated to St. Demetrius, had a population of 800 souls and 72 churches, as many as there were families. Nowadays the best preserved of these is the church of St. Barbara. Perched on the cliffs of the east coast of the island is the monastery known as Aghia Moni, dedicated to the Virgin. In the church, dated 1840, there is the miraculous two-sided icon: on one face the Virgin (Hope of All) and on the other St. George.

One of the most interesting regions is that of **Avlemonas** (32 km. northeast of Chora), site of Palaiopolis which was a quarter in the city of ancient Skandeia, located at present-day Kastri. The church of St. Cosmas at Palaiopolis is constructed of ancient building material taken from the temple of Aphrodite. There are remnants of a Venetian fortress beside the harbour of Avlemonas and above the village stands the Byzantine chapel of St. George on the Mountain which dates to the 6th century, the mosaic floors inside are preserved.

Places of scenic beauty on Kythera include **Livadi**, **Mylopotamos**, **Diakofti** and there are therapeutic springs, as well as wonderful beaches for swimming, mainly on the east side and the bay of **Aghios Nikolaos**, **Kapsali**, **Avlemonas**, **Diakofti**, **Aghia Pelagia**. One may explore the coast best by boat and even visit Antikythera. There is a refuelling station at Kapsali. There are rooms to let for visitors.

Antikythera

Antikythera is in fact a cluster of islands between Kythera and the Cretan Sea, about 16 miles from Crete (Gramvousa). Surface area 20 sq. km., length of coast 24 km., population 115 and capital Potamos. There is a boat connection with Piraeus (once a week) and with Kasteli (Kissamos). In antiquity the island was known as *Aigila* and was apparently first settled by Cretans and Dryopes. Much later, the Romans and Byzantines arrived, followed by the Venetians who called it *Tsirigoto*. The present inhabitants came from Sfakia at the end of the 18th century. A target and haven for pirates, the island is renowned for the ships sunk in its waters. In 1900 a shipwreck was recovered from the depths of the sea and a hoard of objects retrieved, including the wonderful bronze statue of the Ephebe of Antikythera, a work of the mid-4th century BC nowadays on display in the National Archaeological Museum, Athens. This is an island only for those seeking escapism from civilisation.

Elafonisos

A tiny islet off the southeast coast of the Peloponnese, in the Vatikiotikos gulf, 18 sq. km. in area, 26 km. of coastline, Elafonisos belongs administratively to the Prefecture of Lakonia. There are small local craft linking it with Neapolis and a boat to Piraeus once a week. In ancient times it was actually a peninsula, the narrow isthmus of which was subsequently submerged, and until 1677 there was a shallow causeway linking it with the Peloponnese. Excavations here have brought to light finds from the Bronze Age. Its sparkling clear sea and sandy beaches entice an ever-growing number of visitors who prefer holidays off the beaten track, since there are no organised facilities for tourists.

KEY TO MAPS

ROAD NETWORK

══════ ASPHALT-PAVED ROAD

══════ NON-ASPHALT ROAD

━━ ═ ═ ROAD UNDER CONSTRUCTION

── ─── CART TRACK - FOOTPATH

⬆8⬆ DISTANCES IN KILOMETRES

✈ AIRPORT

✈ AIRFIELD

⬇ PORT

⛺ CAMPING

♨ SPA RESORT

⋂ CAVE

🏊 SWIMMING AREA

⛳ GOLF COURSE

⚑ PREHISTORIC SITE

♟ ARCHAEOLOGICAL SITE

☖ BYZANTINE SITE

▣ MEDIEVAL SITE

⛪ MONASTERY

⛪ CHURCH

•350 ALTITUDE IN METRES